D1159751

SOCIAL CLASS AND THE URBAN SCHOOL

The Impact of Pupil Background on Teachers and Principals

SOCIAL CLASS AND THE URBAN SCHOOL

The Impact of Pupil Background on Teachers and Principals

ROBERT E. HERRIOTT

The Florida State University

NANCY HOYT ST. JOHN

Harvard University

With a Foreword by

NEAL GROSS

Harvard University

John Wiley & Sons, Inc.
New York · London · Sydney

FOREWORD

One basic assumption made by most sociologists in their analyses of the structure and operation of societies and communities is that patterns of social arrangements and of institutional systems are inter-related and can influence each other directly and indirectly. This premise is also the point of departure for most sociological studies of pressing and persistent social problems; for example, poverty, de-linquency, the disenchantment and alienation of youth, talent loss, and racial, religious, and ethnic conflict. It largely explains why sociol-ogists take into account *multiple* social forces—forces that reflect in-fluences of the family, of religion, of political, economic, and other institutional and social systems—in their efforts to isolate factors that have impact on the stresses and strains experienced by nations, communities, and their citizens.

This central premise of a sociological approach to social systems and their problems underlies the significant theoretical and practical issues that Professors Herriott and St. John explore in these pages. These writers attempt to increase our limited knowledge of possible relationships between the social class composition of the student bodies in large city schools and the attributes, attitudes, and behavior of their teachers and administrators. A basic assumption of their inquiry—one supported by an extensive body of social science research—is that the patterns of in- and out-migration of large Ameri-can cities have resulted in important changes in their ecological ar-rangements and in the socioeconomic composition of different sections of these communities. A second premise, also well documented and of considerable concern to educators and officials at all governmental levels, is that because of population shifts in the metropolitan community, relatively few schools in large cities serve pupils of *varying* socioeconomic (and racial) backgrounds; most schools serve children who come from either lower- or middle-class families, but not both. Thus, changes in the social patterning of cities have important consequences for schools. These changes influence directly the socioeconomic composition of the clients who are served by schools located in different areas of the city.

Certain features in the design of this study are noteworthy because they differ in important respects from most earlier sociological investigations of the relationships between indices of social stratification and educational phenomena. First, previous inquiries of educational correlates of social stratification have generally focused on social class or socioeconomic status as an attribute of *individuals*. The central issues of this inquiry, however, deal with educational variables that may be associated with the socioeconomic status of the clients of *organizations*—in this case the composition of student bodies.

Second, whereas most investigators concerned with the educational consequences of social stratification have focused on variation in the performance or attitudes of students (for example, their academic achievement, level of educational and occupational aspiration, or self concept), the dependent variables of this study deal primarily with indices of the behavior, attitudes, and attributes of key adult personnel in the schools—teachers and principals who can exert "positive" or "negative" influence on students. By examining the relationship between the social class composition of schools and dependent variables of this kind, it is possible to ascertain whether widely held views about differences between educational personnel who work in lower and higher "social class schools" are myth or reality.

Third, whereas most sociological and educational studies have treated social class *solely* as an independent variable, the present authors demonstrate the value of a research strategy that also views social class or socioeconomic status as a contextual or conditional variable. The most significant findings of their study, in my judgment, are those that emerge in Chapter 8 when they view the social class composition of the school from this perspective. Their data indicate that the principal's performance has varying effects on teacher behavior, *depending on* the social class composition of the student body of the school.

For many reasons the findings of this inquiry will interest social scientists, educators, and administrators responsible for developing and implementing public educational policy. First, they demonstrate that differences exist between the background characteristics of personnel and pupils in *both* "lower and higher social class" schools, a finding that does not support the frequently expressed view that there is a greater gap between the social and economic characteristics of pupils and teachers in schools whose students come primarily from low socioeconomic backgrounds. Certain findings bear on a hypothesis that has never before been tested with a body of national data: that teachers in big-city schools tend to be more interested in horizontal than in vertical career mobility. Data presented in this volume also reveal the many similarities, as well as differences, in the attitudes of teachers and principals toward work and toward their associates in schools that vary in the social class composition of their pupils.

Social scientists and educators will find of especial interest the concluding chapter of this book. There the authors candidly appraise the substantive and methodological shortcomings of their study as well as its positive features. Moreover, they consider the types of inquiries that are needed if deeper penetrations are to be made into the problems they explored.

Those who are responsible for the development and implementation of policies that affect public schools will find this book of considerable value. I believe that its findings about the ways in which teachers and principals in schools whose pupils vary in their social class backgrounds tend to perceive and evaluate their clients and their working conditions have important implications for staffing the schools. Of special significance are the authors' data about the differential effects of the principal's behavior on the performance of teachers in schools whose pupils vary in their social backgrounds.

A subject that deserves special stress for those who establish or influence educational policy is the value of a sociological point of view in deliberations about basic problems of urban schools. Perhaps these officials need to be aware of the many ways the social structure and institutional systems of our society are intertwined and influence each other. This book points out some of the ways in which the system of social stratification in cities comes into contact with, and influences, educational institutions, in large part because of changes in residential patterns that are highly correlated with social status variables. The findings suggest that sound and realistic educational planning and effective implementation of programs for the schools in urban America need to be based on an understanding of the social structure and the culture of communities, of schools, and of families. Too frequently, well-intentioned efforts of the schools to provide more services and a "better" education to students in our large cities have been of little value because important sociological facts of life have been overlooked or ignored.

The publication of this book gives me a great deal of personal gratification. The data that serve as the basis for the many valuable analyses and findings presented here were obtained from the national sample of principals and teachers who participated in the National Principalship Study. As Professors Herriott and St. John note in their preface, this research program was designed to explore a number of issues of concern to both sociologists and educational practitioners. Four final reports, each dealing with a major substantive problem involving the role and performance of principals, were submitted to the United States Office of Education during 1964 and 1965. The results of a study of the determinants and organizational effects of the professional leadership of principals were published in Neal Gross and Robert E. Herriott, *Staff Leadership in Public Schools* (New York, Wiley, 1965). The findings of an examination of differences between men and women in the principalship—in their careers, attitudes, performance and in the operation of their organizations—are presented in Neal Gross and Anne E. Trask, *The Sex Factor and the Administration of Schools* (New York: Wiley, in press). As Director of the National Principalship Study, I had to decide in 1962 whether it would be a worthwhile expenditure of limited fiscal and human resources to extend its scope to include an exploration of the data in terms of the relationship between the social class composition of student bodies of schools and many other educational variables. Once the decision was made to venture forth in this area, I also had to decide who could best accomplish the task. After reading the authors' manuscript, I have concluded that both decisions were correctly made.

NEAL GROSS

ACKNOWLEDGMENTS

In 1958 Professor Neal Gross of Harvard University conceived and developed a plan for a nationwide and multifaceted sociological inquiry into the role of public school principals. Later, with the financial support of the United States Office of Education, he and his staff obtained extensive data from principals, their administrative superiors, and their teachers in elementary, junior, and senior high schools in 41 major American cities. The National Principalship Study examined a large number of questions, including these: the effects and determinants of staff leadership exhibited by school principals; sex differences in the careers and backgrounds of principals, in their role behavior, in the performance of their organizations, and in their reactions to work; the incidence and correlates of role conflicts in the principalship; correlates of such dimensions of their administrative performance as closeness of supervision, support of innovation, and client involvement in school affairs; and the job and career satisfaction and level of aspiration of school administrators.

In 1962 Professor Gross invited us as members of the staff of the National Principalship Study to examine the data obtained from personnel in 490 schools from the perspective of their social class composition. Although he participated in our early deliberations about research strategies and made a number of suggestions about possible analyses of the material, we had complete freedom to develop our own design for a "secondary analysis" of the available materials. This book reports the major results of our investigation.

We are greatly indebted to our associates on the National Principalship Study for the part they played in making our research possible, and particularly to the director, Professor Neal Gross. Without his continued interest and stimulation our inquiry could not have materialized. He identified the social class composition of urban schools as an important area in need of intensive sociological study. His encouragement was the major factor in our decision to undertake the analysis reported here, and the wisdom of his frequent counsel has been most valuable throughout all stages of the study.

Peter C. Dodd, Robert Dreeben, Joseph L. Hozid, Paul E. Kelly, Keith W. Prichard, Anne E. Trask, and Dean K. Whitla served as members of the senior staff of the National Principalship Study and in that capacity prepared research instruments, supervised field work activities, and conducted most of the interviews on which our analyses have been based. Their efforts were essential to the success of our undertaking.

Members of the staff of the Institute of Human Learning of the Florida State University were also helpful in the execution of this research. We are particularly grateful to Russell P. Kropp, the director, who facilitated the completion of the research, and to F. J. King who provided counsel on many methodological matters.

Valuable advice on statistical problems was also provided by Hubert M. Blalock, Jr., Richard Cornell, and Frank Wilcoxon. The computer runs and statistical analyses performed at Harvard University were conducted by Larry Weiss and David Napior, and at the Florida State University by Robert Dawson and Robert Michielutte.

Charlene Worth supervised the financial details of the research, and with Marion Crowley, secretary to the National Principalship Study, gave valuable assistance in many other ways. Clerical tasks were performed by Sandi Kinyon, Peggy Phelps, Betty Whaley, and Pauline Worth. We owe a particular debt of gratitude to Prudy DeLuisi who supervised the many details of revising the final draft for publication.

We also wish to express our thanks to the following persons who critically appraised the final draft of this book: Charles E. Bidwell, Ronald C. Corwin, Benjamin J. Hodgkins, F. J. King, Russell P. Kropp, Sam D. Sieber, and Anne E. Trask. Portions of earlier drafts were read and criticized by Hubert M. Blalock, Jr., Robert Dreeben, Wallace Dynes, Charles B. Nam, A. Lewis Rhodes, and Wade M. Robinson. In addition, we owe thanks to Clarissa Atkinson who provided editorial assistance and to Stephen Miles who designed the format for the illustrations. However, in spite of all the help received in the conduct and reporting of this research, we alone are responsible for its limitations.

April, 1966   ROBERT E. HERRIOTT
                                                   NANCY H. ST. JOHN

CONTENTS

SOCIAL CLASS AND THE URBAN SCHOOL

The Impact of Pupil Background on Teachers and Principals

Chapter 1

INTRODUCTION

The American school . . . reflects the socio-economic order in everything that it does; in what it teaches, whom it teaches, who does the teaching, who does the hiring and firing of the teachers, and what the children learn in and out of the classroom.

Warner, Havighurst, and Loeb

The publication in 1944 by Warner, Havighurst, and Loeb of *Who Shall be Educated?: The Challenge of Unequal Opportunities*[1] was a landmark in the sociological study of education. Following by only a few years the pioneering investigations of social stratification in "Middletown" by the Lynds[2] and in "Yankee City" by Warner and his associates,[3] it drew educators into a debate which was already engrossing sociologists and laymen. A quarter of a century later the debate continues. Although few today deny the existence of some form of social differentiation within American society, there is still disagreement as to the nature of social class[4] in America and its influence on our schools. Currently, vast demographic shifts add new urgency to the question and suggest the need for further research.

American cities are changing rapidly and dramatically. The explosive growth of metropolises involves the simultaneous decline of

---

[1] W. Lloyd Warner, Robert J. Havighurst, and Martin B. Loeb, *Who Shall be Educated?* (New York: Harper and Brothers, 1944). Quotation cited above is from page xii.

[2] Robert S. Lynd and Helen M. Lynd, *Middletown in Transition* (New York: Harcourt, Brace and World, 1937).

[3] W. Lloyd Warner, Marcia Meeker, and Kenneth Eels, *Social Class in America* (Chicago: Science Research Associates, Inc., 1949).

[4] Throughout this chapter we have used the term "social class" somewhat uncritically in referring to the phenomena of social stratification in America. Later (in Chapter 2) we shall discuss some of the controversy associated with this term and then adopt the more operational term "socioeconomic status."

1

the central city and the burgeoning of suburbs. It involves, too, a changing urban social class structure. Although migrants are in general apt to be of higher social class than nonmigrants, migrants to the central city are on the average of low status, many of them poorly educated rural workers. On the other hand, migrants to suburbs are apt to be middle-class families. Since cities lose more high-status people to the suburbs than they gain, the net effect is a lowered social class level in the central city and a raised social class level in the suburbs. The racial character of these population changes—many of the in-migrants to the central city are Negro and most of the families who move to the suburbs are white—is important, but not exclusively so: the population is redistributed between city and suburb on the basis of social class as much as of race.[5]

Within the central city, too, there are population shifts with respect to social class. Neighborhoods grow old and decay; second generation ethnic clusters break up; white families leave as Negroes arrive. All of these factors contribute to the general tendency of mobile elements to move to the periphery of the city.[6] Such "natural" processes are both accelerated and reversed by urban renewal. Working class city dwellers are forced to move by the building of parkways, by the conversion of land use from residential to commercial, and by the replacement of slum housing with middle-income apartments. Very often they move to deteriorating areas of the city, bringing overcrowding, lowered social class level, and new slums.[7] Another type

[5] Donald J. Bogue, *Components of Population Change, 1940–1950* (Oxford, Ohio: Scripps Foundation for Research in Population Problems, No. 12, 1957); Otis D. Duncan and Albert J. Reiss, Jr., *Social Characteristics of Urban and Rural Communities, 1950* (New York: John Wiley and Sons, 1956); Morton Grodzins, *The Metropolitan Area as a Racial Problem* (Pittsburgh: University of Pittsburgh Press, 1958); Conrad Taeuber, "Some Recent Population Changes in the United States," *The Journal of Intergroup Relations*, I (1960), pp. 113–122; and Karl E. Taeuber and Alma F. Taeuber, "White Migration and Socio-Economic Differences between Cities and Suburbs," *American Sociological Review*, XXIX (1964), pp. 718–729

[6] Otis D. Duncan and Beverly Duncan, "Residential Distribution and Occupational Stratification," *American Journal of Sociology*, LX (1955), pp. 493–503; Otis D. Duncan and Stanley Lieberson, "Ethnic Segregation and Assimilation," *American Journal of Sociology*, LXIV (1959), pp. 364–374; and Philip M. Hauser, "The Changing Population Pattern of the Modern City," in Paul K. Hatt and Albert J. Reiss, Jr. (Editors), *Cities and Society* (Glencoe, Illinois: The Free Press, 1959).

[7] Davis McEntire, "Government and Racial Discrimination in Housing," *The Journal of Social Issues*, XIII (1957), pp. 60–67; Mel J. Ravitz, "Effects of

of planned social change, the desegregation of school districts, may have the unexpected consequence of driving away the middle-class families who wish to avoid schools in which they believe lower-class children will predominate.[8]

Demographic shifts, planned and unplanned, are thus responsible for a decline in the average social class level of many urban neighborhoods and for a rise in the average social class level of a few neighborhoods. They may also be producing a more fundamental development in our cities—an increase in social class segregation. In the city, the homes of the rich and the homes of the poor have always been more widely separated than in the village or small town. The larger the city, the more possible it is for geographical distance to match social distance. However, the growth of the metropolis, the scale of urban renewal, and the development of urban planning, all facilitate the further splitting of the city by superhighways, commercial districts, and housing projects into islands inhabited almost entirely by people of similar income level.

City schools reflect the changes in the social composition of the city. As the rural poor crowd into cities and become the urban poor, and as middle class families move out from the center, the social class level of central schools falls, and enrollments of middle-class pupils in schools on the periphery increase. It is also probable that there is a decline in the number of neighborhoods in which children from different social strata grow up within sight of each other, play in the same vacant lot, or attend the same neighborhood school.[9] Robert Havighurst has called attention to a decreasing percentage of "mixed

Urban Renewal on Community Racial Patterns," *The Journal of Social Issues* XIII (1957), pp. 38–49; and Robert C. Weaver, "Integration in Public and Private Housing," *Annals of the American Academy of Political and Social Science* CCCIV (1956), pp. 87–97.

[8] S. Joseph Fauman, "Housing Discrimination, Changing Neighborhoods, and Public Schools," *Journal of Social Issues*, XIII (1957), pp. 21–30; Robert J. Havighurst, "Social Class Influences on American Education," in Nelson B. Henry (Editor), *Social Forces Influencing American Education* (Chicago: University of Chicago Press, 1961), pp. 120–143; and Eleanor P. Wolf, "The Invasion-Succession Sequence as a Self-Fulfilling Prophecy," *The Journal of Social Issues*, XIII (1957), pp. 7–20.

[9] Bobby J. Chandler, "Forces Influencing Urban Schools," in Bobby J. Chandler, Lindley J. Stiles, and John I. Kitsuse, *Education in Urban Society* (New York: Dodd, Mead and Company, 1962), pp. 3–35; and Jane Jacobs, *The Death and Life of Great American Cities* (New York: Random House, 1961).

class schools" and an increasing percentage of either lower or middle-class schools.[10]

Particularly affected by these changes are the schools attended only by the children of the very poor. Usually located in the oldest sections of the city, where building costs are high and play space at a premium, faced with rising enrollments of the children of multiproblem, migrant families, these schools report the difficulties that might be expected. They suffer from generally low achievement, high rates of transiency, antisocial behavior, dropouts, overcrowded classrooms, and teacher shortages. Each year there are more urban schools with such problems.[11]

The popular press as well as the educational literature of recent years reveals a growing awareness on the part of laymen and professionals of the special problems of the "slum schools." Their awareness has been demonstrated since 1959 by the initiation in many large school systems of special remedial programs. These programs try to meet the specific needs of some pupils or to raise the productivity of all pupils.[12] However, projects for the "culturally deprived" involve large outlays of resources—in money, in skilled manpower, and in the imagination and time of administrators—and systematic research evidence to guide the allocation of these resources is still scarce.[13]

RESEARCH ON SOCIAL CLASS AND EDUCATION

During the past 20 years there has been much valuable research on the relation of social class to education in America, and sound data have been amassed. However, the relevance of this research for the solution of contemporary problems is greatly limited by its emphasis on the social class of the *child*, instead of the social class composition of the *school;* on *slum schools* only, rather than *contrasting*

[10] Robert J. Havighurst, "Urban Development and the Educational System," in A. Harry Passow (Editor), *Education in Depressed Areas* (New York: Bureau of Publications, Teachers College, Columbia University, 1963), pp. 24–45.

[11] James B. Conant, *Slums and Suburbs* (New York: McGraw-Hill Book Company, Inc., 1961); and Educational Policies Commission, *Education and the Disadvantaged American* (Washington, D. C.: National Education Association, 1962).

[12] Educational Research Service, *School Programs for the Disadvantaged* (Washington, D. C.: American Association of School Administrators, 1963); and Carl L. Marburger, "Considerations for Educational Planning," in Passow, *op. cit.*, pp. 298–321.

[13] Miriam L. Goldberg, "Factors Affecting Educational Attainment in Depressed Urban Areas," in Passow., *op. cit.*, pp. 68–99.

schools of low, medium, and high social class levels; and on the *pupils* in slum schools, instead of their *teachers* and *principals*. In particular, we do not know enough about the effect on school staff of the social class *composition* of the schools in which they are situated.

Social Class and the Pupil

The heterogeneous school, typical of a small community, is the ideal locale in which to compare pupils of different social class backgrounds in a single classroom. Most of the early studies of the influence of social class on learning used this approach. Their findings are in substantial agreement with one another; they attest to the strong correlation between an individual pupil's social class level and many aspects of his school career.

For instance, in midwestern Elmtown in the mid-forties, Hollingshead found that Class V students (at the bottom of the social hierarchy) were rated significantly lower on all measures of achievement than Class I students. They received lower test scores, lower grades, fewer prizes, and more failures, and were less apt to enroll in the college preparatory curriculum.[14] These findings on the relation between social class and achievement are corroborated by the work of many researchers, both in single classrooms and in samples of schools.[15] It has been well established that early withdrawal from high school is characteristic of lower-class youth, while plans for post-high school education and high level occupations are characteristic of middle-class youth.[16] Participation in extracurricular activities, election to student offices, and membership in high-ranking peer-group cliques

[14] August B. Hollingshead, *Elmtown's Youth* (New York: John Wiley and Sons, 1949).

[15] Hubert A. Coleman, "The Relationship of Socioeconomic Status to the Performance of Junior High School Students," *Journal of Experimental Education,* IX (1940), pp. 61–63; Robert J. Havighurst, *et al., Growing Up in River City* (New York: John Wiley and Sons, 1962); Stephen Abrahamson, "Our Status System and Scholastic Rewards," *Journal of Educational Sociology,* XXV (1952), pp. 441–450; Horace M. Bond, "Talent- and Toilets," *Journal of Negro Education,* XXVIII (1959), pp. 3–14; and Duane C. Shaw, "The Relation of Socio-economic Status to Educational Achievement in Grades Four to Eight," *Journal of Educational Research,* XXXVII (1943), pp. 197–201.

[16] James S. Davie, "Social Class Factors and School Attendance, *Harvard Educational Review,* XXIII (1953), pp. 175–185; William H. Sewell, Archie O. Haller, and Murray A. Strauss, "Social Status and Educational and Occupational Aspiration," *American Sociological Review,* XXII (1957), pp. 67–73; and Richard M. Stephenson, "Mobility Orientation and Stratification of 1,000 Ninth Graders," *American Sociological Review,* XXII (1957), pp. 204–212.

are among the other variables that are regularly found to be related to the individual pupil's social class background.[17]

We suggested above that, as cities have grown, stratification has increased between schools, rather than within them. This trend has led recent investigators to study the effect on the achievement and aspiration of pupils of the social class *composition* of the school as a whole, as distinct from the social class of the individual pupil. The depressing effect on pupil performance of the very low social class level of a school as a whole has been documented through a number of careful case studies of schools in city slums,[18] as well as through more generalized descriptions of typical schools in such neighborhoods.[19] But the peculiar qualities of a phenomenon can best be understood when it is compared with its opposite. For this reason Conant's report on schools in slums and suburbs has been a contribution to general understanding of the phenomenon.[20] Two "ideal types" were dramatically contrasted, and although empirical evidence was not supplied, a number of key variables, such as public expenditure for schools, were suggested.

Recently, investigators have begun to relate a systematic characterization of the social class composition of a school to aspects of pupil behavior within that school. Sexton was able to relate average family income in the census tract in which a school is located to many measures of pupil achievement.[21] But Wilson carried the inquiry a big step further. He not only demonstrated that the achievement level of a school varies according to its social class composition, but showed that an individual's achievement and aspiration levels are related both to his own social class and to the average social class of the school

---

[17] Hollingshead, *op. cit.;* C. Wayne Gordon, *The Social System of the High School* (Glencoe, Illinois: The Free Press, 1957); Bernice L. Neugarten, "Social Class and Friendship Among School Children," *American Journal of Sociology,* LI (1946), pp. 305–313; and Celia B. Stendler, *Children of Brasstown* (Urbana: University of Illinois, Bureau of Research and Service, College of Education, 1949).

[18] Fern H. Jacobi, "Changing Pupils in a Changing School," *Educational Leadership,* XVII (1960), pp. 283–287; Martin Mayer, "The Good Slum Schools," *Harper's Magazine* (April, 1961), pp. 46–52; and Charles E. Silberman, "The City and the Negro," *Fortune* (March, 1962), pp. 88–91, 139–154.

[19] Conant, *op. cit.;* Educational Policies Commission, *op. cit.;* and Frank Riessman, *The Culturally Deprived Child* (New York: Harper and Row, 1962).

[20] Conant, *op. cit.*

[21] Patricia Sexton, *Education and Income* (New York: The Viking Press, 1961); see also Allen H. Barton and David E. Wilder, "Research and Practice in the Teaching of Reading: A Progress Report," in Matthew B. Miles (Editor), *Innovation in Education* (New York: Bureau of Publications, Teachers College, Columbia University, 1964).

that he attends. The social class "climate" of a school apparently makes its own contribution to the achievement and aspiration of its pupils, in addition to that made by the social class climate of the home.[22] This important finding is corroborated in a study by Turner of a single city and in one by Michaels, who employed a national sample of schools.[23]

Social Class and the Teacher

Research on the influence of social class on learning has thus begun to turn from a focus on the social class of the individual child to a focus on the social class of the school, and from a preoccupation with the slum school to a comparison of schools of different social class levels. It has also begun to shift the spotlight from the effect of social class on the pupil to its effect on his teacher. A number of writers have urged a new look at the relation between a school's social class composition and its teachers. Riessman and Clark, for instance, have both argued that instead of studying the pupils in a disadvantaged neighborhood and asking why their academic achievement is so low, one should study the teachers and ask why they are not more successful with these pupils.[24]

There have been three dominant and related themes in sociological thinking as to the relation of pupil social class and the public school teacher. One might be called the "culture-gap hypothesis," another the "horizontal mobility hypothesis," and the third the "inequality hypothesis."

The *culture-gap hypothesis,* associated with writers like Burton[25] and Davis,[26] proposes that teachers are not only middle class in origin, but completely middle class in occupational status and values. In contrast, pupils are from all social classes, but (the occupational pyramid being what it is) predominantly from the lower class. The middle-

---

[22] Alan B. Wilson, "Residential Segregation of Social Classes and Aspirations of High School Boys," *American Sociological Review,* XXIV (1959), pp. 836–845; and Alan B. Wilson, "Social Stratification and Academic Achievement," in Passow, *op. cit.,* pp. 217–235.

[23] Ralph H. Turner, *The Social Context of Ambition* (San Francisco: Chandler Publishing Company, 1964); and John A. Michaels, "High School Climates and Plans for Entering College," *Public Opinion Quarterly,* XX (1961), pp. 585–595.

[24] Riessman, *op. cit.,* pp. 4–5; and Kenneth B. Clark, *Dark Ghetto* (New York: Harper and Row, 1965).

[25] William H. Burton, "Education and Social Class in the United States," *Harvard Educational Review,* XXIII (1953), pp. 243–256.

[26] Allison Davis, *Social-Class Influences upon Learning* (Cambridge, Massachusetts: Harvard University Press, 1952).

class family is said to be child-centered, future-oriented, and interested in achievement and mobility. It teaches children to respect property and to value neatness, thrift, and punctuality. The lower-class family, on the other hand, is described as adult-centered, present-oriented, and interested in enjoying life with extended family and peers. It teaches children to admire toughness, physical prowess, generosity, and practicality. Since these values of the middle and lower classes differ widely, there is, it is argued, a culture gap between teachers and pupils in most schools (or between teachers and most of their pupils, if the school is heterogeneous).[27]

This generalization may be less accurate today than when it was proposed a decade or so ago. In the first place, the shape of the occupational pyramid is changing and we are becoming a more middle-class nation. In the second place, there is evidence that in recent years an increasing percentage of public school teachers are the children of skilled workers.[28] But regardless of whether teachers (on the average) are of higher social class origin than pupils (on the average), we still do not know whether teachers in one type of school are very different in background from teachers in other types of schools. It is tacitly assumed that the origin of the *average* teacher is identical from school to school, regardless of the social class composition of the school in which he works. But this may not be true.

Discussion of a culture gap has concentrated on whether or not middle-class status inevitably means inability to understand and respect the values of working-class children and their parents, producing favoritism for middle-class children in a mixed-class situation. There is considerable evidence that this is often the case.[29] However, the

[27] Riessman, *op. cit.*; Martin Deutsch, *Minority Group and Class Status as Related to Social and Personality Factors in Scholastic Achievement* (Ithaca, New York: Society for Applied Anthropology, Monograph No. 2, 1960); Herbert J. Gans, *The Urban Villagers* (Glencoe, Illinois: The Free Press, 1962), Chapter VI; Warner, Havighurst, and Loeb, *op. cit.*; and Sloan R. Wayland, "Old Problems, New Faces, and New Standards," in Passow, *op. cit.*, pp. 46–67.

[28] Wilbur B. Brookover, "Teachers and the Stratification of American Society," *Harvard Educational Review*, XXIII (1953), pp. 257–267; Robert J. Havighurst and Bernice L. Neugarten, *Society and Education*, (Boston: Allyn and Bacon, Inc., 1957); Ward S. Mason, *The Beginning Teacher* (Washington, D. C.: Government Printing Office, 1961); and W. W. Charters, Jr., "The Social Background of Teaching," in Nathaniel L. Gage (Editor), *Handbook of Research on Teaching* (Chicago: Rand McNally and Company, 1963), pp. 715–813, see especially pp. 719–722.

[29] Abrahamson, *op. cit.*; Howard S. Becker, "Social-Class Variations in the Teacher-Pupil Relationship," *Journal of Educational Sociology*, XXV (1952), pp. 451–465; Helen H. Davidson and Gerhard Lang, "Children's Perceptions of their

relationship of the social class of the student body as a whole to the attitudes, behavior, or morale of teachers is relatively unknown.

The *horizontal mobility hypothesis* was the product of a series of studies of the school as a formal organization conducted at the University of Chicago in the early 1950's. Chief among these were the investigations of Becker and Winget.[30] Becker, for instance, found that because of problems of teaching, of discipline, and of pupils with unacceptable morals, most teachers eventually transferred away from the lower-class school in which their careers typically began. For these teachers, career mobility lay in geographical movement to a teaching position in a more middle-class school, rather than in promotion to an administrative position. Becker also found that some teachers stayed on in slum schools and adapted their expectations and methods to the capabilities of their pupils, but this was the career pattern of a minority. The majority, through horizontal mobility, eventually reduced (or reversed) the gap between their own social class and that of their pupils.

In view of the interest in Becker's findings in educational circles, it is surprising that his study has not been replicated in other cities. Scattered reports from various cities indicate that it is customary in some school systems to reward faithful service with the option of transfer to a more "desirable" school. In others, such transfers may be frowned upon in theory but in fact allowed. Many writers assume that, regardless of official policy, horizontal mobility from schools of low social class to schools of high social class is the dominant career pattern in large cities.[31] But the evidence on this matter is far from conclusive.

The *inequality hypothesis* asserts that school systems do not distribute their resources equitably, but favor middle-class schools in the

---

Teachers' Feelings toward Them Related to Self-Perception, School Achievement and Behavior," *Journal of Experimental Education,* XXIX (1960), pp. 107–117; and Patrick J. Groff, "Dissatisfactions in Teaching the Culturally Deprived Child," *Phi Delta Kappan,* XLV (November, 1963), p. 76.

[30] Howard S. Becker, "The Career of the Chicago Public Schoolteacher," *American Journal of Sociology,* LVII (1952), pp. 470–477; and John A. Winget, *Teacher Inter-School Mobility Aspirations, Elementary Schools, Chicago Public School System, 1947–48* (unpublished doctoral dissertation, University of Chicago, 1952).

[31] Chandler, Stiles, and Kitsuse, *op. cit.,* pp. 3–35; Helen E. Amerman, "Perspective for Evaluating Intergroup Relations in a Public School System," *Journal of Negro Education,* XXVI (1957), pp. 108–120; and Hermine I. Popper, *How Difficult are the Difficult Schools?* (New York: Public Education Association, 1959).

assignment of staff, as well as in the building and maintenance of plant and in the allocation of teaching materials and special resources.[32]

The definition of equity is a matter of opinion. Strict equality may be inequitable if the needs of certain school children are seen as greater than those of others. If resources are scarce, should the needs of talented children for superior teaching come first? Or should preferential treatment be given to potential dropouts? In any case, regardless of which group of children stands in "greatest need," it is possible that both the children and their requirements are very different. This being true, it follows that it may be neither equal nor equitable if the teachers, their interests, and methods, are exactly alike in schools of different social class composition.

Studies such as Sexton's seem to suggest that the quality of teaching performance may vary according to the social class composition of the school.[33] However, her evidence, and that of a number of others,[34] is inferential and based on such indices as the proportion of substitute or inexperienced teachers in a school. It could be that the younger teachers are as effective as the older teachers, in spite of their lack of formal teaching experience. Whether, in general, the quality of teaching performance is lower in slum schools is really not known. Nor is it known whether, by and large, there are differences in the interests, training, or methods of teachers from one school setting to another which match the different needs of the children they teach.

Social Class and the Principal

The characteristics of public school principals, in relation to the social class of their pupils, has been little studied. We do not know, for example, whether the gap between the social class or values of principals and pupils is generally greater or smaller than that thought

[32] Amerman, *op. cit.;* Sexton, *op. cit.;* Public Education Association, *The Status of the Public School Education of Negro and Puerto Rican Children in New York City* (New York: Public Education Association, 1955); and for a theoretical discussion of equality of educational opportunities, see Myron Lieberman, "Equality of Educational Opportunity," *Harvard Educational Review,* XXIX (1959), pp. 167–183.

[33] Sexton, *op. cit.,* pp. 116–122.

[34] Matthew J. Pillard, "Teachers for Urban Schools," in Chandler, Stiles, and Kitsuse, *op. cit.,* pp. 193–210; and Public Education Association, *The Status of the Public School Education of Negro and Puerto Rican Children in New York City, op. cit.*

to exist between teachers and pupils. It is likely that a principal's career shows horizontal as well as vertical mobility, but it has not been established whether such mobility is related to the social class composition of the school. Similarly, the quality of performance of principals from schools of one social class level to another is unrecorded.

Certain writers have recently suggested that the principal may prove to be the key to the successful slum school. They cite individual cases in which morale and productivity in a difficult school improved after the arrival of a strong and imaginative administrator.[35] It is possible, although not proved, that the slums demand a different kind of leadership or administrative style than the suburbs.

OVERVIEW

In the chapters which follow, our interest in the social class composition of schools and the characteristics, attitudes, and behavior of school personnel can be viewed as a concern with the effect of the "input" of a formal organization on its "workers." In the typical model of an organization, *workers* perform certain operations on *inputs* and transform them into desired *outputs*. Classical theory viewed the worker as an instrument of production, whose performance is affected primarily by his physiological skill and the appropriateness of his instructions.[36] Recent theoretical developments have noted limitations to such a conceptualization and have introduced considerations of cognitive processes and the motivational and affective components of human behavior.[37]

Of central importance to recent formulations is the proposition that the relationships which the worker has with his superiors and his co-workers can affect his job performance. However, what such formulations often fail to consider is that in many organizations having human *inputs* (for example, hospitals, prisons, colleges, and particularly public schools) the relationship of the worker to these *inputs* may be even more crucial and may affect his relationships to superiors and co-workers, as well as his job performance.

School teachers and principals are employed to "affect" the pupils

---

[35] Educational Policies Commission, *op. cit.*, p. 11; Marburger, *op. cit.*, p. 17; Silberman, *op. cit.*; Mayer, *op. cit.*; and Passow, *op. cit.*, p. 242.

[36] James G. March and Herbert A. Simon, *Organizations* (New York: John Wiley and Sons, 1958), Chapter 2.

[37] *Ibid.*, Chapter 3.

assigned to them in certain socially desirable ways. But it is possible that an effect exists in the opposite direction and that the pupils affect the teachers in certain undesirable ways. Furthermore, as Becker's observations suggest,[38] the relative strengths of these directed effects may vary with the social class composition of the school. It may be that in schools with a preponderance of pupils from one type of background, the "teacher to pupil" effect is relatively large, and the "pupil to teacher" effect relatively small; whereas in schools with a preponderance of pupils from another type of background the reverse may be true.

Our major focus will therefore be on the extent to which the social class composition of the pupils in urban schools is associated with characteristics of the staff of these schools, in terms of the individuals who are assigned to work in them, their job-related attitudes and behavior, and their relationships to each other. We have taken the data from a national survey which in 1960 investigated the role of the principal in 501 public schools in 41 American cities with populations of 50,000 or more, and have performed a reanalysis in terms of the social class composition of the schools. In this "secondary analysis" of existing data we have, in general, found it necessary to approximate the relationships that we desired to study. Given the pressing need for definitive answers to our questions, this weakness is unfortunate. However, we feel that the advantage of obtaining even partial answers to questions of great educational and sociological importance with data from a national sample of urban schools outweighs the disadvantage of incompleteness. Any research inquiry raises questions as well as answers them. This study may have raised more than it has answered, since our techniques are far from precise. It is hoped, however, that the data and discussions which follow will provide some partial answers to important questions and will establish guidelines for the asking and answering of the many important questions still unanswered.

[38] Becker, "Social-Class Variations in the Teacher-Pupil Relationship," *op. cit.*, pp. 451–465.

Chapter 2

BACKGROUND OF THE SCHOOL SOCIOECONOMIC STATUS STUDY

During the years 1959 to 1964, Harvard University, with the support of the Cooperative Research Branch of the United States Office of Education, conducted a research program called the National Principalship Study. This study, directed by Neal Gross, was designed to examine many aspects of the public school principalship in cities with populations of 50,000 or more.[1] The School Socioeconomic Status (SES) Study was an extension of the National Principalship Study and utilized the data collected by it from 501 principals and 3367 teachers in 41 cities throughout the United States in order to consider the impact of the socioeconomic composition of schools upon the characteristics, attitudes, and behavior of their principals and teachers.

[1] One of the investigations undertaken by the study focused on the determinants and effects of the staff leadership of elementary school principals, and another on the effects of the sex of the principal on his behavior. Other inquiries of the study considered the role conflicts experienced by principals and the relation of their administrative behavior to organizational performance. For the results of these inquiries, see Neal Gross and Robert E. Herriott, *Staff Leadership in Public Schools* (New York: John Wiley and Sons, 1965); Neal Gross and Anne E. Trask, *The Sex Factor and the Administration of Schools* (New York: John Wiley and Sons, forthcoming, title tentative); Robert Dreeben and Neal Gross, *The Role Behavior of School Principals,* Final Report No. 3, Cooperative Research Project No. 853 (Cambridge, Massachusetts: Graduate School of Education, Harvard University, 1965); and Peter C. Dodd, *Role Conflicts of School Principals,* Final Report No. 4, Cooperative Research Project No. 853 (Cambridge, Massachusetts: Graduate School of Education, Harvard University, 1965).

13

SAMPLING AND DATA COLLECTION

The technical aspects of the research design and data collection procedures of the National Principalship Study have been described in detail by Gross and Herriott.[2] The target population consisted of all supervising principals in cities with a population of 50,000 or more during the 1960 to 1961 school year. In selecting a sample, the 11,000 principalships in cities of that size were classified on the basis of geographical region, system per-pupil expenditure, and size of city. Through a cluster-sampling procedure designed to obtain a 5 per cent sample of the population, 41 cities were selected and the number of principals to be sampled in each city was determined. To select the actual sample, all schools of a nonspecialized nature[3] in each of the 41 communities were classified according to level (elementary, junior high, or senior high), and again by the average socioeconomic characteristics of their pupils (high, medium, or low) as estimated by the superintendent of schools. Then approximately one-ninth of the required number of principals were selected randomly from each of the nine classifications.

The National Principalship Study required data from school principals, their immediate administrative superiors, and a sample of teachers on their staffs. The School SES Study utilized only data obtained from the principals and their teachers. The collection of data from principals was divided into three phases. In the first, each of the principals in the sample was mailed a personal letter notifying him of his selection, explaining the aims and design of the study, and requesting that he provide information about his personal characteristics (for example, age, sex, education), his family background (for example, father's occupation, mother's education), his job history (for example, number of years as a principal), and the school which he was currently administering (for example, size of its student body, characteristics of its teachers). In addition, while attending a luncheon meeting held in his city by the study staff, each principal completed a questionnaire about his role. Later he was interviewed by a member of the staff for approximately four hours. Of the 508 principals selected to participate in the study, 501 (99 per cent) completed all three of these phases.

The School SES Study also analyzed data obtained through a 21-page teacher questionnaire which was mailed to a random sample

[2] Gross and Herriott, op. cit., pp. 15–21.

[3] Such "single purpose" institutions as vocational, technical, and detention schools were excluded from the universe.

of 10 teachers in each of 476 of the 501 participating schools.[4] In this questionnaire, the teachers were asked to provide background information, to answer a set of questions concerning their attitudes, and to characterize (on the basis of previous observations) their principal, their fellow teachers, and their pupils. Seventy-one per cent of the teachers to whom the teacher questionnaire was sent completed it. The personal characteristics of the teachers who returned the questionnaire were checked and found to be representative of those of all teachers in their schools.[5]

THE DEFINITION AND MEASUREMENT
OF SCHOOL SOCIOECONOMIC STATUS

The major concern of the School SES Study, as distinct from that of other investigations utilizing the data of the National Principalship Study, has been the effect on staff of the different social and economic characteristics of the groups of pupils attending the 501 schools. As noted in Chapter 1, a focus on the social class "composition" or "mix" of schools is relatively new. The problems of definition and measurement of the social class level of both households and larger collectivities had therefore to be considered.

We mentioned in Chapter 1 the controversy that followed early research on social class in this country and the fact that many issues remain unresolved.[6] It may be useful, therefore, to review briefly some of these issues and the position we take in relation to them.

[4] In one of the 41 school systems the higher administration, although willing to have the principals participate in the National Principalship Study, was unwilling to have the teachers participate. Consequently, the 13 schools in this system do not appear in any analyses based upon data obtained from the teacher questionnaire. In addition, no teacher questionnaires were sent to 12 schools in which the principal had either died or been transferred to another position between the time of the principals' interviews and the mailing of the teacher questionnaire.

[5] To check the representativeness of the teacher sample, the relationship of School SES to such teacher characteristics as sex, age, highest degree held, years of teaching experience, and years of tenure in current school was examined for both the teacher sample and the teacher population. In all five instances, the decision with respect to the null hypothesis was identical for the two groups of elementary school teachers. Similar tests were made for the junior and senior high school teachers. See Chapter 4, footnote 3, for further discussion of this point.

[6] For general discussions as to the existance of social stratification in America, as well as the problems of definition and measurement, see Kurt B. Mayer, *Class and Society* (Garden City, New York: Doubleday, 1955); Bernard Barber, *Social Stratification* (New York: Harcourt, Brace, 1957), or Joseph A. Kahl, *The American Class Structure* (New York: Rinehart and Company, Inc., 1957).

With respect to the nature of the phenomenon, the debate has centered around such questions as the following:

1. Is social stratification a reality in America?
2. Is stratification in this country in the nature of a continuum, or a set of ordered levels?
3. If a set of ordered levels, how many?
4. Does our system of stratification have a single dimension, or is it a composite of many dimensions?
5. Does each locality have its own system of stratification, or is there a national system?
6. Are there, then, social classes in America?

In answer to these questions, it is our position that:

1. Social stratification is an important characteristic of American society.
2. Stratification is a continuum.
3. This continuum can be divided conceptually into any desired number of levels, but these levels are not clearly distinct from one another.
4. Stratification is complex, a composite of at least the economic, the prestige, and the power dimensions, and each dimension is capable of subdivision.
5. Systems of social status are more highly developed in small communities where residents are known to each other and form status groups, but the features of these systems are general from community to community. Moreover, the economic hierarchy is not community-bound, since it is made up of aggregates of people of similar economic position, and therefore of similar opportunities, values and sub-culture. It is thus realistic to speak of a national stratification system, especially with respect to large urban communities.
6. Contemporary American sociologists vary in their use of the term *social class*. A few adhere strictly to Weber's practice,[7] reserving the term for the economic order of stratification. Some use the term loosely to refer to all dimensions of social stratification. Others, like ourselves, prefer to avoid semantic problems by abandoning the term in favor of the more opera-

---

[7] Max Weber, "Class, Status, Party," in *From Max Weber: Essays in Sociology,* translated and edited by Hans H. Gerth and C. Wright Mills (New York: Oxford University Press, 1946), pp. 180–195. Published in German in 1925.

tional one, *socioeconomic status,* which represents whatever is measured by the indices used.

Given the above decisions with respect to definition, there remained the important issue of measurement. Of particular relevance were two questions: What are the most appropriate indicators of the socioeconomic composition of schools, and how can the necessary data best be obtained?

In his studies of the status of individuals, Warner identified six variables (occupation, amount of income, source of income, house type, dwelling area, and level of education), which in combination correlated with the reports of social status provided by local judges.[8] Other researchers have tested combinations of these and other indicators and have found them to be correlated with measures of attitudes and behavior. In general, occupation, education, and income have been found to be three important components of social status. Therefore, in attempting to differentiate among schools in terms of their socioeconomic composition, we decided to focus upon variation in: the occupation of the pupils' fathers, the level of educational attainment of fathers and mothers, and the total family income.[9] Within each school, we focused on the *average* socioeconomic status of the households from which the pupils come, rather than on its variability.[10] To obtain this average we chose to rely on a factor analysis of the reports of a single expert for each school, and we selected the school principal as the person best suited to make such judgements.[11]

We have noted that as a part of the technique used to select a sample of schools, the National Principalship Study asked the superintendents in the 41 cities to provide a list of all schools in the system and to indicate their relative socioeconomic status. The intention was not to define the SES of the different schools, since what is considered

---

[8] W. Lloyd Warner, Marcia Meeker, and Kenneth Eels, *Social Class in America* (Chicago: Science Research Associates, Inc., 1949). For a discussion of the use of occupation as an index of social status, see Albert J. Reiss, *Occupations and Social Status* (New York: The Free Press of Glencoe, 1961).

[9] The decision to use only occupation, education, and income as indicators of socioeconomic status is consistent with that made by the Bureau of the Census with respect to the analysis of the data from the 1960 Census. See U. S. Bureau of the Census, *Methodology and Scores of Socioeconomic Status,* Working Paper No. 15 (Washington, D. C.: U. S. Bureau of the Census, 1963).

[10] For a further discussion of this distinction, see Chapter 11.

[11] For a discussion of some of the limitations of this procedure as well as of several alternatives, see Chapter 11.

to be "high" SES in one system may be "low" in another, but rather to insure that the sample of schools would vary widely in socioeconomic characteristics.

The actual measurement of the SES of the schools took place during the personal interview with the school principal. At that time, each principal was asked to estimate the percentage of pupils in his school from homes where:

1. The father is an unskilled or semiskilled worker.
2. The father is a professional person, business executive, or manager.
3. Neither parent has received any education beyond high school.
4. At least one parent is a college graduate.
5. The combined family income is less than $5000.
6. The combined family income is $10,000 or more.

Many principals responded without hesitation to these questions and acknowledged that they had made rough estimates of this kind before. Others found the task more difficult. When a principal was unable to give a specific figure, he was encouraged to indicate the mid-point of the range within which the exact value probably lay. If a principal had no idea as to the appropriate figure or range for his school, his response was coded as "don't know."

Of the 501 principals who were interviewed by the staff of the National Principalship Study, 490 (98 per cent) were able to provide an estimate for each of the six indices of SES. These principals and the teachers in their schools who completed the teacher questionnaire are the subjects of the School SES Study.

The variability in the socioeconomic composition of urban public school attendance districts is clearly shown in Figure 2-1. It presents a distribution of the principals' estimates in answer to the question regarding the percentage of pupils from homes where the father is an unskilled or semiskilled worker. Thirty-eight of the principals estimated that for their school the percentage is less than 10, while 71 estimated that it was at least 90 (Figure 2-1).

A more stable summary of the SES of each school than that provided by a single estimate of the principal was needed. Therefore, the six estimates of the 490 principals were combined through the statistical procedure of factor analysis, and the resulting weights on the first principal component were used to compute a "School SES Score"

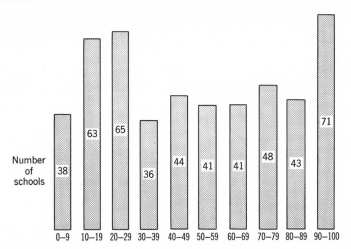

FIGURE 2-1. Frequency distribution of 490 elementary, junior, and senior high schools according to the percentage of pupils whose fathers are unskilled or semiskilled workers.

for each school.[12] As a check on its validity, the School SES Score was compared with information obtained by the 1960 United States Census. We were well aware that, for many reasons, census data are not a perfect criterion for use in evaluating the estimates of principals about their schools. Such factors as the lack of congruency between census tract and school attendance district boundaries, the enrollment of some children at parochial and private schools, and the variation between the socioeconomic characteristics of the general adult population and those adults who are the parents of school-age children can all converge to weaken such a comparison. It was, therefore, encouraging to find that for the 42 elementary schools in which the school attendance district and census tract boundaries were both known and reasonably similar, the rank order correlation between the pooled principals' estimates and the pooled census figures was .81.[13]

[12] For the means, standard deviations, and correlation coefficients, as well as the resulting factor matrix, see Appendix Tables 2A-1 and 2A-2. For a discussion of the statistical technique of factor analysis see Harry H. Harman, *Modern Factor Analysis* (Chicago: University of Chicago Press, 1960).

[13] The corresponding figures for 32 junior high schools and 28 senior high schools are .68 and .64 respectively. The design and execution of these three comparisons was conducted by Dean K. Whitla and Joseph Hozid, two of our colleagues with the National Principalship Study. We are indebted to them for permission to refer to their unpublished work.

The School SES score is a continuous variable running from a low of 1 to a high of 20 with an average value of 8.00 and a standard deviation of 4.27.[14] The SES of the 490 schools varies widely, more notably at the high end of the scale than at the low (Figure 2-2). This is not surprising, since within American society there is in general much greater range in wealth than in poverty. Minimum education and wage laws, unemployment compensation, and aid to dependent children, for example, all support a minimum socioeconomic status, and although graduated income and inheritance taxes tend to limit

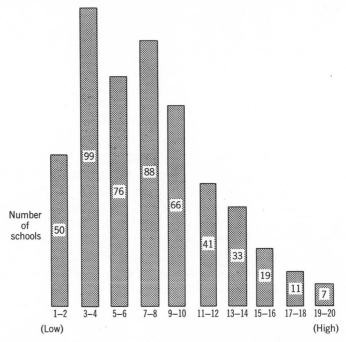

FIGURE 2-2. Frequency distribution of 490 schools according to the value of their school socioeconomic status (SES) score.

high incomes, incomes do not approach the mean as much at the higher as at the lower end of the socioeconomic scale.

Another factor which may be reflected in the small number of schools of very high SES (Figure 2-2) is the general migration of middle-class families from the central city to the more desirable

[14] The actual score resulting from the factor analysis and scoring procedure is continuous with a mean of 0.00 and a standard deviation of 4.27. In order to avoid a discussion of negative score values, the constant 8.00 was added to all scores.

suburbs, many of which have populations of less than 50,000 and, therefore, would not have been involved in the National Principalship Study.

Secondary schools are larger and draw students from more hetero-

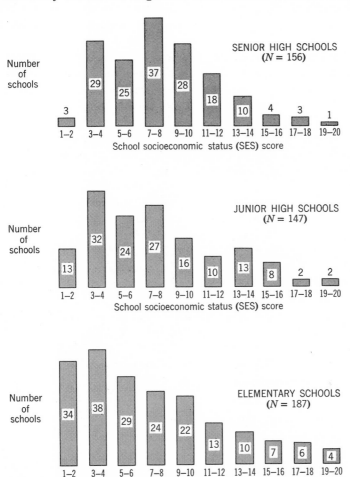

FIGURE 2-3. Frequency distribution, by level, of 490 schools according to the value of their school socioeconomic status (SES) score.

geneous backgrounds than do elementary schools; they also lose many students of low SES who "drop out" before graduation. It is therefore not surprising to find that although there are roughly equal numbers of elementary, junior, and senior high schools in the School SES Study,

34 (68 per cent) of the 50 schools assigned the very low School SES score of 1 or 2 are at the elementary level, whereas only 13 (26 per cent) are junior high schools and 3 (6 per cent) senior high schools (Figure 2-3). Similarly, of the 7 schools with the very high SES score of 19 or 20, 4 (57 per cent) are elementary, whereas only 2 (38 per cent) and 1 (15 per cent) are junior or senior high schools respectively (Figure 2-3).

Because the socioeconomic status of schools is related to their school level, we found it desirable to consider the effects of School SES upon school personnel separately in elementary, junior and senior high schools. In this way, the variable of school level could not confuse us about the impact of School SES. In order to simplify our consideration of the relationship of School SES to the characteristics, attitudes, and behavior of pupils, teachers, and principals, we shall in general confine our presentation in the text to the elementary schools. In Chapter 9, however, we shall consider whether the level of a school affects many of the relationships under consideration, while in the detailed tables which are appended to this monograph (Appendix A), the summary statistics and tests of significance for most of the variables are presented for all three levels.

For purposes of simplifying the presentation of our data it was also decided, in general, to limit the number of categories of School SES by dividing the 187 elementary schools into 4 groups of approximately 47 each, according to their position on the School SES variable. These groups have been named "highest," "moderately high," "moderately low," and "lowest" School SES. Similarly, the 147 junior high schools were divided into 4 groups of approximately 37 each and the 156 senior high schools into groups of 39.

CHARACTERISTICS OF FOUR TYPES
OF ELEMENTARY SCHOOLS

The SES of a school is not necessarily the same as the SES of the neighborhood in which a school is located. Many people live near a school but have no children in attendance there. Moreover, a school's attendance roster may include pupils who reside in other sections of the city. In this study School SES refers to the socioeconomic status of the aggregated clients of a school, rather than to the residents of its geographical area.

What are the characteristics of the 187 urban elementary schools which have been classified as "highest," "moderately high," "moderately low," and "lowest" in School SES? Since these schools have been operationally defined in terms of their relative positions on the School SES continuum, we already know, for example, that they differ in the proportion of pupils whose fathers are unskilled or semiskilled workers. We do not know the magnitude of these and the other differences implied by the School SES score.

However, on examination we find that in the average elementary school of highest SES only 17 per cent of the fathers of pupils are unskilled or semiskilled workers; in the average school in the lowest category, 89 per cent are unskilled or semiskilled (Figure 2-4). Similarly, in the average school of highest SES in only 20 per cent of the families neither parent has gone beyond high school; in the average school of lowest SES the figure is 94 per cent (Figure 2-5). With respect to income, in the average school of highest SES 13 per cent

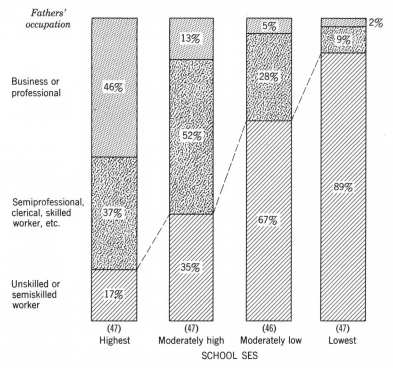

FIGURE 2-4. Occupational level of pupils' fathers, by school SES. (This and all subsequent figures in this chapter present data comparing the average *elementary* school in each of the four SES categories. Unless otherwise indicated, the reporter is the school principal. The figures in parentheses indicate the number of schools in that category.)

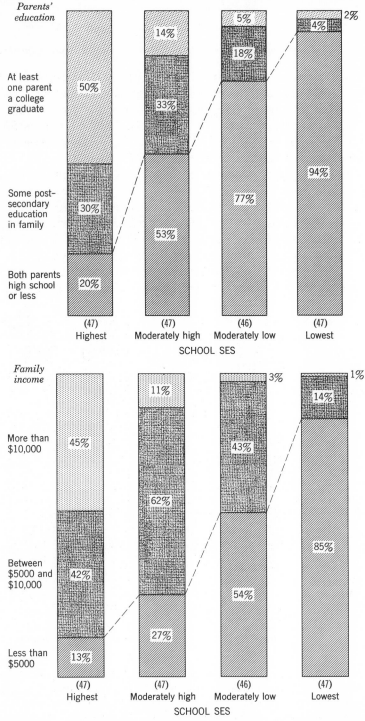

FIGURE 2-5 (*top*). Educational level of pupils' parents, by school SES.
FIGURE 2-6 (*bottom*). Income level of pupils' parents, by school SES.

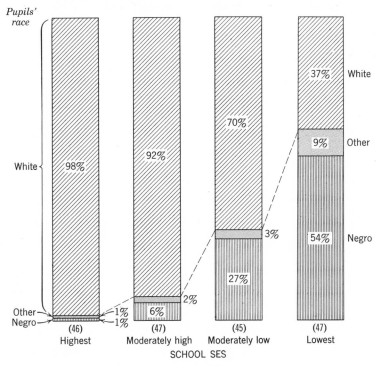

FIGURE 2-7. Race of pupils, by school SES.

of the families have incomes of less than $5000; in the lowest, 85 per cent (Figure 2-6).

Such differences are equally pronounced when one examines the percentages for the high categories of occupation, education, and income. (For similar data on junior and senior high schools, see Appendix Table 2A-3.) Clearly, the four categories of School SES reflect rather different socioeconomic contexts. What factors in addition to education, occupation, and income are reflected by these categories?

Race and socioeconomic status are highly intertwined.[15] In the School SES study we deliberately omitted racial characteristics from our definition of SES so that we could study them separately and, if possible, control for their association. That such an association exists, is seen in Figure 2-7. Whereas, according to the reports of princi-

[15] E. Franklin Frazier, *The Negro Family in the United States* (Chicago: University of Chicago Press, 1939); Gunnar Myrdal, *An American Dilemma* (New York: Harper and Brothers, 1944); Eli Ginzberg, *The Negro Potential* (New York: Columbia University Press, 1956); and Thomas F. Pettigrew, *A Profile of the Negro American* (Princeton, New Jersey: D. Van Nostrand Company, Inc., 1964), pp. 168–176.

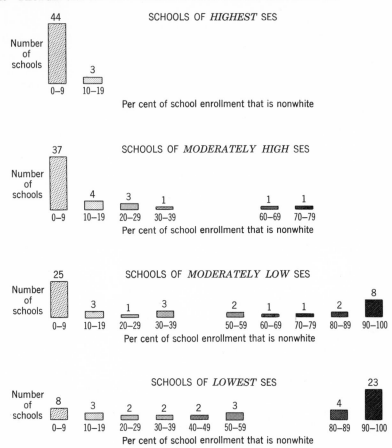

FIGURE 2-8. Frequency distribution of the proportion of school enrollment that is nonwhite, by school SES.

pals, only 2 per cent of the pupils in the average school of highest SES are nonwhite,[16] in the lowest 63 per cent are nonwhite (Figure 2-7). This distribution in the racial characteristics of schools of different SES is best seen in Figure 2-8. Of the 47 elementary schools in

[16] For the purposes of this study, we have grouped together and designated as "nonwhite" all Mexican, Oriental, and Puerto Rican individuals as well as those who are Negro. As Figure 2-7 indicates, the proportion of "nonwhite" pupils who are not Negro is very small.

the highest SES category, 44 have fewer than 10 per cent nonwhite students (22 have none), while in the 47 schools of lowest SES only 8 have fewer than 10 per cent nonwhite (3 have none). At the other end of the racial continuum, no school of highest SES is more than 19 per cent nonwhite while 23 of the schools of lowest SES are more than 90 per cent nonwhite (10 are 100 per cent). (Similar statistics for junior and senior high schools as well as tests of significance for all three levels are presented in Appendix Table 2A-4).

Although our major interest is the socioeconomic status of schools irrespective of racial differences, such racial distinctions as can be observed in Figures 2-7 and 2-8 suggest that relationships between the SES of schools and the characteristics, attitudes, and behavior of teachers and principals *may be* produced by the strong association between School SES and the racial composition of the student body.

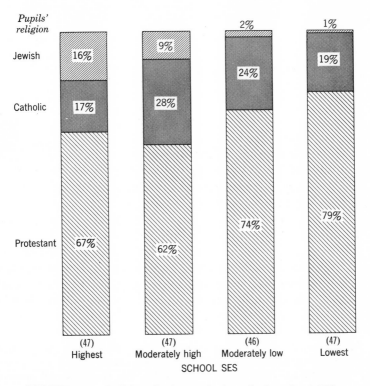

FIGURE 2-9. Religious background of pupils, by school SES.

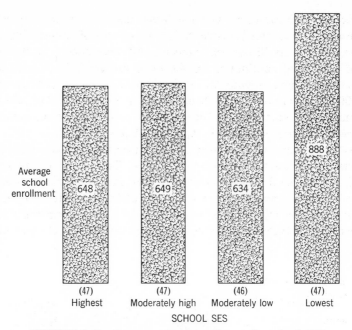

FIGURE 2-10. Average school enrollment, by school SES.

However, in the light of evidence to be presented in Chapter 10, this is unlikely to be the case.

The difference in the religious composition of schools of different SES as reported by the principals is slight in comparison with that of race. In general, the proportion of pupils from Jewish homes declines from the highest to the lowest SES groups and that of the Protestant pupils increases. More pupils are Catholic in schools of moderate than in those of highest or lowest SES (Figure 2-9).[17]

The size of the pupil enrollment of the schools of lowest and highest SES also varies. Whereas the average urban elementary school of highest, moderately high, and moderately low SES each has an enrollment of less than 650 pupils, that of the lowest SES enrolls 888 pupils (Figure 2-10).[18] To some extent this difference may be attribut-

[17] See Appendix Table 2A-3 for the similar data on junior and senior high schools, as well as for all tests of statistical significance.

[18] See Appendix Table 2A-5 for the similar data on junior and senior high schools, as well as for all tests of statistical significance.

able to overcrowding in the schools of lowest SES. Although the enrollment in the average school of highest SES is only 98 per cent of that
for which the building was designed (according to the principals), that
in the school of lowest SES is 109 per cent (Figure 2-11).[19] No doubt
the migration of middle class families to the suburbs and the influx
of lower status families to the slum areas has contributed to this
discrepancy.

The differences in the size of the schools of different SES and
in the extent to which their buildings are utilized are not, however,
reflected in their pupil-teacher ratios. The 47 elementary schools of
lowest SES contain 41,749 pupils and 1369 teachers, a pupil to teacher
ratio of 30.50. In the 47 elementary schools of highest SES, the 30,449
pupils are instructed by 1009 teachers for an average of 30.18 pupils
per teacher (Figure 2-12).[20] Thus, on the average, there appears to
be no "socioeconomic bias" in the pupil-teacher ratio in schools of
different SES.[21]

The sample schools are found in all four major regions of the

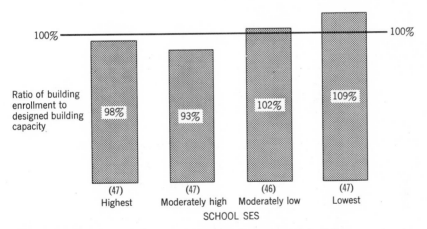

FIGURE 2-11. Ratio of building enrollment to designed building capacity, by
school SES.

[19] See Appendix Table 2A-6 for the similar data on junior and senior high
schools, as well as for all tests of statistical significance.

[20] See Appendix Table 2A-7 for the similar data on junior and senior high
schools, as well as for all tests of statistical significance.

[21] Figure 2-12 does not reflect the number of part-time or assistant teachers
assigned to elementary schools of different SES, nor the extent to which subject
matter specialists are used to relieve teaching loads.

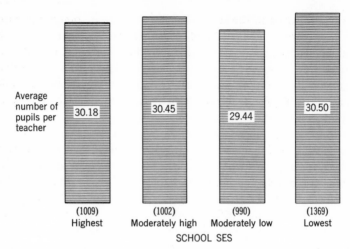

FIGURE 2-12. Pupil-teacher ratio, by school SES.

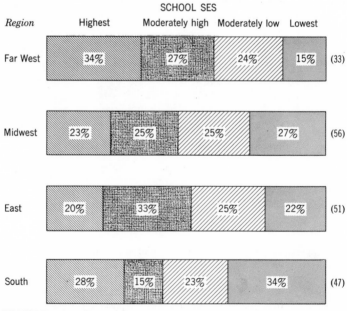

FIGURE 2-13. Proportion of elementary schools in each school SES category, by region.

United States (Figure 2-13). Although within each region the four categories of School SES are not equally represented (the Far West is "overrepresented" with schools of highest SES and "underrepresented" with those of lowest SES) the over-all differences are not significant statistically and probably reflect actual differences in the varied socioeconomic structure of the several regions of the United States, as well as differences in the extent to which parents choose to send their children to "nonpublic" schools.[22]

With respect to the size of the city in which the elementary schools of different SES are located, a larger percentage of those of lowest SES are, as might be expected, in cities of more than 1 million inhabitants than are in cities of between 50,000 and 250,000 inhabitants. The converse is true for schools of highest SES (Figure 2-14). However, the over-all association of School SES and size of city is not significant statistically.[23] Just as the findings of the School SES Study are unlikely to be merely a function of the different racial com-

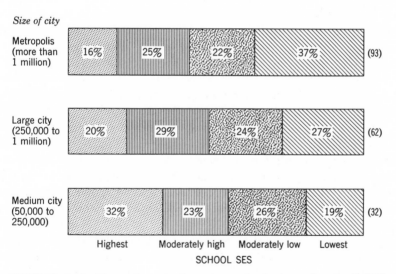

FIGURE 2-14. Proportion of elementary schools in each school SES category, by size of city.

[22] See Appendix Table 2A-8 for similar data on junior and senior high schools, as well as for all tests of statistical significance.

[23] See Appendix Table 2A-9 for the similar data on junior and senior high schools, as well as for all tests of statistical significance.

positions of the schools, they are unlikely to be merely a function of the particular cities in which the schools are located.[24]

SOME ADDITIONAL METHODOLOGICAL NOTES

In the interest of readability, most statistical considerations and all tests of statistical significance have been deleted from the tables and text of this monograph and inserted in a technical appendix. Through this research we are attempting to discover, within a sample, relationships that are likely to hold for a universe of schools in cities with populations of 50,000 or more. It is therefore appropriate to assess the probability that associations which we find in this sample are unrepresentative, and would not have been found if we had studied all 11,000 schools. However, because of the very complex multistage cluster sampling design used by the National Principalship Study we have been unable to do more than simply make rough estimates of the sampling error associated with the many statistics we report.[25]

Unless otherwise noted, all relationships reported in this book are *estimated* to be statistically significant at below the .05 level. This, of course, does not necessarily mean that they have *practical* significance. With large samples (such as that of our teachers), "small" differences among categories of School SES are frequently significant statistically; while with small samples (such as that of our principals), "large" differences are frequently not significant statistically.

In order to simplify our discussion we focus on differences between only the highest and lowest categories of School SES, rather than on differences among all four categories. Although for illustrative purposes we shall present data for the moderately high and moderately low categories of the elementary schools, the tests of statistical significance for all data presented in Chapters 3 through 7 have compared only the two extreme groups. Occasionally, when a particularly interesting pattern with respect to the two middle groups emerges within our data, we shall note it in order to make clear that the relationship between School SES and other variables is not always monotonic.

---

[24] Of the six tests of statistical significance involving the relationship of School SES and region or size of city, only that between School SES and size of city within the senior high schools was statistically significant (Appendix Tables 2A-8 and 2A-9).

[25] For a further discussion of this point, see Chapter 11.

Two basic types of comparison among schools of different SES are employed in this book. In one type of comparison the unit of analysis is the *school* while in the other it is the *individual*. This distinction is particularly relevant with respect to our examination of pupils and teachers, since in each case there is more than one individual per school. In general, when using data about pupils or teachers to characterize their school, these characterizations have involved averaging within each school and thus the unit of analysis becomes the school. However, when using data about pupils or teachers to characterize themselves, no averaging within schools is necessary and the unit of analysis remains the individual.

It is essential to note that many of our comparisons of schools of different SES are based on averages within each of the SES categories. In general, for each variable considered, as many schools will be above the average of their SES category as below, although most will be fairly close to it. One of the purposes of our tests of statistical significance is to take into account such variability *within* the categories of highest and lowest SES when making judgements about differences *between* them.

In all graphs and tables, schools of the highest, moderately high, moderately low, and lowest SES are presented in that order from left to right. We have arranged the categories in this way in order to view the schools of lower SES within the frame of reference of those of higher SES. In addition, the scales of the bar and line graphs presented here are not always identical. Therefore, small differences may appear larger in some figures than they do in others. This has been done to make all graphic representation as readable as possible. When it is intended that the reader make comparisons between graphs, we have been careful to place them in the same figure and to represent all units with an identical scale.

One final methodological note: almost all of the relationships examined in this book are between two variables, School SES and each of many factors thought to be associated with it. Obviously, many of these bivariate relationships could be elaborated through the introduction of additional variables. Since so little is known about the effects of School SES on teachers and principals, we have defined our objective as one of considering as many bivariate relationships as can be handled effectively in one monograph. Because of this goal of "exploration" rather than "explanation," we have generally been unable to examine in detail variables which may place conditions upon our findings, or which may intervene between School SES and the effects we have chosen to study.[26] However, we have considered in some detail such variables as School Race and School Level which might lead us to make a spurious interpretation of an observed relationship, and on occasion we have introduced other third variables for purposes of clarification. We hope that, with "aerial surveys" such as this in hand, future investigators can begin to map in greater detail the "topography" of the urban school from the perspective of the socioeconomic status of its clientele.

[26] For discussions of the logic and method for the introduction of third variables into two variable analyses, see Patricia L. Kendall and Paul F. Lazarsfeld, "Problems of Survey Analysis, Part 1: Accounting for Statistical Relationships," in Robert K. Merton and Paul F. Lazarsfeld (Editors), *Continuities in Social Research* (Glencoe, Illinois: The Free Press, 1950), pp. 135–167; Paul F. Lazarsfeld, "Interpretation of Statistical Relations as a Research Operation," in Paul F. Lazarsfeld and Morris Rosenberg (Editors), *The Language of Social Research* (Glencoe, Illinois: The Free Press, 1955), pp. 115–125; Herbert H. Hyman, *Survey Design and Analysis: Principles, Cases and Procedures* (Glencoe, Illinois: The Free Press, 1955); or Paul F. Lazarsfeld, "The Algebra of Dichotomous Systems," in Herbert Solomon (Editor), *Studies in Item Analysis and Prediction* (Stanford: Stanford University Press, 1961), pp. 111–157.

Chapter 3

SOME PUPIL AND PARENTAL
CORRELATES OF SCHOOL SES

In the previous chapter we described the schools which we have called "highest," "moderately high," "moderately low," and "lowest" in SES in terms of three indicators of SES (occupation, education, and income) and in terms of several other demographic variables. In this chapter we shall elaborate our discussion of the socioeconomic composition of urban schools by considering some of the attitudes and behavior of pupils and parents often found to be correlated with SES. We will not introduce data with respect to the "realities" of these attitudes and behavior, but rather with respect to how principals and teachers *perceive* them. If our major focus were the pupils in schools of different SES, then it would be essential to report data obtained from the pupils themselves, but our major focus is the schools' staffs. If we are to understand why staff attitudes and behavior may vary with the socioeconomic composition of the schools in which they work, we must gain insight into how they *view* the pupils and parents with whom they interact. The fact that these reports yield results which are highly consistent between principals and teachers and with the research of other investigators suggests that, although no doubt affected by perception, they may also be fairly realistic. In the eyes of the principals and teachers, what are the pupil and parental characteristics of schools at different SES levels?

Inferences about the nation as a whole cannot be made from research utilizing local samples, nor can direct inferences about staff perceptions be made through data gathered from the pupils themselves. But, arguing from what is known through such research, we would expect to find great differences in the way principals and teachers in schools different in SES perceive the attitudes and behavior of parents and pupils. In particular, we predict that the lower the School SES, the more family instability, the weaker the parental encouragement, the lower the pupils' achievement, and the less desirable their behavior, as perceived by principals and teachers.

To test these predictions, we turned first to those interviews and questionnaires of the National Principalship Study in which principals were asked to estimate the percentage of pupils or parents exhibiting certain background and behavioral characteristics. The replies to more than 50 relevant questions, when averaged within each category of schools, showed that over 90 per cent of the characteristics of pupils and parents vary significantly and, for the most part, monotonically by School SES. Moreover, the direction of the variation is without exception as predicted: that is, to the "disadvantage" of pupils in schools of low SES. Thus, the lower the School SES, the greater the proportion of pupils who are believed to come from unstable homes, whose pace of learning and behavior in school do not meet standards and whose parents allegedly fail to support the school program so as to stimulate their children to a greater achievement and better behavior.[1]

HOME BACKGROUND

One variable which might be taken to represent all of the others here considered is the reply of the principals to the question: "What per cent of the students in your school have emotional or social problems?" The question is far from precise. Some principals may have understood it to refer to grave personality maladjustment or serious family disorganization. Indeed, there is ample evidence that these phenomena are related to social and economic status[2] so that their asso-

---

[1] Within this chapter all reported differences are statistically significant. See Appendix Tables 3A-1 through 3A-4 for the complete data referred to in this chapter. This includes that referred to in the text and that omitted due to space limitations, as well as data for all tests of statistical significance.

[2] August B. Hollingshead, *Elmtown's Youth* (New York: John Wiley and Sons, 1949), Chapter V; Lee G. Burchinal, Bruce Gardner, and Glenn R. Hawkes, "Children's Personality Adjustment and the Socio-economic Status of Their Families," *Journal of Genetic Psychology*, XCII (1958), pp. 149–159; Emile Heintz, "Adjustment Problems of Class Status," *Phi Delta Kappan*, XXX (1949), pp. 290–293; and James V. Mitchell, Jr., "Identification of Items in the California

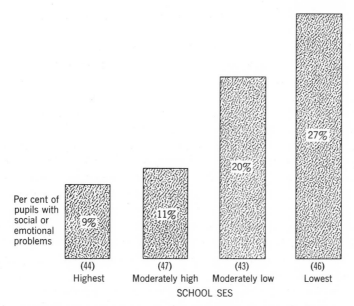

FIGURE 3-1. The lower the school SES, the greater the proportion of pupils with social or emotional problems. (All figures
and tables in this chapter present data comparing the average
elementary school in each of the four school SES categories.
Unless otherwise indicated, the reporter is the school principal.)

ciations with School SES in the present study would not be surprising.
Others probably took the item as a short-hand reference to any handicap a child may bring to school. In either case, we would expect to
find that significantly more children in schools of lowest SES (than
in schools of highest SES) are perceived to suffer from social or emotional problems. This is borne out by the data: the average percentage
reported by the principals rises from 9 in the elementary schools in
the highest SES category to 27 in the schools in the lowest category
(Figure 3-1).[3] In other words, in schools in the poorest neighborhoods
three times as many children are believed by their principals to have

Test of Personality that Differentiate between Subjects of High and Low SES
at the Fifth and Seventh Grade Levels," *Journal of Educational Research*, LI
(1957), pp. 241–250.

[3] See Appendix Table 3A-1 for similar data on junior and senior high schools,
as well as for all tests of statistical significance. For a consideration of this
variable with the effect of race held constant, see Table 10-4. The effect of
race on a number of other variables discussed in this chapter is also examined
in Chapter 10.

social and emotional problems as in schools in the most favored neighborhoods.

The tables and figures which follow suggest some of the problems which are seen to plague more of the children in schools of lowest SES than their contemporaries.

If the school's SES is low, its pupils are more apt than other children to suffer deprivation. Their homes lack both tangibles and intangibles—adequate food, clothing, medical attention, as well as educated parents and cultural stimulation. How well, in the view of the principals, are such specific needs met among pupils attending schools in the four categories of SES? They report that in the average school of lowest SES over one-third of the children are without adequate diet and one-fifth are without adequate clothing, as compared with 13 per cent and 1 per cent, respectively, in the average school of highest SES. The difference in the proportion of children with poor teeth is in the same direction, probably a reflection of SES differences in diet and medical attention (Figure 3-2).

School personnel may be more troubled by the family instability than by the physical deprivation suffered by their pupils. The principals were asked to estimate the percentage of their pupils who come from broken homes, from homes receiving some type of welfare or relief payment, from homes where the mother is employed full time, and the percentage who had transferred from other schools in the previous school year. It was found that the lower the SES, the greater the reported incidence of each type of instability. Thus, although 90 per cent of the children in the average elementary school of highest SES are reported by the principal to be living with both mother and father, this is true of only 63 per cent in the schools of lowest SES. Similarly, on the average, 21 per cent of the mothers of pupils in the highest SES category, but 39 per cent in the lowest, hold full-time jobs. Although practically no families are reported to be on any type of welfare in the average school of highest SES, one-quarter are reported to be receiving some form of public assistance in the schools of lowest SES (Table 3-1). All of these differences were predictable, in direction and magnitude, from previous research.[4]

The average SES difference in both inter- and intrapupil transiency as reported by elementary school principals is not as large for

---

[4] James B. Conant, *Slums and Suburbs* (New York: McGraw-Hill Book Company, Inc., 1961); Martin Deutsch, *Minority Group and Class Status as Related to Social and Personality Factors in Scholastic Achievement* (Ithaca, New York: Society for Applied Anthropology, Monograph No. 2, 1960); Patricia Sexton *Education and Income* (New York: The Viking Press, 1961).

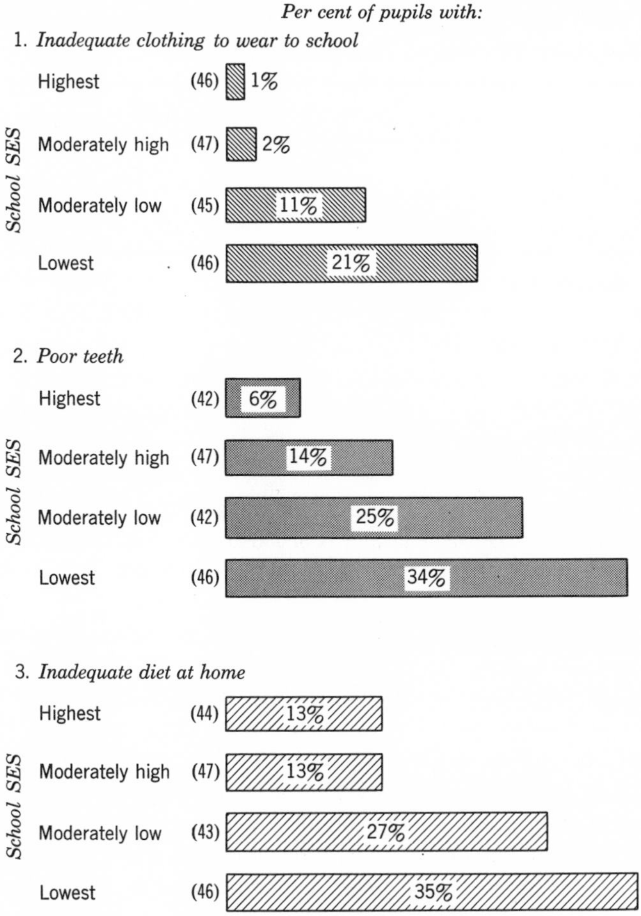

Per cent of pupils with:

1. *Inadequate clothing to wear to school*

School SES

Highest (46) 1%

Moderately high (47) 2%

Moderately low (45) 11%

Lowest (46) 21%

2. *Poor teeth*

School SES

Highest (42) 6%

Moderately high (47) 14%

Moderately low (42) 25%

Lowest (46) 34%

3. *Inadequate diet at home*

School SES

Highest (44) 13%

Moderately high (47) 13%

Moderately low (43) 27%

Lowest (46) 35%

FIGURE 3-2. The lower the school SES, the greater the proportion of pupils who suffer from deprivation.

the nation as a whole as it has been found to be from time to time in certain cities.[5] Nevertheless, the fact that *twice* as many pupils are reported to have transferred into the average school of lowest (as compared to highest) SES during the 1960 to 1961 school year (Table 3-1) probably makes a considerable difference in the impression of stability perceived by principals and teachers.

[5] Sexton, *op. cit.*, p. 96; Hermine I. Popper, *How Difficult Are the Difficult Schools?* (New York: Public Education Association, 1959), p. 13; and Benjamin C. Willis, "The Quest for Quality Education in a Major City," in Bobby J. Chandler, Lindley J. Stiles, and John I. Kitsuse, *Education in Urban Society* (New York: Dodd, Mead and Company, 1962), pp. 211–232.

TABLE 3-1. The Lower the School SES, the Greater the Proportion of Pupils Who Have Experienced Home Instability

	School SES			
Per cent of pupils in the average school who:	Highest $(N_m = 46)$[a]	Moderately High $(N_m = 46)$[a]	Moderately Low $(N_m = 46)$[a]	Lowest $(N_m = 46)$[a]
1. Come from broken homes.	10%	16%	23%	37%
2. Come from families on welfare.	1	4	13	26
3. Have mothers employed full-time.	21	29	40	39
4. Transferred into your school this year.	11	16	18	24

[a] N_m stands for the *median* number of schools for which data are available on these four items. See Appendix Table 3A-1 for exact Ns.

PARENTAL REINFORCEMENT

Just as differences in School SES mean great differences in the economic and social security of the average child, so, too, differences in School SES reflect differences in the part played by parents in his socialization and in the support they give to the values of the school.

A number of studies have found that parental values, aspirations for their children, modes of discipline, and patterns of child rearing, all vary according to social class.[6] Our data lead to a similar conclu-

[6] Richard A. Cloward and James A. Jones, "Social Class: Educational Attitudes and Participation," in A. Harry Passow (Editor), *Education in Depressed Areas* (New York: Bureau of Publications, Teachers College, Columbia University, 1963), pp. 190–216; Allison Davis and Robert J. Havighurst, "Social Class and Color Differences in Child-Rearing," *American Sociological Review,* XI (1946), pp. 698–710; Herbert H. Hyman, "The Value Systems of Different Classes: A Social Psychological Contribution to the Analysis of Stratification," in Reinhard Bendix and Seymour M. Lipset (Editors), *Class, Status and Power* (Glencoe, Illinois: The Free Press, 1953), pp. 426–442; Melvin L. Kohn, "Social Class and the Exercise of Parental Authority," *American Sociological Review,* XXIV (1959), pp. 352–366; George Psathas, "Ethnicity, Social Class, and Adolescent Independence from Parental Control," *American Sociological Review,* XXII (1957), pp. 415–423; Albert J. Reiss, Jr. and Albert L. Rhodes, "Are Educational Norms and Goals of Conforming, Truant and Delinquent Adolescents Influenced by Group Position in American Society?" *Journal of Negro Educa-*

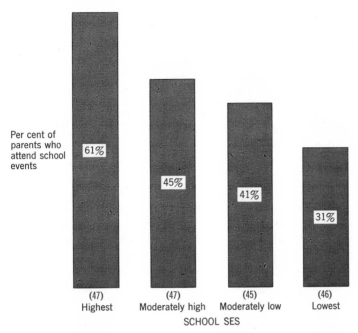

Per cent of
parents who
attend school
events

61%

45%

41%

31%

| (47) | (47) | (45) | (46) |
| Highest | Moderately high | Moderately low | Lowest |

SCHOOL SES

FIGURE 3-3. The lower the school SES, the lower is parental attendance at school events.

sion: we found that the principals' perceptions of the frequency of parental visits to the schools, the percentage of parents who supervise their children adequately, and the percentage who show interest in their children's school work all vary with School SES. In the first place, the lower the SES, the lower the parental attendance at school events. According to the principals, nearly two-thirds of the parents usually attend events in the average elementary school of highest SES; the proportion drops to under one-third in the average school of lowest SES (Figure 3-3).[7] Not only is parental attendance at school events related to School SES, but so too is the frequency with which parents come to school of their own initiative to discuss their children's problems. Thus, in the average school of highest SES, 53 per cent of the

tion, XXVIII (1959), pp. 252–267; Bernard C. Rosen, "Race, Ethnicity and the Achievement Syndrome," *American Sociological Review*, XXIV (1959), pp. 47–60; and Bernard C. Rosen, "The Achievement Syndrome: A Psychocultural Dimension of Social Stratification," *American Sociological Review*, XXI (1956), pp. 203–211.

[7] See Appendix Table 3A-2 for similar data on junior and senior high schools, as well as for all tests of statistical significance.

parents of children with learning problems, 52 per cent of the parents of those with social or emotional problems, and 34 per cent of the parents of those who misbehave are reported to initiate conferences. In contrast, in the group of schools of lowest SES, the comparable percentages drop to 14, 10, and 8 (Figure 3-4).

Whatever may contribute to decreasing parental attendance as SES drops—for example, a higher proportion of working mothers or large families, fatigue, ill health, and inability to pay for baby sitters or transportation—it would seem natural for principals and teachers to view the parents' poor attendance as an indication of indifference. But parental interest in their children's "academic achievement" was rated high by almost all these principals. Moreover, the differences in the percentage interested in academic achievement (86 per cent in the schools of highest SES and 61 per cent in those of lowest) are smaller than differences in the percentage interested in other aspects of school work (Figure 3-5). It is noteworthy that principals perceive that even in schools in the most disadvantaged areas, a large majority

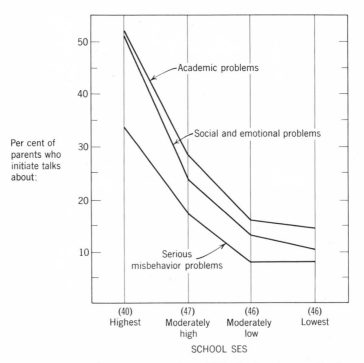

FIGURE 3-4. The lower the school SES, the less frequently do parents initiate talks with school staff about their children's problems.

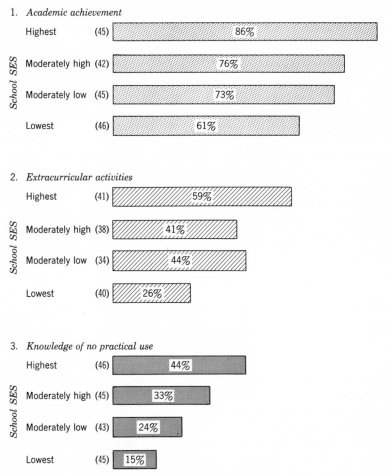

Per cent of parents reported interested in:

1. *Academic achievement*

School SES

Highest (45) 86%

Moderately high (42) 76%

Moderately low (45) 73%

Lowest (46) 61%

2. *Extracurricular activities*

School SES

Highest (41) 59%

Moderately high (38) 41%

Moderately low (34) 44%

Lowest (40) 26%

3. *Knowledge of no practical use*

School SES

Highest (46) 44%

Moderately high (45) 33%

Moderately low (43) 24%

Lowest (45) 15%

FIGURE 3-5. The lower the school SES, the smaller the proportion of parents "interested in their children's school work."

of the parents are interested in their children's performance. Apparently, the infrequency of parental visits to schools low in SES is, in the eyes of the administration, not an evidence of lack of interest; their conviction that the parents are concerned is corroborated by other research.[8]

[8] Cloward and Jones, *op. cit.;* Reiss and Rhodes, *op. cit.;* and Frank Riessman, *The Culturally Deprived Child* (New York: Harper and Row, 1962), Chapter II.

TABLE 3-2. The Lower the School SES, the Less Close the Parental Supervision

	School SES			
Per cent of parents in the average school who:	Highest $(N_m = 46)$	Moderately High $(N_m = 46)$	Moderately Low $(N_m = 45)$	Lowest $(N_m = 46)$
1. Adequately supervise their children during out-of-school hours.	80%	74%	58%	42%
2. Are overprotective of their children.	28	15	10	8
3. Push their children too hard.	21	13	11	7
4. Are able to control the behavior of their children.	83	86	77	69

Observers have frequently commented on the utilitarian conception of education of working-class people in contrast to that of white-collar or professional workers.[9] Our principals report that large numbers of parents in all strata place little value on knowledge that is of no practical use, but there is a significant difference between one SES category and another on this point. On the basis of his own observation, the principal of the average school in the highest category of SES estimates that 44 per cent of the parents are interested in having their children acquire "knowledge of no practical use"; in contrast, the principal in the average school in the lowest group puts the figure at 15 per cent (Figure 3-5).

Parental interest in the extracurricular activities of their children varies widely according to School SES. The percentage of interested parents as reported by the principals drops from 59 in the schools of highest SES to 26 in the schools of the lowest (Figure 3-5). It is possible that the utilitarian orientation of parents in the most deprived elementary school neighborhoods leads them to define extracurricular

[9] Herbert J. Gans, *The Urban Villagers* (Glencoe, Illinois: The Free Press, 1962), pp. 129–136; Riessman, *op. cit.,* p. 28; and Joseph A. Kahl, "Educational and Occupational Aspirations of 'Common Man' Boys," *Harvard Educational Review,* XXIII (1953), pp. 186–203.

activities as unnecessary luxuries, in comparison with the pressing need for learning how to earn bread and butter.

Parent-child relations also vary with School SES: the lower the SES, the weaker is parental supervision. In the average school of highest SES, principals report that 80 per cent of the parents provide "adequate" supervision and 83 per cent are able to control their children. But in the average school of lowest SES, principals estimate that only 42 per cent adequately supervise and only 69 per cent are in control. The record of the parents of high SES is, however, qualified by the fact that about one-quarter of them are reported to be "overprotective" or to "push their children too hard"; less than a tenth of the parents in schools at the other end of the SES spectrum are accused of being overzealous in supervision of their offspring (Table 3-2).

PUPILS' PERFORMANCE

As indicated in Chapter 1, the relation of School SES to staff characteristics can be considered the effect of the "input" of a formal organization on its workers. From this point of view, differences in home background and parental reinforcement of the school, such as those reviewed in this chapter, would indicate differences in the "raw material" with which teachers work. Pupil achievement and discipline, on the other hand, are the product of the school as much as its raw material. The output of the same pupils placed in a different school situation could be quite different. The input of one school year is thus a function of the output of the previous school year, as well as a function of forces outside of the school.

Nevertheless, the studies cited in Chapter 1 indicate that academic achievement and classroom behavior are usually related both to the SES of the individual and to the SES composition of the school he attends. We would therefore predict significant differences by School SES in the reports of staff on these characteristics of their pupils.

Achievement

The principals' reports as to the mean and range of the IQs of their pupils are probably fairly reliable, since these statistics are generally available to school officials. As expected, the lower the School SES, the lower the mean IQ: whereas the average pupil in the average school of highest SES has an IQ of 109, his counterpart in the typical school of lowest SES has an IQ of 94 (Figure 3-6).[10] Similarly, the lower the School SES, the smaller the proportion of pupils with IQs of over 120 and the greater the proportion with IQs under 90 (Figure 3-7). Studies of the possible cultural bias of IQ tests suggest that many circumstances may contribute to the differences noted here: among these are social class differences in motivation and speed on tests, in familiarity with the testing situation, with the language used, and with the items referred to.[11]

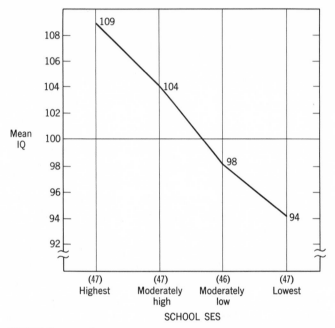

FIGURE 3-6. The lower the school SES, the lower the mean IQ of its pupils.

Retardation is a phenomenon relatively rare in the school of high SES and common where the SES is low. The principals were asked for the percentage of pupils in their schools who "have stayed back one year or more," "are one year or more behind in arithmetic,"

[10] See Appendix Table 3A-3 for similar data on junior and senior high schools as well as for all tests of statistical significance.

[11] Kenneth W. Eels, *Intellectual and Cultural Differences: A Study of Cultural Learning and Problem Solving* (Chicago: University of Chicago Press, 1951); and Ernest A. Haggard, "Social-Status and Intelligence: An Experimental Study of Certain Cultural Determinants of Measured Intelligence," *Genetic Psychological Monographs*, XLIX (1954), pp. 141–186.

and "are one year or more behind in reading." In the average school in the lowest SES category, 20 per cent had stayed back one year or more, 36 per cent were behind in arithmetic, and 43 per cent (close to one-half) were lagging in reading. In the average school of highest SES, these percentages are all 10 or below (Figure 3-8).[12] It is also clear that less than one-half of the students of any given SES category who are reported to be retarded in one of the basic skills have on

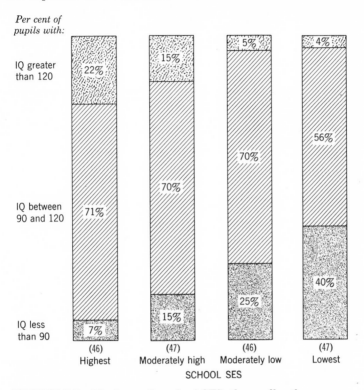

FIGURE 3-7. The lower the school SES, the smaller the proportion of pupils with IQs greater than 120, and the larger the proportion of pupils with IQs less than 90.

those grounds been made to repeat a school year. Moreover, differences by SES are greater in the percentage reported to be behind in arithmetic than in the percentage reported to have repeated, and in the

[12] For a similar finding with respect to reading retardation in schools of different SES, see Allen H. Barton and David E. Wilder, "Research and Practice in the Teaching of Reading: A Progress Report," in Matthew B. Miles (Editor), *Innovation in Education* (New York: Bureau of Publications, Teachers College, Columbia University, 1964), Table 9.

Per cent of pupils who:

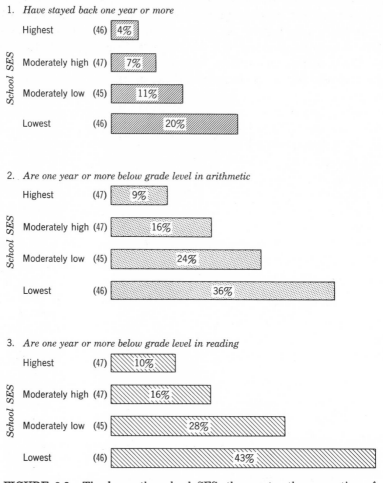

1. *Have stayed back one year or more*

<table>
<tr><td>Highest</td><td>(46)</td><td>4%</td></tr>
<tr><td>Moderately high</td><td>(47)</td><td>7%</td></tr>
<tr><td>Moderately low</td><td>(45)</td><td>11%</td></tr>
<tr><td>Lowest</td><td>(46)</td><td>20%</td></tr>
</table>

2. *Are one year or more below grade level in arithmetic*

<table>
<tr><td>Highest</td><td>(47)</td><td>9%</td></tr>
<tr><td>Moderately high</td><td>(47)</td><td>16%</td></tr>
<tr><td>Moderately low</td><td>(45)</td><td>24%</td></tr>
<tr><td>Lowest</td><td>(46)</td><td>36%</td></tr>
</table>

3. *Are one year or more below grade level in reading*

<table>
<tr><td>Highest</td><td>(47)</td><td>10%</td></tr>
<tr><td>Moderately high</td><td>(47)</td><td>16%</td></tr>
<tr><td>Moderately low</td><td>(45)</td><td>28%</td></tr>
<tr><td>Lowest</td><td>(46)</td><td>43%</td></tr>
</table>

FIGURE 3-8. The lower the school SES, the greater the proportion of pupils who are retarded.

percentage who are slow in reading than in the percentage who are behind in arithmetic.

The previous data that we have introduced have been based upon the reports of the 187 elementary school principals in our sample. As noted in Chapter 2, in the course of the National Principalship Study, ten teachers in each of the sample schools were asked a series of questions; their answers to one set of questions described their pupils by estimating the percentage with certain characteristics. Although, because of their different vantage points, principals and teachers may differ in their perception of the average proportion of pupils who share a given characteristic, we would not expect the reports of teachers to differ by School SES from those of principals.

Teachers and principals were both asked to estimate the proportion of pupils that they felt were not interested in learning. The teachers' replies are probably based on better evidence than those of the principals; nevertheless, both are subjective. Although principals are more favorable in their estimates than teachers, this discrepancy does not affect the relationship of the estimates of either to the schools' SES. In the average school of highest SES, 9 per cent of the pupils, according to the principals, and 14 per cent, according to the teachers, are not interested in learning. But in the average school in the category of lowest SES, 22 and 29 per cent, respectively, are felt to be uninterested (Figure 3-9).

Table 3-3 presents by School SES the replies of teachers to four additional questions which call for more objective data about the aca-

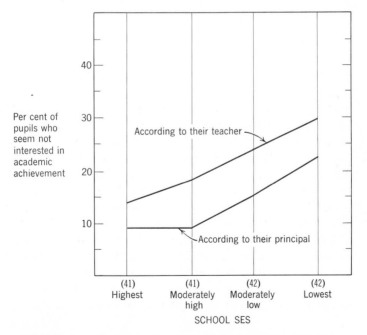

FIGURE 3-9. The lower the school SES, the greater the proportion of pupils "not interested in academic achievement."

TABLE 3-3.   The Lower the School SES, the Greater the Proportion of Pupils Whose Academic Performance Fails to Come up to the Expectations of Their Teachers

	School SES			
Per cent of pupils in the average school who:	Highest $(N = 38)$	Moderately High $(N = 35)$	Moderately Low $(N = 39)$	Lowest $(N = 39)$
1. Were not adequately prepared to do the grade level work you expected of them.	17%	21%	27%	38%
2. Are not mastering skills at minimum level of satisfactory performance.	11	13	19	27
3. Do not work up to their intellectual capacities.	43	49	46	51
4. Are one or more years behind grade level in reading ability.	12	19	31	39

demic performance of pupils. As in the case of the subjective item reported above, the replies to each are significantly related to School SES.[13] In schools lowest in SES, 39 per cent of the pupils are reported to be below grade level in reading, whereas this is true of only 12 per cent in the schools highest in SES. The difference is almost as great in the case of questions as to the percentage of pupils who "were not adequately prepared to do the level of work you expected of them when they entered your class," and "are not mastering the skills you teach at the minimum level of satisfactory performance." However, the difference between schools in the percentage who "do not work up to their intellectual capacities" appears to be of considerably less magnitude than was found for other questions. "Underachievers," it would seem, are perceived to be a frequent phenomenon in all schools.

[13] See Appendix Table 3A-4 for similar data on junior and senior high schools, as well as for all tests of statistical significance.

Discipline

We turn now to a presentation of SES differences in the reports of school behavior. In view of the widespread belief in the difficulty of maintaining discipline in slum schools, what is striking about the data to be presented is that differences by SES, while statistically significant, are nevertheless not as great as might be expected. Pupils in elementary schools of highest and lowest SES are apparently less different in nonacademic than in academic behavior.

Figure 3-10 shows that, as with academic performance, the reports of principals as to pupil classroom behavior are more favorable than are those of teachers. Could it be that principals feel more responsible and vulnerable on matters of the pupils' performance than do teachers and so, unconsciously or consciously, color their estimates accordingly? Or do teachers frequently handle discipline themselves with the result that principals are not aware of the extent of misbehavior in the classrooms? Also, it could be that the teachers' defensiveness works in the opposite direction from that of the principals; they may tend to describe their pupils in somewhat darker terms than is warranted by the facts, thereby removing the onus for lack of success from their own shoulders.

Be that as it may, the fact remains that neither optimism nor pessimism interferes with the relationship of the estimates of both principals and teachers to School SES. Thus the percentage of pupils who are reported to present constant problems in discipline is put by the average principal in schools of highest SES at 4 and by the average principal where SES is lowest at 9. Similarly, the percentages according to teachers are 9 and 16, respectively (Figure 3-10).

Table 3-4 presents the teachers' estimates in the average school in each SES category of the percentage of pupils whose behavior is undesirable or unacceptable. The greatest SES difference is among the percentage who seem lacking in self-discipline: 31 per cent in the average school of highest SES and 44 per cent in the average school of lowest SES. Although the differences by SES appear to diminish as we consider other items, they continue to be significant in the percentage who "are tolerant of fellow students from different backgrounds," "appear socially immature," or "have engaged in vandalism at school during the current school year."

Finally, we turn to the association of School SES with the replies of principals to the questions: "What percentage of the students in your school will probably drop out before they graduate from high

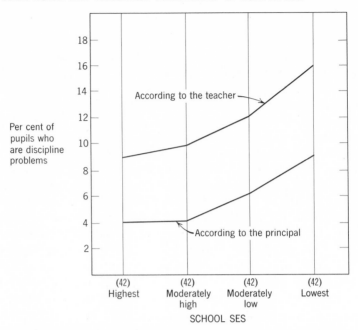

FIGURE 3-10. Teachers report more discipline problems than do principals, but according to both, the lower the school SES the greater the incidence of problems.

TABLE 3-4. The Lower the School SES, the Greater the Proportion of Pupils Whose Behavior is Sub-standard, as Reported by Teachers

	School SES			
Per cent of pupils in the average school who:	Highest (N = 38)	Moderately High (N = 35)	Moderately Low (N = 39)	Lowest (N = 39)
1. Do not show a sense of self-discipline.	31%	37%	42%	44%
2. Are not tolerant toward fellow students from different backgrounds.	14	15	18	23
3. Appear socially immature for their age.	12	15	20	21
4. Have engaged in vandalism at school during the current school year.	1	2	3	5

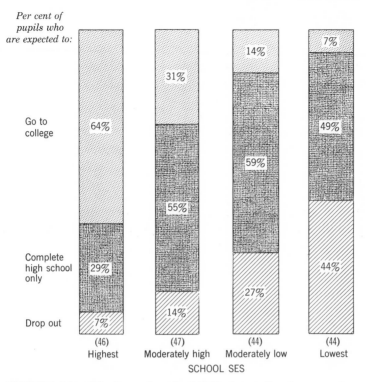

*Per cent of
pupils who
are expected to:*

Go to
college

Complete
high school
only

Drop out

(46)
Highest

(47)
Moderately high

(44)
Moderately low

(44)
Lowest

SCHOOL SES

FIGURE 3-11. The lower the school SES, the smaller the proportion
of pupils who "will go to college," and the greater the proportion
who "will drop out."

school?" "What percentage of the students in your school will probably go to college?" Some principals in the elementary schools may
have had at their disposal follow-up studies of the careers of former
pupils, but this would certainly not be true of many. Therefore, their
replies are likely to be subjective and derived from impressions rather
than facts and from their estimates of all the circumstances already
discussed: home conditions, parental interest and guidance, motivation,
achievement, and behavior in grade school. Since these are known to
exert a cumulative effect on learning and since many studies have
found that withdrawal from school and attendance at college are
closely related to SES, it is not surprising that our data reveal great
differences by School SES in the percentage of pupils expected by the
principals not to finish high school, to finish high school only, or to go
on to institutions of higher learning. In the average school of highest
SES, these elementary principals estimate that 64 per cent of the pu-

pils will go to college and 7 per cent will drop out; at the other end of the SES scale, however, only 7 per cent will go to college and 44 per cent will drop out (Figure 3-11).

Such are the differences, among schools categorized in terms of their social class composition, in principals' and teachers' perceptions of the characteristics of pupils and their parents. The lower the school in SES, the greater the proportion of pupils characterized in terms of economic deprivation, home instability, parental apathy, inadequate supervision, academic retardation, low motivation, and unacceptable behavior. As we turn to consider the association of School SES and school staff, it is important that the full meaning of the School SES variable, in terms of the characteristics of pupils, be kept in mind. Although their school buildings may be in sight of one another, the pupil inputs with which these four groups of principals and teachers work seem to be very different.

Chapter 4

SCHOOL SES AND THE CHARACTERISTICS AND ORIGINS OF TEACHERS

As we mentioned in Chapter 1, there are those who argue that school systems do not distribute their resources equally among schools of different SES, but favor middle-class schools in the building and maintenance of plant, in the allocation of teaching materials and special resources, and particularly in the assignment of staff.[1] Some evidence from our data in support of this "hypothesis of inequality" has been presented in Chapter 2, where it was shown that the elementary schools of lowest SES were larger and more apt to be "overutilized" than schools of higher SES.

In this chapter we shall consider a series of teacher variables which have often been introduced in discussions of inequality; variables such as the age of the teachers, their formal training, their years of experience, and their salary. It is usually assumed that teachers who are young and less experienced are also less effective in the classroom. On this basis one might argue that a predominance of younger and less experienced teachers in the schools of lowest SES constitutes evidence of a socioeconomic bias in the assignment of teacher resources.

However, it could also be argued that teaching in the schools of lowest SES demands greater energy and—particularly—a willingness to use novel approaches to instruction. In this case it could well

---

[1] See, for example, Patricia Sexton, *Education and Income* (New York: The Viking Press, 1961).

be that the young and inexperienced are best suited for such schools. Because so little is known about the characteristics of effective teachers in general or at different SES levels, we have decided to avoid assumptions as to which type of teacher is best. In considering the characteristics of teachers in schools of different SES, we shall not attempt to test the hypothesis of inequality, but rather the null hypothesis that the distribution of teacher characteristics is random. Thus all statistical tests reported in this chapter will be two-tailed.[2]

Chapter 1 made reference to the arguments of writers such as Davis and Burton that most teachers are middle class in origin. According to this position, a cultural gap exists between middle-class teachers and their predominantly working-class pupils. Later in this chapter we will test an assumption implicit in the culture-gap hypothesis: that, regardless of the SES of the school, its teachers are middle class, or in other words that the socioeconomic origins of the average teacher in schools of different SES are identical. In testing this *assumption of identical origins*, we shall compare, across schools of different SES, such characteristics of teachers as the type of community in which they grew up and the socioeconomic standing of their parents. Again our tests will be two-tailed. Finally, to test a variant of the culture-gap hypothesis, we shall consider the racial and religious congruency of the teachers and pupils in schools of different SES.

The data used in this chapter were obtained from two sources. As a part of the personal and school-background questionnaire of the National Principalship Study, each principal was asked to provide detailed information about the number of teachers in his school, recorded according to their sex, age, years of experience in education, years of experience in current school, and highest degree held. These questions and many others were also asked of the sample of ten teachers in each school, 71 per cent of whom complied. When the data on the entire faculty of the schools of different SES (as reported by their principals) are available, they are presented here. When such data are not available, the reports of the sample of teachers who completed and returned the teacher questionnaire will be used.[3]

---

[2] For the benefit of others who may be willing to make assumptions which we find tenuous, we have presented in Appendix A the data upon which our analyses have been conducted.

[3] In order to establish empirically the validity of the sample of teachers who returned the teacher questionnaire as representative of all teachers in their schools, we compared a series of personal characteristics of both the sample

TEACHER CHARACTERISTICS

Sex

Figure 4-1 (next page) presents the proportion of male and female teachers in elementary schools of different SES. Of the 1009 teachers in the 47 elementary schools of highest SES, only 11 per cent are men. In the 47 schools of lowest SES almost twice as many teachers (19 per cent) are men. The difference of 8 percentage points between the two types of schools is statistically significant,[4] and suggests that, in the large group of schools of which these are but a sample, there are proportionately more male teachers in the schools of lowest SES than in those of highest SES. Perhaps in many city school districts a special effort is made to hire men to teach in slum schools where discipline is a problem and where boys are reported to need male role models.[5]

Experience in Teaching

Teachers in schools of highest and lowest SES differ significantly with respect to their years of formal teaching experience. In the former, only 1 teacher in 25 is in his first year of teaching; in the latter, the figure is more than 1 in 10. Furthermore, in schools of highest SES, only 23 per cent of the teachers have been teaching for five years or less, while in those of lowest SES the corresponding percentage is 43 (Figure 4-2).

Similar monotonic differences exist in all classifications of years of experience used to compare the four levels of School SES. However,

---

and population within each of twelve categories of schools (that is, four categories of School SES times three of School Level). The results of the analysis comparing the sex distribution of the sample with that of the population is presented in Appendix Table 4A-16. There it can be seen that with respect to the variable of teacher sex the teacher sample is an adequate representation of the population in all twelve categories.

As a further validation of the teacher sample, parallel tests of the statistical significance of their relationship with School SES were run for five variables (sex, age, years of experience in education, years of experience in current school, and highest degree held) for which comparable data were available for both the teacher sample and the teacher population. In 13 of the 15 tests (five variables times the three school levels) the same decision with respect to the null hypothesis was made.

[4] See Appendix Table 4A-1 for similar data on junior and senior high schools, as well as for all tests of statistical significance.

[5] Frank Riessman, *The Culturally Deprived Child* (New York: Harper and Row, 1962), p. 34; and Sexton, *op. cit.*, p. 278.

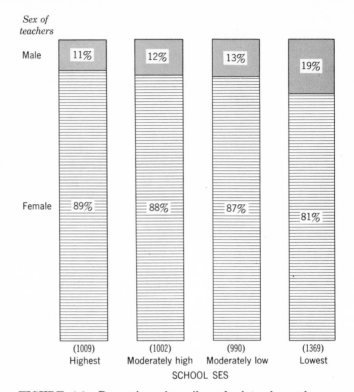

FIGURE 4-1. Proportion of pupils and of teachers who are male or female in schools of different SES. (All tables and figures in this chapter refer to *elementary* schools only.)

these differences are most pronounced in a comparison of different types of schools phrased in terms of the proportion of teachers who have taught for 10 years or more. In schools of highest SES it is 61 per cent, while in those of moderately high, moderately low, and lowest SES, the corresponding percentages are 52, 49, and 37, respectively (Figure 4-2).

These data of the School SES Study suggest that experienced teachers are not distributed uniformly among schools of different SES. It appears from Figure 4-2 that more beginning teachers are assigned to schools of lower SES, and that those who are so assigned (if they do not leave teaching altogether) later transfer to schools of higher SES.[6]

[6] See Appendix Table 4A-2 for similar data on junior and senior high schools, as well as for all tests of statistical significance.

*Experience
of teachers*

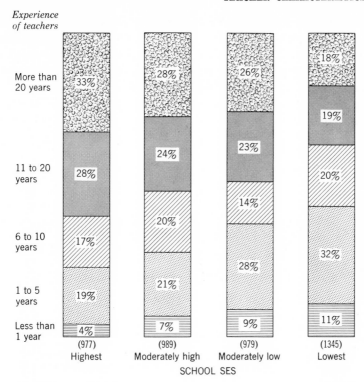

FIGURE 4-2. The lower the school SES, the more brief the total experience of teachers.

Experience in Current School

We find that teachers in schools of lowest SES have been in their current schools for a shorter time than their colleagues in schools of higher SES. Whereas 11 per cent of the teachers in the schools of highest SES are in their first year *in that school,* in schools of lowest SES the figure is 20 per cent. The monotonic trend noted with respect to total experience in teaching exists too for years of experience in current school. Forty-eight per cent of the teachers in elementary schools of highest SES have been teaching in that school for more than five years, while in the schools of moderately high, moderately low, and lowest SES, the corresponding figures are 45, 42, and 38 per cent, respectively (Figure 4-3). The difference between the schools of highest and lowest SES is significant statistically.[7]

[7] See Appendix Table 4A-3 for similar data on junior and senior high schools, as well as for all tests of statistical significance.

Figures 4-2 and 4-3 considered together suggest the typical career experience of teachers in schools of different SES. In schools of highest SES, 52 per cent of the teachers have taught in that school for five years or less (Figure 4-3), but only 23 per cent have been teachers for five years or less (Figure 4-2). In schools of lowest SES, the corresponding percentages are 62 and 43. Whereas in schools of highest SES approximately one-half (23/52) of the "new" teachers are also

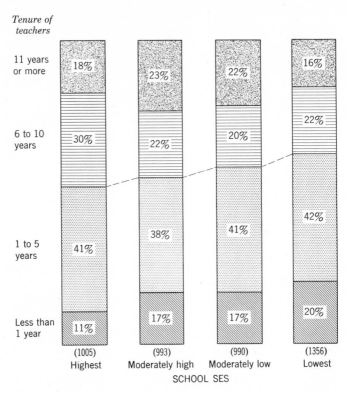

FIGURE 4-3. The lower the school SES, the more brief the tenure of teachers in their current schools.

new to education, in the schools of lowest SES the proportion is over two-thirds (43/62). In Chapter 5 we shall consider the possibility that this discrepancy is due to horizontal mobility in the career of teachers.

Age

Given the distinct relationship between SES and number of years of teaching experience, it is not surprising to find that teachers in the elementary schools of lowest SES are in general younger than those in schools of higher SES. Ten per cent of the 1009 teachers in the 47 elementary schools of highest SES, but 18 per cent of those in the 47 schools of lowest SES, are less than 25 years old (Figure 4-4). The corresponding percentages for the number of teachers less than 35 years of age are 30 and 48, and their difference is statistically significant.[8]

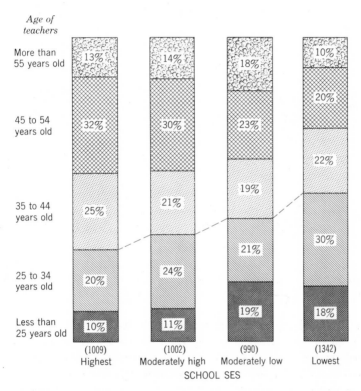

FIGURE 4-4. The lower the school SES, the greater the proportion of young teachers.

Highest Degree Held

On the four variables thus far considered, teacher sex, age, experience, and tenure, we have been able to reject the null hypothesis that the distribution of teacher characteristics is random. Significant differences by School SES have been found. With respect to highest aca-

[8] See Appendix Table 4A-4 for similar data on junior and senior high schools, as well as for all tests of statistical significance.

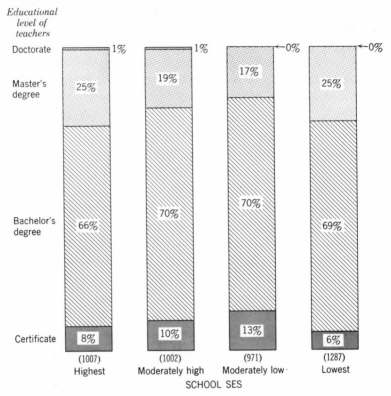

FIGURE 4-5. There is no significant difference between schools of highest and lowest SES in the academic degrees held by the teachers.

demic degree, however, this is not the case. Eight per cent of the teachers in elementary schools of highest SES hold a teaching certificate as their highest degree. In the schools of lowest SES the corresponding percentage is 6 (Figure 4-5). Neither this difference nor that between the proportion of teachers holding a bachelor's or master's as their highest degree is significant statistically.[9]

In the light of our findings on the experience, age, and tenure of teachers in schools of different SES, the absence of any general difference in the highest degree they hold is puzzling at first. It could be that although more young and inexperienced teachers are assigned to schools of lowest SES, a concerted effort is made not to discriminate in the formal training of teachers assigned. The expected difference

[9] See Appendix Table 4A-5 for similar data on junior and senior high schools, as well as for all tests of statistical significance.

in the formal training of teachers between schools of different SES may be masked by the recent increase in the number of young teachers who obtain higher degrees. Since there are more young teachers in the schools of lower SES than in those of higher SES (Figure 4-4), we should compare the highest degree held by teachers in schools of different SES *within selected age categories*. We could then see, for example, if more of the beginning teachers assigned to schools of highest SES hold a master's degree than do those assigned to schools of lower SES.

Unfortunately, it is not possible to explore this question with all of the teachers in the schools of highest and lowest SES as subjects. The principals reported to the National Principalship Study the distribution of their faculties with respect to age and highest degree held, but they were not asked to put the information together. We do not know, for example, anything about the ages of the 25 per cent of the 1009 teachers in the schools of highest SES who hold the master's degree.

However, we do have such information for the sample of teachers who returned the teacher questionnaire (see Chapter 2). Each teacher was asked to state his year of birth (in five-year categories) and the highest degree he held (certificate, bachelor's, master's, master's plus 30 hours, and doctor's). Through a simultaneous cross-tabulation of these variables and School SES, we can consider further the association of highest degree and School SES.

It will be noted (Table 4-1) that 25 per cent of the 1265 elementary teachers in the sample hold a degree higher than the bachelor's. As expected, this percentage varies with age. Few (2 per cent) of the teachers younger than 25 years old hold a master's or doctor's degree. The percentage rises with age to a high of 33 per cent for teachers in the 35–44 age range and then falls to 21 per cent for those 55 years or older. The curvilinear pattern probably reflects within the 35–44 age range the recent tendency for teachers to seek higher degrees. As for those less than 25 years old, urban elementary teachers seldom complete their work for a master's degree in their first few years of teaching.

Table 4-1 also shows the percentage of elementary school teachers in the sample in each SES category who hold an advanced degree. These percentages, although slightly larger than those in Figure 4-5 for all teachers in these 187 schools, suggest the same absence of a direct relationship to School SES: 29 per cent of the teachers in both the schools of highest and lowest SES hold a degree higher than the

TABLE 4-1. Proportion of Teachers Who Have Earned a Master's or Doctor's Degree, by Teacher Age and School SES

Age of Teacher	School SES				
	Highest	Moderately High	Moderately Low	Lowest	All Schools
Less than 25 years old	0%(20)a	0%(27)	0%(33)	8%(26)	2%(106)
25 to 34 years old	29 (65)	29 (80)	17 (69)	33 (78)	27 (292)
35 to 44 years old	39 (67)	29 (59)	27 (44)	35 (77)	33 (247)
45 to 54 years old	32 (102)	20 (97)	22 (98)	33 (84)	27 (381)
More than 54 years old	23 (57)	22 (51)	20 (77)	20 (54)	21 (239)
All ages	29 (311)	23 (314)	19 (321)	29 (319)	25 (1265)

a Figures in parentheses refer to the number of cases upon which the associated percentage was based.

bachelor's. This lack of difference in highest degree is unlikely to result from age differences, as can be seen by examining the percentages for each of the several age groups. With the exception of a few cases in the youngest age group, the difference between the percentage of teachers in elementary schools of highest and lowest SES who hold a higher degree is always less than 5, with two differences in favor of the schools of highest SES and two favoring those of lowest SES. We must conclude that the absence of a difference by School SES in the highest degree held by elementary teachers cannot be explained by differences in age.

Quality of College Work

We have no objective evidence as to the quality of the academic preparation of teachers in our sample. We do, however, have the replies of the teachers to this question: "In general, what was the quality of your work when you were in college?"—"graduated with honors," "above average," "average," and "somewhat below average."

*Quality of
teachers'
college work*

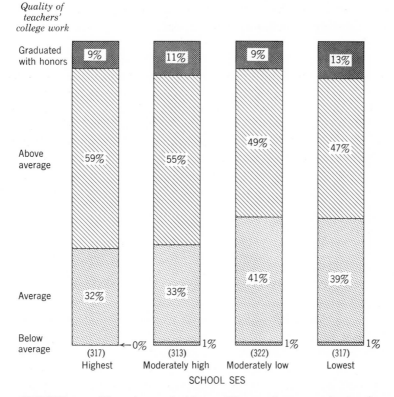

FIGURE 4-6. There is no significant difference between schools of highest and lowest SES in the quality of their college work, as reported by teachers.

To a subjective question of this type, we expect respondents to give an answer more favorable to themselves than is justified by the facts. The natural reluctance to admit to being "below average" is borne out by Figure 4-6. In conflict with studies which report that college students preparing to teach perform academically below those preparing for most other professions,[10] less than one per cent of these elementary teachers report their college performance to be below average.

However, the apparent distortion of the answers does not invalidate them as a means of comparing the academic performance of teachers in schools of different SES. In fact if this inflation is a uni-

[10] See, for example, Dael L. Wolfle, *America's Resources of Specialized Talent* (New York: Harper and Row, 1954) or Myron Lieberman, *Education as a Profession* (Englewood Cliffs: Prentice-Hall, 1956).

form trait, rather than a trait of teachers in one type of school alone, these estimates, inflated as they are, can be quite valid. Do these "inflated reports" vary with School SES?

A further examination of Figure 4-6 shows that the teachers in the schools of lowest SES have more frequently reported the quality of their college work to be "average" and less frequently reported it to be "above average." However, this difference is not statistically significant.[11] This index, as in the case of the more objective index of the highest degree held by these teachers, fails to suggest differences in the population of which these teachers are a sample. Unfortunately we have no way of assessing how differences in the academic standards of the colleges they attended affect these measures of academic preparation.

Salary

In any organization, although the workers' financial reward may not be an accurate measure of the quality of his performance, it is indicative of the value placed upon his performance by the organization. No question concerning teacher salary was asked of the principals, but only of the sample of teachers, again through the teacher questionnaire of the National Principalship Study. When the replies are examined according to the SES of their schools no evidence of salary differences is found. Although teachers in elementary schools of lowest SES often receive higher salaries than those in schools of highest SES, none of the differences presented in Figure 4-7 is statistically significant.[12]

This lack of relationship is strange indeed. The teachers in the schools of lowest SES are less experienced than their counterparts in schools of higher SES (Figure 4-2) and, in general, higher salaries are paid to more experienced teachers. Yet this does not appear to be the case with respect to our sample. Regional differences in salary schedules evidently do not produce this anomaly, for the Far West which, in general, pays the highest salaries to teachers, is, if anything, overrepresented rather than underrepresented within the schools of highest SES (Figure 2-13).

It is more likely that the expected trend is being masked by the size of the city in which these teachers are located. In general, larger

[11] See Appendix Table 4A-6 for similar data on junior and senior high schools, as well as for all tests of statistical significance.

[12] See Appendix Table 4A-7 for similar data on junior and senior high schools, as well as for all tests of statistical significance.

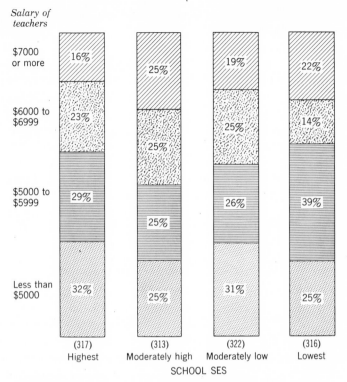

FIGURE 4-7. There is no significant difference between schools of highest and lowest SES in the current salary of teachers.

cities pay higher salaries than smaller ones, and it was seen in Chapter 2 (Figure 2-14) that the largest cities are somewhat overrepresented with schools of lowest SES and underrepresented with schools of the highest SES. To explore this possibility, the relationship of School SES and teacher salary was examined within each of the three categories of size of city: metropolis (more than 1 million), large city (250,000 to 1 million) and medium city (50,000 to 250,000).

As expected, a teacher's salary is clearly related to the size of the city in which he teaches. Whereas 70 per cent of the teachers in cities with populations of one million or over receive a salary of $6000 or more, in those of 250,000 to 1 million, and 50,000 to 250,000 inhabitants, the percentages are 46 and 33, respectively (Table 4-2). Further, when we consider the relationship of School SES and salary within each of the three categories of city size, we find that for all three the difference is in favor of the teachers in schools of highest

TABLE 4-2. Proportion of Teachers Receiving Salaries of $6000 or Greater, by Size of City and School SES

	School SES				
Size of City	Highest	Moderately High	Moderately Low	Lowest	All Schools
Metropolis (more than 1 million)	90%(10)a	91%(32)	56%(43)	67%(70)	70%(155)
Large city (250,000 to 1 million)	38 (97)	57 (122)	50 (108)	36 (107)	46 (434)
Medium city (50,000 to 249,999)	37 (210)	36 (159)	36 (171)	19 (139)	33 (679)
All cities	39 (317)	50 (313)	43 (322)	36 (316)	43 (1268)

ᵃ Figures in parentheses refer to the number of cases upon which the associated percentage was based.

SES. Two of these differences (those for the "metropolis" and the "medium city") are statistically significant. We must conclude, therefore, that there is an SES difference with respect to teacher salary when size of city is controlled. No doubt this is affected by the differences observed earlier in the experience of teachers in the schools of highest and lowest SES (Figure 4-2). A more extended consideration of salary differences by School SES should, no doubt, take into account such differences in experience.

Up to this point, we have examined the association between seven characteristics of teachers and the socioeconomic composition of the schools to which they have been assigned. We found no differences that are statistically significant with respect to the highest degrees held by these teachers or their self-reports of the quality of their college work. The teachers do differ in terms of their sex, age, experience as teachers, tenure in their current school, and salary: the teachers in the schools of lowest SES are somewhat more apt to be male, and are on the average younger, less experienced, and less well paid than their counterparts in the schools of highest SES. We turn now from background and professional characteristics to four indicators of the social origins of teachers.

TEACHER ORIGINS

According to the assumption of identical origins, one would predict that the schools of lowest SES would not differ from those of highest SES in the socioeconomic characteristics of their teachers. In this section we shall examine whether empirical evidence supports this assumption, using as indicators of the socioeconomic characteristics of a teacher the type of community in which he spent the major part of his youth, his father's occupation and educational level, his mother's educational level, and the income position of his family at the time he graduated from secondary school.

Community of Their Youth

The teacher questionnaire of the National Principalship Study asked the sample of teachers the question: "In what type of community did you spend the *major* part of your youth?" The response alternatives were: "farm," "village or town" (under 10,000), "small city" (10,000 to 50,000), or "city" (50,000 or more). To what extent is the community of origin of elementary teachers related to the SES of the schools in which they are teaching?

Sixty-four per cent of the teachers in schools of highest SES grew up in communities smaller than the one in which they now teach, but only 49 per cent of those in schools of lowest SES did so (Figure 4-8, next page). This difference of 15 per cent is statistically significant.[13] In terms of the community of their youth, the origins of teachers in schools of highest and lowest SES are clearly not identical. Those in schools of highest SES are more apt to be rural or small-town in-migrants to the city.

Father's Occupation

The teachers were also asked a question about the major lifetime occupation of their fathers. The response alternatives were: (1) education, (2) professional (other than education) or scientific, (3) managerial, executive, or proprietor of large business, (4) small business owner or manager, (5) clerical or sales, (6) farm owner or renter, (7) skilled worker or foreman, (8) semiskilled worker, or (9) unskilled worker or farm laborer. If we combine the first five categories as "white collar," and the last three categories as "blue collar," we see

[13] See Appendix Table 4A-8 for similar data on junior and senior high schools, as well as for all tests of statistical significance.

again that the assumption of identical origins receives no support. Whereas only 30 per cent of the teachers in schools of highest SES have fathers whose occupation has been classified as "blue collar," in the case of schools of lowest SES the figure is 43 per cent (Figure 4-9). This difference is also statistically significant.[14]

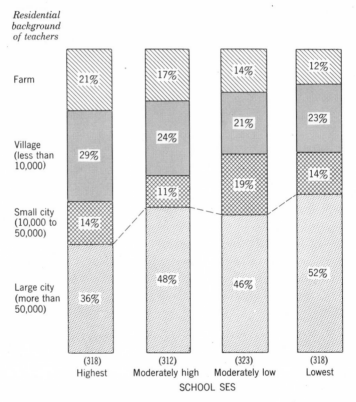

FIGURE 4-8. The lower the school SES, the greater the proportion of teachers who grew up in a city.

Father's Education

The teachers in the sample were asked: "What was your father's highest educational attainment?" They could respond with eight answers running from "no formal education" to "graduate or professional school." When these replies are classified according to School SES,

[14] See Appendix Table 4A-9 for similar data on junior and senior high schools, as well as for all tests of statistical significance.

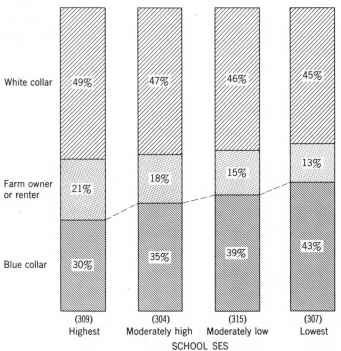

FIGURE 4-9. The lower the school SES, the greater the proportion of teachers with fathers in blue collar occupations.

no relationship is apparent. Within the schools of highest SES, 26 per cent of the teachers report that their fathers attended (but not necessarily completed) college, while within the schools of lowest SES, the figure is 22 per cent (Figure 4-10, next page). Neither this comparison nor any of the other seven comparisons which can be made between the educational level of the teachers' fathers and the SES of the schools in which they now teach is statistically significant.[15]

Mother's Education

The educational level of the teachers' mothers was questioned too. Again, although the trend of the data suggests that the mothers of teachers in the schools of lowest SES have had less formal education

[15] See Appendix Table 4A-10 for similar data on junior and senior high schools, as well as for all tests of statistical significance.

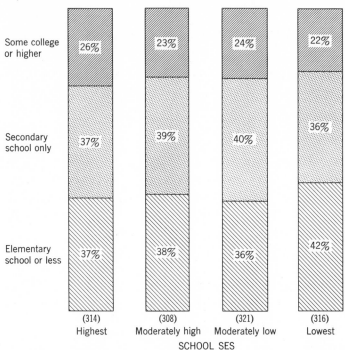

FIGURE 4-10. There is no significant difference between schools of highest and lowest SES in the educational level of the *fathers* of teachers.

than those of the teachers assigned to the schools of highest SES (Figure 4-11), the difference is not statistically significant.[16]

Income Position of Family

No completely reliable measure of family income was available to the National Principalship Study. However, the teachers were asked: "What was the income position of your parents at the time of your graduation from high school?" The teachers replied by indicating either "highest 25% of our community," "second highest 25% of our community," "third highest 25% of our community," or "lowest

[16] See Appendix Table 4A-11 for similar data on junior and senior high schools, as well as for all tests of statistical significance.

*Education
of teachers'
mothers*

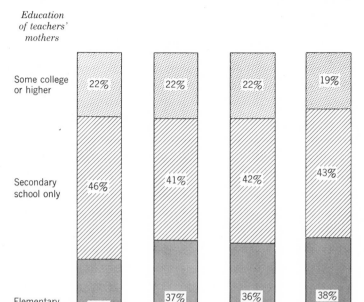

FIGURE 4-11. There is no significant difference between schools of highest and lowest SES in the educational level of the *mothers* of teachers.

25% of our community." Unfortunately, this rough estimate of family income fails to consider possible differences in the economic levels of the communities in which the teachers grew up. Although it seems that the teachers in the schools of lowest SES come from families of relatively low income (Figure 4-12, next page), the differences are not statistically significant.[17]

We have examined five indices of the origins of teachers in schools of different SES in order to test the assumption that, on the average, their origins are identical. The five indices suggest that teachers in the schools of lowest SES have come from family backgrounds

[17] See Appendix Table 4A-12 for similar data on junior and senior high schools, as well as for all tests of statistical significance.

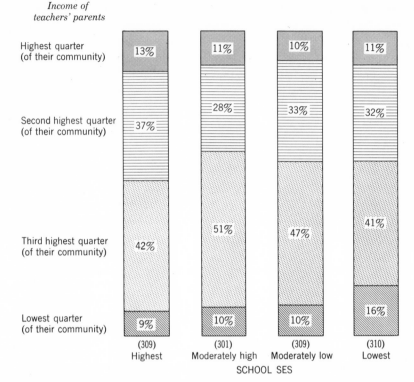

Income of teachers' parents

FIGURE 4-12. Teachers in schools of highest and lowest SES did not differ significantly at the time they completed high school in the income position of their families.

which can be characterized as more urban, more "blue collar," with less formal education and lower income than those of the teachers from schools of highest SES, but only in the case of the community of their youth and their fathers' occupation was the difference statistically significant. But even though teachers in schools of lowest SES are of somewhat lower socioeconomic background than teachers in the schools of higher SES, even here they are not, by and large, of very low socioeconomic origin. Hence, it appears likely that regardless of the level of School SES, there is a gap between the background of teachers and pupils in these schools.

Careful exploration of the culture-gap hypothesis requires detailed measurement not only of the indicators of socioeconomic background considered here, but also of the values and attitudes which these indicators are assumed to portend. Unfortunately, we do not have available the comparable data on the teachers and pupils essential to such an exploration. However, we do have comparable data with respect to their racial and religious characteristics (two variables which are generally found to be related to values and attitudes as well as to socioeconomic status), and it is to these that we now turn.

TEACHER–PUPIL CONGRUENCY

There is currently some disagreement with respect to the ideal ethnic, religious, and racial composition of the faculty of public schools. On the one hand, some maintain that in order to insure that schools are staffed with teachers who understand their pupils and can serve as role models for their development, the social characteristics of the teachers in any school should resemble those of their pupils. On the other hand, it is argued that in order to encourage children to respect the many diverse social and ethnic groups within American society, the teachers within each public school should be representative, not of the pupils they teach, but of some larger collectivity (whether it be the city, the state, or the nation) of which their pupils are but a part.

The first point of view we shall call one of *microcongruency*, for the term suggests that teachers and pupils should be matched in terms of a small unit of organization—their own school. The second point of view we shall call *macrocongruency*, for the term suggests that such matching should be defined in terms of a larger collectivity. Since the School SES Study deals only with data from schools in cities with populations of 50,000 or greater, we shall, for illustrative purposes, develop the argument of macrocongruency in terms of "urban America," and our estimates of the socioeconomic composition of this collectivity will be made from our own data. This does not mean that for these same schools different criteria of macrocongruency or different estimates of social and economic composition (for example, census data) could not be used.

In exploring the distinction between the two bases for definitions of congruency we shall, again for illustrative purposes, consider only two characteristics of teachers: proportion nonwhite and proportion Jewish. This selection by no means exhausts the pool of possible social and economic characteristics on which to compare teachers and pupils, but it does enable us to focus upon two somewhat scarce attributes.

Elementary teachers who are nonwhite or Jewish are clearly in the minority in urban America. In addition, these characteristics are relatively easy to define and identify for both teachers and pupils.

Race

From the perspective of *microcongruency* based on race, the school is "most favored" whose teachers most closely match their pupils in racial characteristics. That is, for example, if a school has 70 per cent nonwhite enrollment, it would be "most favored" if its faculty was also 70 per cent nonwhite. From the perspective of *macrocongruency,* if we use our sample of urban America as the standard, that school is "most favored" where the faculty is 21 per cent nonwhite (the per cent of all the pupils in our sample who are nonwhite), regardless of the racial composition of its own student body. Which type of congruency is there in the elementary schools in our sample, and how is it related to School SES?

Table 4-3 presents for each of 185 elementary schools the proportion of teachers who are nonwhite according to the proportion of pupils who are nonwhite. Also plotted are the lines of micro- and macrocongruency. In terms of microcongruency those 60 schools falling along the line of microcongruency are "most favored," with an approximately equal percentage of nonwhite pupils and teachers, regardless of whether the percentage is 0 or 100. Those 3 schools located farthest from the line, with 90–99 per cent nonwhite pupils and no nonwhite teachers, are "least favored." It is also apparent that the majority of the schools in the sample (116/185) have a higher proportion of nonwhite pupils than of nonwhite teachers. In only 7 schools does the proportion of nonwhite teachers exceed that of nonwhite pupils.

In terms of macrocongruency those 8 schools located along the line of macrocongruency (with 20 to 29 per cent nonwhite faculty) are "most favored" and those 8 schools located farthest from it (with all nonwhite teachers and over 90 per cent nonwhite pupils) are "least favored." Clearly, in respect to race neither micro- nor macrocongruency is common in the distribution of elementary school teachers in our cities. However, it appears that, on the average, the fit between the race of teachers and the race of *their* pupils is closer than that between the race of teachers and the race of pupils in the cities in which the schools are located. Let us now see how this phenomenon varies with the SES of the school.

TABLE 4-3.   Distribution of 185 Schools, According to the Proportion of Teachers and the Proportion of Pupils Who Are Nonwhite

	Per Cent of Teachers Who Are Nonwhite												
	0	1 to 9	10—19	20—29	30—39	40—49	50—59	60—69	70—79	80—89	90 to 99	100	All Schools
100						1		1		1		6	11
90–99	3	1	2	2	1	1		2		2	2	2	18
80–89			3	1	1	1							6
70–79				1	1								2
60–69	1				1								2
50–59	2			1	1	1							5
40–49	1	1											2
30–39	2			3	1								6
20–29	2		4										6
10–19	10	2	1										13
1–9	56	7	2	1									66
0	44	4											48
All schools	121	22	11	8	2	2	1	3	—	3	4	8	185[a]

(Per Cent of Pupils Who Are Nonwhite on vertical axis)

Line of microcongruency

Line of macrocongruency

[a] Data on race of teachers are unknown for two of the 187 elementary schools.

Figure 4-13 contrasts in the aggregate (rather than in terms of the individual schools) the proportion of pupils and teachers who are white or nonwhite according to the four levels of School SES. The pupils in the schools of lowest SES have a far greater proportion of nonwhite teachers than do those in the schools of higher SES. In gen-

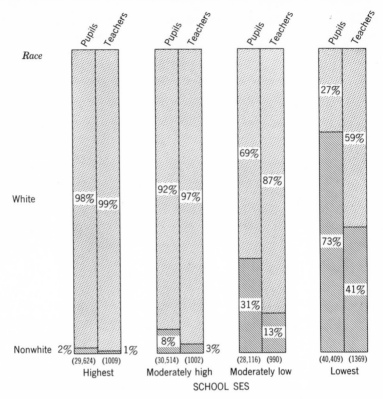

FIGURE 4-13. Proportion of pupils and of teachers who are white or nonwhite, by school SES.

eral the proportion of teachers who are nonwhite is less than that of the pupils, and this "underrepresentation" becomes greater as School SES becomes lower. Thus, whereas in the schools of highest SES, 2 per cent of the pupils and 1 per cent of the teachers are nonwhite, in the schools of lowest SES, 73 per cent of the pupils, but only 41 per cent of the teachers are nonwhite (Figure 4-13).[18]

This relationship, noted here in the aggregate, is true for almost every school at every level of School SES, as can be seen in Appendix Tables 4A-17 through 4A-20. Some elementary schools of highest SES achieve microcongruency, since with few or no nonwhite pupils they also have no nonwhite teachers, but all these fall short of macrocongruency, since in no case does a school of highest SES have as many

[18] See Appendix Table 4A-13 for similar data on junior and senior high schools, as well as for tests of statistical significance.

nonwhite teachers as does the larger collectivity to which it is compared. As School SES falls, the proportion of schools that achieve microcongruency falls too, for the proportion of nonwhite teachers does not increase as rapidly as does the proportion of the nonwhite pupils. Nor do most schools of lowest SES achieve macrocongruency; they have either far more nonwhite teachers than the proportion of nonwhites in urban America (if the pupils are largely nonwhite) or far fewer nonwhite teachers (if the pupils are largely white).

Religion

From the perspective of microcongruency based on religion, one must argue that those pupils are "most favored" whose teachers most closely represent their own religious characteristics. For example, if 40 per cent of its student body is Jewish, a school would be most favored if its faculty was 40 per cent Jewish, and less favored if its faculty was either less or more than 40 per cent Jewish. From the perspective of macrocongruency, those pupils are most favored whose teachers most represent the religious characteristics of our urban American society. That is, since approximately 12 per cent of urban pupils (as indicated by our sample) are Jewish, that school is most favored whose faculty is 12 per cent Jewish, regardless of the religious composition of its own student body, and is less favored if its faculty is either less than or greater than 12 per cent Jewish. Which type of religious congruency exists within the elementary schools of our sample, and how does it vary with School SES?[19]

Table 4-4 presents for each of 183 elementary schools the proportion of teachers who are Jewish in relation to the proportion of pupils who are Jewish. Also plotted are the lines of micro- and macrocongruency. In terms of the objective of microcongruency the "most favored" schools are the 75 which fall along the line which indicates that the percentage of Jewish pupils and teachers is roughly equal. The great majority of these are schools in which no pupil and no teacher is of the Jewish faith. Of the remaining 108 schools in the sample, 63 have more and 45 have fewer Jewish pupils than Jewish teachers.

[19] A complete answer to the question of religious congruency would consider separately each of the major religious categories. However, for illustrative purposes, one will suffice. As was seen in Figure 2-9 the proportion of pupils who are Jewish is the smallest of the three categories and varies with School SES more than that of those who are Catholic or Protestant. Therefore, in exploring the question of micro- and macrocongruency, it seemed most interesting to focus on that group.

TABLE 4-4. Distribution of 183 Schools, According to the Proportion of Teachers and the Proportion of Pupils Who Are Jewish

Per Cent of Pupils Who Are Jewish	Per Cent of Teachers Who Are Jewish												
	0	1 to 9	10 to 19	20 to 29	30 to 39	40 to 49	50 to 59	60 to 69	70 to 79	80 to 89	90 to 99	100	All Schools
100													—
90–99						1	1	1			1		4
80–89						1							1
70–79						1							1
60–69			1	1									2
50–59													—
40–49													—
30–39	1	2	2										5
20–29		3	2	1					1				7
10–19	7	2	3				1	1					14
1–9	37	16	6	5			2						66
0	54	23	4	1	1								83
All schools	99	46	18	8	1	3	4	2	1	—	1	—	183[a]

Line of macrocongruency · Line of microcongruency

[a] Data on religion of both pupils and teachers are unknown for four schools.

In terms of the macrocongruency criterion, the 18 schools with 10 to 20 per cent Jewish teachers are "most favored" and the one school with 90 to 99 per cent Jewish teachers and pupils is "least favored." In the great majority of schools in the sample (145/183) less than 10 per cent of the teachers are Jewish. But again we must ask how this varies with School SES.

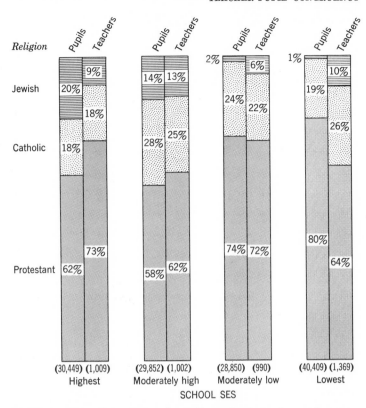

FIGURE 4-14. Proportion of pupils and of teachers who are Jewish, Catholic, or Protestant, by school SES.

Figure 4-14 contrasts in the aggregate the proportion of pupils and teachers who are Jewish according to the four levels of School SES. There it is shown that the proportion of Jewish teachers to Jewish pupils is far less than half in schools of highest SES, but 10 to 1 in those of lowest SES.[20] The lower the School SES, the greater, not only the proportion of Jewish teachers to Jewish pupils, but also the number of schools in which the two proportions are roughly equal, that is, with microcongruency. (See Appendix Tables 4A-21 to 4A-24.) In terms of macrocongruency, School SES appears to make no difference.

As a means of contrasting the trends with respect to racial and religious pupil-teacher congruency, the average ratio of nonwhite

[20] See Appendix Tables 4A-14 and 4A-15 for similar data on junior and senior high schools, as well as for all tests of statistical significance.

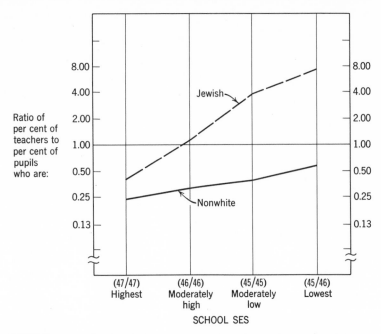

FIGURE 4-15. Ratio of the per cent of teachers who are Jewish to the per cent of pupils who are Jewish, and of the per cent of teachers who are nonwhite to the per cent of pupils who are nonwhite, by school SES.

teachers to nonwhite pupils and of Jewish teachers to Jewish pupils has been computed for each of the four categories of School SES. The ratios have been presented in Figure 4-15. Although, as School SES falls, the ratios of the proportion of teachers (to the proportion of pupils) who are Jewish and nonwhite both increase, the Jewish ratio increases more rapidly than the one for nonwhites and eventually becomes greater than 1.00. Particularly noteworthy is the fact that although there are levels of School SES in which the proportion of Jewish teachers is greater than the proportion of Jewish pupils, such a disparity does not exist for nonwhite teachers and pupils. With respect to the racial characteristic, the "gap" between teachers and pupils is in the direction of proportionately fewer teachers than pupils at all levels of School SES.

Clearly the issue of teacher-pupil congruency is extremely complex. We have chosen to focus on only one category each for the variables of race and religion because these are the minority categories of each variable; we have emphasized these two variables because they lend themselves fairly readily to definition and measurement. Teacher-pupil congruency in socioeconomic background could also be examined in similar fashion, but before this can be done properly, problems of definition and measurement that are beyond the scope of our data will have to be solved. Further exploration of the culture-gap hypothesis should include the measurement of the attitudes and values of both teachers and pupils. In Chapter 11 we shall return to some of the questions left unanswered by the analysis described in this chapter. In the meantime, with some understanding of the characteristics of teachers in these schools of different SES, in comparison to each other and to their pupils, we turn to their attitudes toward their work and their job performance.

Chapter 5

SCHOOL SES AND TEACHER SATISFACTION AND MORALE

Many observers and a number of research studies agree that teachers in slum schools are, in general, dissatisfied.[1] Both objective and subjective factors account for this condition. In the first place, slum schools are usually located in old and dilapidated sections of the city and are often housed in antiquated buildings with limited space for pupils and teachers. Rates of pupil transiency, truancy, delinquency, and retardation indicate that teaching in slum schools requires more effort and is less likely to be rewarded by standard pupil performance than is the case in more prosperous neighborhoods.

In the second place, if the values and norms of teachers are very unlike those of their pupils, a "culture gap" may make them long for a less alien environment. Reports of other observers as well as our own findings on staff perceptions of pupil characteristics in schools of different SES levels (Chapter 3), and the evidence of horizontal mobility based on differential teacher experience and tenure at the four SES levels (Chapter 4), all lead us to predict that the lower the School SES, the greater, in general, is the dissatisfaction of teachers.

[1] Howard S. Becker, "Social-Class Variations in the Teacher-Pupil Relationship," *Journal of Educational Sociology*, XXV (1952), pp. 451–465; Patrick J. Groff, "Dissatisfactions in Teaching the Culturally Deprived Child," *Phi Delta Kappan*, XLV (1963), p. 76; Vernon F. Haubrich, "The Culturally Different: New Context for Teacher Education," *The Journal of Teacher Education*, XIV (1963), pp. 163–167; and Clemmont E. Vontress, "Our Demoralizing Slum Schools," *Phi Delta Kappan*, XLV (1963), pp. 77–81.

It would not be surprising, however, if the relation between School SES and teacher satisfaction varied with different aspects of a teacher's vocation. The more closely a particular aspect of teaching is related to characteristics of the pupils themselves, the greater the difference we would expect to find in the satisfaction expressed by teachers in schools of highest and lowest SES. For this reason, satisfaction with teaching as a career, or preference among the various tasks in which a teacher must engage, should not show as marked differences by School SES, as should satisfaction with the present job or the desire to change jobs. However, we would expect dissatisfaction with present job to influence total attitude toward work and career; thus, teachers in lowest SES schools may be on the whole less satisfied with teaching and all its aspects than teachers in highest SES schools.

Six sets of questions and answers from the National Principalship Study provide data on the satisfaction of teachers. The elementary, junior and senior high school teachers answered questions concerning their own job aspiration, job satisfaction, career satisfaction, and work satisfaction. In addition, both teachers and principals answered a number of questions pertaining to the percentage of teachers in their schools who exhibited certain characteristics, among which are items referring to satisfaction. These latter questions refer to the satisfaction of the teacher work *group* and will be called teacher "morale." We will turn first to the results of the analysis, according to School SES category, of the 60 items in the 4 sets of questions about teacher satisfaction, and then we will consider the responses to 12 items measuring teacher morale.[2]

JOB ASPIRATION

In Chapter 1, we referred to Becker's hypothesis of horizontal mobility as the typical career pattern of teachers.[3] Although there have been few replications of Becker's study, it is assumed in educational literature that this pattern prevails in large cities. According to the hypothesis, the typical beginning teacher is first assigned to a school in a depressed neighborhood, is dissatisfied with this assignment, and sooner or later, if he stays in teaching, transfers to a school in a more prosperous neighborhood.

[2] For the research instruments, see Appendix B, Sections B-2, B-3, B-4, and B-5.
[3] Howard S. Becker, "The Career of the Chicago Public Schoolteacher," *American Journal of Sociology*, LVII (1952), pp. 470–477.

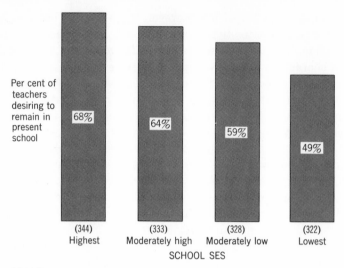

FIGURE 5-1. The lower the school SES, the smaller the proportion of teachers who desire to remain in their present school for the remainder of their educational careers. (All figures and tables in this chapter refer to *elementary* schools only. Unless otherwise noted, the reporters are in each case the teachers.)

In Chapter 4 we saw how our study found that teachers in the lowest SES group are younger and less experienced than teachers in the highest SES group. The evidence lends support to the first half of the Becker hypothesis: that big city teachers typically begin their careers in slum schools. What about the second half of the hypothesis? Are teachers in the disadvantaged schools more eager than other teachers to leave their present situations, through transfer to a teaching position in a different neighborhood, or through promotion to an administrative post?

The answer is apparently "yes." The replies of teachers to a series of questions as to whether or not they desire a change of job reveals, as predicted, a negative relation between School SES and dissatisfaction with their present situation. For each of ten items, the lower the SES of elementary schools, the greater is the teacher's desire to move, and eight of these relationships are statistically significant.[4] Thus, 68 per cent of the teachers in the highest School SES group hope to remain in their present schools for the rest of their educational careers. In contrast, less than half (49 per cent) of those in the lowest School SES group give this answer (Figure 5-1).

[4] See Appendix Table 5A-1 for the data on the full 10 items, similar data on junior and senior high schools, and all tests of statistical significance.

The difference in the attitude of teachers toward their present situation shows even more clearly in their answers to the question: "How desirous are you of remaining a teacher in this school system for the remainder of your educational career, but of moving to a school in a 'better neighborhood?' " In reply, 42 per cent in the lowest SES group but less than half that percentage (18 per cent) in the highest group indicate that this is what they desire (Figure 5-2).

Apparently, teachers want "horizontal mobility" whether or not it is encouraged by their school systems. Not many appear to be interested in "vertical mobility"—that is, in becoming a principal or superintendent. Nevertheless, the proportion who wish these administrative posts is significantly greater among teachers in schools in the most depressed areas than among those in the most privileged areas (Table 5-1).

What is it about their present teaching situation that teachers in slum schools wish to escape? Is it the undisciplined behavior of their pupils? Or is it a lack of teaching supplies, or the low level of competence of fellow teachers or principal? Some clues as to the source of the discontent of teachers in slum schools with their

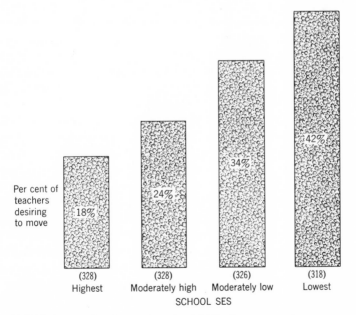

Per cent of teachers desiring to move

18%   24%   34%   42%

(328)   (328)   (326)   (318)
Highest   Moderately high   Moderately low   Lowest
SCHOOL SES

FIGURE 5-2. The lower the school SES, the greater the proportion of teachers who would like to move to a school in a "better neighborhood."

TABLE 5-1. Teachers in Schools in the Lowest SES Category Are More Desirous of a Different Job than Teachers in the Highest School SES Category

Per cent of teachers who say they "have some desire to," "would very much like to," or "are extremely anxious to":	School SES			
	Highest $(N_m = 344)$	Moderately High $(N_m = 332)$	Moderately Low $(N_m = 328)$	Lowest $(N_m = 324)$
1. Become an assistant principal.	14%	20%	17%	23%
2. Become principal of an elementary school.	16	21	16	21
3. Become principal of a junior high school.	4	6	5	10
4. Become principal of a senior high school.	3	3	3	6
5. Become associate superintendent.	5	6	5	7
6. Become superintendent.	4	6	7	7

situations are afforded by their answers to a series of questions dealing with their job satisfaction.

JOB SATISFACTION

All teachers were asked to indicate whether they felt satisfied (very, moderately, slightly) or dissatisfied (very, moderately, slightly) with 14 aspects of their present teaching situation. Most of these indices of "job satisfaction" relate specifically to their present school, its pupils, and its staff. A few refer to central office administration or to the system as a whole. Although our prediction of a positive relation between School SES and teacher job satisfaction covered all 14 items, we expected the relationship to be more pronounced for the 9 items which referred to the school than for the 5 items referring to the school system. When the replies of teachers to these items are analyzed according to School SES, it becomes apparent that there is a positive relation. On 11 of the 14 items, teachers in the schools of lowest SES are less satisfied than their colleagues in schools of highest SES. Moreover, on 8 of the 9 items referring to school alone, the direc-

TABLE 5-2. Teachers in Schools in the Lowest SES Category Tend to Be Less Satisfied than Teachers in the Highest SES Category

Per cent of teachers who say they are "very satisfied," "moderately satisfied," or "slightly satisfied" with:	School SES			
	Highest ($N_m = 344$)	Moderately High ($N_m = 332$)	Moderately Low ($N_m = 325$)	Lowest ($N_m = 324$)
1. Academic performance of students in their schools.	91%	85%	61%	52%
2. Adequacy of supplies available for use in their teaching in the school.	84	82	72	70
3. Attitude of students toward faculty in the school.	86	86	84	74
4. Method employed in the school for making decisions on pupil discipline matters.	76	79	78	68
5. Level of competence of most other teachers in the school.	94	94	92	87
6. Educational philosophy which seems to prevail in the school.	89	86	85	84
7. Manner in which teachers and administrative staff work together in these schools.	87	87	85	83
8. Amount of time which is available at the school for professional growth.	51[a]	53	50	50[a]
9. The method employed in the school for making decisions on curriculum matters.	79[a]	78	83	81[a]

[a] This highest-lowest difference is *not* significant at the .05 level.

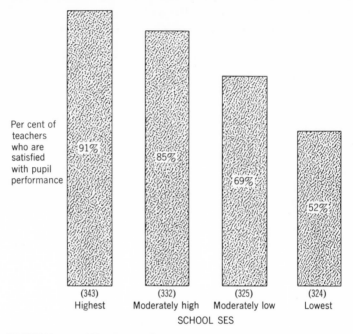

FIGURE 5-3. The lower the school SES, the smaller the proportion of teachers who are satisfied with the academic performance of the students.

tion is as predicted (Table 5-2), and on 7 of these the difference is statistically significant.[5]

A major cause of dissatisfaction appears to be the difference in the academic performance of pupils. We reported in Chapter 3 that the lower the School SES, the smaller the proportion of pupils whose academic work was reported by teachers as meeting grade-level standards. It now appears that substandard academic performance is a source of great dissatisfaction to teachers. Of all the items measuring job satisfaction, the one referring to the academic performance of pupils distinguishes most clearly among teachers in different SES categories. Ninety-one per cent of the teachers in the highest SES group but only 52 per cent of those in the lowest group, indicate that they are satisfied with pupil academic performance (Figure 5-3).

Other items, in descending order of difference, on which teachers in schools of low SES are significantly less satisfied than their col-

[5] See Appendix Table 5A-2 for the data on the full 14 items, similar data on junior and senior high schools, and all tests of statistical significance.

TABLE 5-3. Cumulative Proportion of Teachers Who Desire to Move to a School in a "Better Neighborhood," by Their Degree of Satisfaction with the Academic Performance of the Pupils in Their School

Desire to remain in this school system but move to a school in a "better neighborhood":	Satisfaction with Academic Performance of Pupils						
	Very Satisfied	Moderately Satisfied	Slightly Satisfied	Slightly Dissatisfied	Moderately Dissatisfied	Very Dissatisfied	All Teachers
Would not want to.	2%	2%	3%	4%	4%	12%	3%
Not especially anxious to.	7	11	12	12	18	29	12
Some desire to.	13	25	36	34	36	48	29
Very much like to.	48	62	72	69	70	75	64
Extremely anxious.	100	100	100	100	100	100	100
Number of teachers	182	539	240	157	94	83	1295

leagues are those referring to: the adequacy of teaching supplies, the attitude of students toward faculty, the method employed for making decisions on pupil discipline, the level of competence of other teachers, the educational philosophy of the school, and the cooperation of teachers and administrative staff (Table 5-2).

In order to explore whether the teachers' desire to move to a school in a better neighborhood (Figure 5-2) is functionally related to their dissatisfaction with the academic performance of the pupils (Figure 5-3), the two variables were related across all schools irrespective of their SES. Whereas only 13 per cent of the 182 teachers who are "very satisfied" with the academic performance of the pupils in their school express at least "some desire" to move to a school in a better neighborhood, 48 per cent of the "very dissatisfied" teachers so desire (Table 5-3). This difference is statistically significant.

The data on job aspiration and job satisfaction thus indicate that teachers in schools of lowest SES are, of all teachers, the least anxious to remain in their present positions and the least satisfied with various aspects of their teaching situation, particularly the academic performance of their pupils. In addition, dissatisfaction with pupil performance would appear to be a cause of this desire to move. We will now consider whether this dissatisfaction with present job is likely to color the attitude of teachers toward their total career.

CAREER SATISFACTION

The teachers were asked to indicate the extent of their satisfaction or dissatisfaction with such aspects of their career as its effect on social life, family life, and time for leisure activities. Other items referred to the chances of salary increase and the top salary available to teachers, to the recognition teachers receive from other professionals and the general public, and to the professional standards and capabilities of their fellow teachers.

When the replies of the teachers to 14 such items were related to the SES of the schools in which they taught, it was found that, in general, there was no significant difference between the satisfaction of teachers in schools of lowest and highest SES. As School SES falls, there is increasing satisfaction with eight aspects of the career and decreasing satisfaction with six aspects. Only one item in either direction shows a statistically significant difference:[6] satisfaction with their

---

[6] See Appendix Table 5A-3 for the data on the full 14 items, similar data on junior and senior high schools, and all tests of statistical significance.

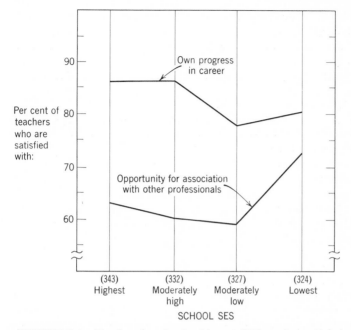

FIGURE 5-4. Teachers in schools of lowest SES are less satisfied than teachers in schools of highest SES with their own progress in their careers, but more satisfied with their opportunities for association with other professionals.

own progress in their careers is expressed by 86 per cent of the teachers in the highest SES group, but by only 80 per cent of those in the lowest group; on the other hand, 63 per cent in the highest group and 72 per cent in the lowest group are satisfied with the opportunity to associate with other professionals (Figure 5-4).

Thus the prediction of significantly lower career satisfaction for teachers in schools of lowest SES is *not* upheld. The present job difficulties of teachers in slum schools do not seem to affect their appraisal of the professional aspects of their careers. But do they affect their preferences among the various types of work in which they and all teachers, regardless of school, must engage?

WORK SATISFACTION

The role of a teacher is many-sided. Although instructing is central to the role, in the course of any day or even hour, a teacher may also be called upon to be a disciplinarian, a counsellor, a judge, or

TABLE 5-4. Proportion of Teachers Who Enjoy Five Aspects of Their Role, by School SES

Per cent of teachers who say that they enjoy "a great deal" or "very much":	School SES			
	Highest ($N_m = 343$)	Moderately High ($N_m = 327$)	Moderately Low ($N_m = 327$)	Lowest ($N_m = 324$)
1. Working with curriculum specialists.	48%	50%	52%	58%
2. Evaluating pupil progress.	62	58	64	71
3. Having to schedule one's time carefully.	27	31	31	36
4. Working with a committee of teachers on a common problem.	55	61	65	61
5. Preparing lessons.	63	60	66	66

a curriculum-planner. Some pupils are able students; others are not. Some adjust easily to the demands of school; others need guidance. Although teachers work primarily with pupils, they must also work with parents, specialists, administrators, and other teachers. In some respects a teaching job is similar to other jobs; in others, it is unique. Long vacations and the annual turnover in clientele are features which are characteristic of, if not peculiar to, this occupation.

Do teachers in schools of lowest SES find less satisfaction in various aspects of their role than teachers in schools of highest SES? This is what we expected to find. However, the prediction of lower work satisfaction—that is, lower enjoyment of the various aspects of the teacher's role—with lower School SES is not supported by the data. On 19 of the 26 items designed by the National Principalship Study to measure work satisfaction, teachers in the least privileged schools indicate *greater* enjoyment than other teachers and on 5 of these the difference is statistically significant.[7] For instance, while 48 per cent of the teachers in schools of highest SES "Enjoy working with curriculum specialists," 58 per cent of the teachers in schools of lowest SES enjoy this aspect of their role (Figure 5-5). There are significant differences in the same direction for "Evaluating pupil progress,"

[7] See Appendix Table 5A-4 for the data on the full 26 items, similar data on junior and senior high schools, and all tests of statistical significance.

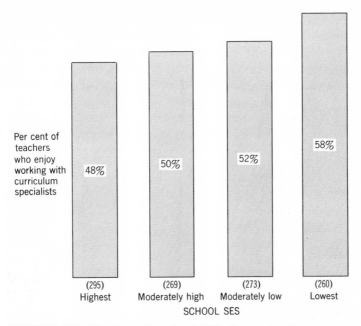

FIGURE 5-5. The lower the school SES, the greater the proportion of teachers who enjoy working with curriculum specialists.

"Having to schedule one's time carefully," "Working with a committee of teachers on a common problem," and "Preparing lessons" (Table 5-4). These tasks appear to be central to a teacher's role, and yet the teacher in the low SES school enjoys them more than does the teacher in the high SES school.

It is also instructive to consider the items on which teachers in the more middle-class schools indicate greater enjoyment than teachers in slum schools. Most of these items do not seem basic to the job of a teacher and only two show significant differences by School SES. Thus 87 per cent of the teachers in the schools in the highest SES category like teaching different groups each year, as compared with 80 per cent in the schools in the lowest SES category (Figure 5-6), and 86 per cent of the teachers in the highest SES group enjoy exceptionally able pupils, as opposed to 79 per cent of the teachers in the lowest SES group (Figure 5-7). The nonsignificant items refer to such matters as attending teachers' meetings, changing work routine, a long summer vacation, teaching different groups each year, or teaching average or slow pupils.

Thus, contrary to prediction, teachers in schools of lowest (and in some cases moderately low) SES indicate greater satisfaction with all but six of the specified aspects of their role than do teachers in schools of highest SES. Is this because these teachers, being of low SES background themselves, or being nonwhite, have fewer alternative careers open to them and are, therefore, satisfied with teaching, in spite of their present teaching situation? As we reported in Chapter 4, there is some tendency for teachers in schools of lowest SES to have lower SES origins than teachers in schools of highest SES.

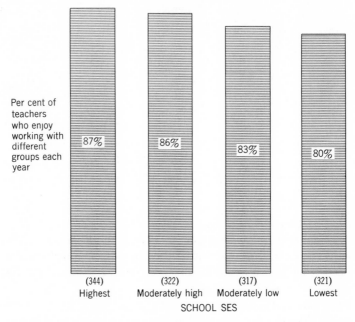

FIGURE 5-6. The lower the school SES, the smaller the proportion of teachers who enjoy working with different groups of pupils each year.

Moreover, almost a third of the teachers in the most deprived schools are nonwhite, which if interpreted by means of the concept of "relative deprivation" may explain, to some degree, their greater work satisfaction.

An alternative explanation, and one that seems equally plausible, suggests that a selective process governs the type of teachers who remain in the low SES schools. Teachers who are willing to put up with the low level of pupil performance which they themselves describe as typical of schools in the lowest SES category (see Chapter 3), may, indeed, be teachers who particularly like most facets of teaching. In other words, these teachers may be more committed to the career than other teachers. This interpretation does not necessarily conflict with the lack of relation between School SES and the items in the career satisfaction instrument. Even though a teacher may be dissatisfied with the state of the profession in certain respects, he might still feel that it is the only career in which he personally wants to engage. Possibly, therefore, the reason for the lack of over-all relation between

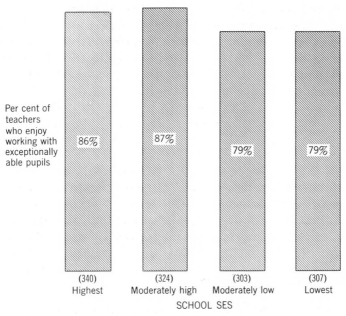

FIGURE 5-7. A larger proportion of teachers in schools of high SES than in schools of low SES report that they enjoy working with exceptionally able pupils.

School SES and career satisfaction as measured here is that teachers in the lowest SES group are caught between the influence of greater devotion to teaching as a career and greater cause for dissatisfaction with their present jobs.

TEACHER MORALE

In social science and educational literature the concept "morale" has been defined in a number of ways. Some use the term to designate a characteristic of an individual. Thus Bates, in reporting on his study of the attitudes of teachers, writes: "Morale is the resultant of the teacher's attitudes, expectations, and feelings related to all factors in the present teaching situation which affect his hopefulness, energy, and devotion to his teaching participation in the school."[8]

But morale has also been defined as a property of a group. An example of this use of the concept is found in the work of Landis, who writes: "Morale is a term to be applied to a state of mind shared by members of a group and moving them to make the fullest use of their strength and skill to obtain their objective. It is not a state of mind existing in one man alone, but in many; it is close to *esprit de corps.*"[9]

The latter conception of morale, as a characteristic of a group, is the one followed in this study. We define the morale of the teaching staff of a school in terms of the proportion of the staff who display great commitment to the school and its tasks.[10]

To measure this phenomenon of teacher "morale," we asked the principals and teachers to characterize their faculties in a variety of ways, and in each case it is our expectation that the lower the School SES the lower is the morale of the teachers. One question asked principals to estimate the percentage of the teachers in their schools who complain about how difficult their students are to work with. In the average school in the highest SES category, 7 per cent were said to make this complaint; in the average school in the lowest SES category, over twice as large a percentage (19 per cent) were said to complain (Figure 5-8).[11] Complaints concerning the physical plant rise from 6 to 14 per cent and complaints as to lack of stimulation in their work rise in percentage from 3 to 9.

[8] Delbert Bates, *The Morale of Teachers of the Public High Schools* (unpublished doctoral dissertation, University of Chicago, 1950), p. 14.

[9] Judson M. Landis, "Morale and Civilian Defense," *American Journal of Sociology,* XLVII (1941), pp. 331–339.

[10] For a consideration of problems connected with the definition and measurement of morale, see James A. C. Brown, *The Social Psychology of Industry* (London: Penguin Books, 1954); Henry Durant, "Morale and Its Measurement," *American Journal of Sociology,* XLVII (1941), pp. 406–414; William E. Hocking, "The Nature of Morale," *American Journal of Sociology,* XLVII (1941), pp. 302–320; Goodwin B. Watson (Editor), *Civilian Morale* (New York: Reynal and Hitchcock, 1942); and Iago Galdston (Editor), *Panic and Morale* (New York: International Universities Press, 1958). For a general discussion of the morale of teachers, see Ronald G. Corwin, *A Sociology of Education* (New York: Appleton-Century-Crofts, 1965), pp. 294–299.

[11] See Appendix Table 5A-5 for the full elementary school data, and the tests of statistical significance.

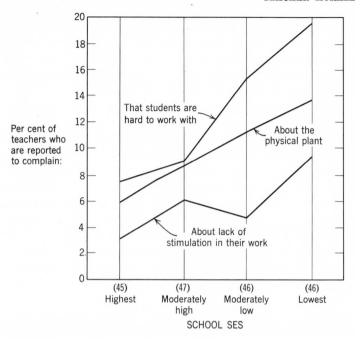

FIGURE 5-8. The lower the school SES, the greater the proportion of teachers who are reported by the principal to complain about three aspects of their work.

In addition, principals and teachers were asked to estimate the proportion of teachers in their schools who appeared to enjoy their jobs. According to both sets of observers, the proportion drops from about 90 per cent in the most privileged schools to about 80 per cent in the least privileged schools (Figure 5-9). Although the magnitude of the difference is less great in the proportion of teachers who, in the opinion of their fellows, "Display a sense of pride in the school," "Display a sense of loyalty to the school," or "Accept the educational philosophy underlying the curriculum," nevertheless, on each of these three items a significantly higher percentage of teachers in the schools of highest than of lowest SES are reported to hold to these attitudes (Table 5-5).[12]

Finally, we have the estimates of the principals and teacher-observers as to the personal loyalty of teachers to their principals. (It seems likely that this attitude contributes substantially to morale

[12] See Appendix Table 5A-6 for the full elementary school data, and the tests of statistical significance.

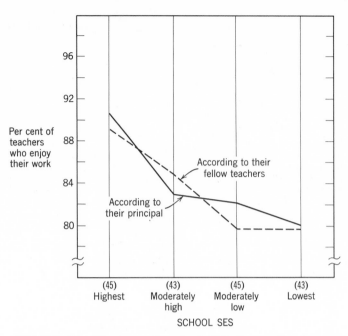

FIGURE 5-9. The lower the school SES, the smaller the proportion of teachers who are reported to enjoy their work.

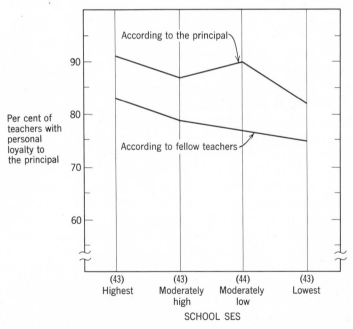

FIGURE 5-10. The lower the school SES, the fewer the teachers who are reported to have personal loyalty to the principal.

TABLE 5-5.   The Lower the School SES, the Lower the Morale of Teachers in Six Respects, According to Teacher-observers

Per cent of teachers in schools who are reported to:	School SES			
	Highest ($N = 43$)	Moderately High ($N = 41$)	Moderately Low ($N = 44$)	Lowest ($N = 41$)
1. Enjoy working in their school.	88%	85%	79%	79%
2. Display a sense of pride in school.	89	89	83	81
3. Display a sense of loyalty to school.	90	88	86	83
4. Accept the educational philosophy underlying the curriculum.	88	87	86	85
5. Respect the judgment of the administrators of the school.	83[a]	81	81	79[a]
6. Work cooperatively with their fellow teachers.	88[a]	90	88	87[a]

[a] This highest-lowest difference is *not* significant at the .05 level.

since the proportions of "loyal" and "satisfied" teachers vary with School SES in a similar fashion.) Principals of schools in the highest SES category believe that 91 per cent of their teachers have a sense of personal loyalty; those in the lowest SES category believe 82 per cent to be loyal (Figure 5-10). Teachers, by and large, place the figure somewhat lower, but their estimates are as closely related to School SES, with 83 per cent reported as loyal in the highest SES category and 75 per cent in the lowest.

To sum up: all of the six principal and seven teacher reports relating to the aggregate satisfaction, or morale, of teachers in their schools are in the direction of lower satisfaction with lower School SES, and all except three of these thirteen differences are statistically significant. Although in absolute terms no single difference is dramatic, the regularity of these results supports our interpretation that these differences are not random. We conclude, therefore, that teacher morale bears a positive relationship with School SES.

This chapter began by predicting a positive relationship between School SES and all measures of teacher satisfaction. The data that we have presented indicate that we must distinguish between satisfaction with career and satisfaction with present job situation. Contrary to prediction, teachers in the lowest SES category appear to enjoy many aspects of the work of teachers *more* than do teachers in higher SES categories, and they are not on the whole more critical than other teachers of professional aspects of the career. However, the data suggest that the difficulties of the present job—particularly the low academic performance of their pupils—produce teachers who, as predicted, have relatively low morale as a group, and as individuals are dissatisfied with many aspects of their job and are relatively more eager to find different positions within the field of education. Apparently, the specific job situation, and not the career, is the source of dissatisfaction to these teachers. In Chapter 8 we shall return to consider this point in the context of the role of the principal in the school of low SES.

Chapter 6

SCHOOL SES AND TEACHER PERFORMANCE

We have shown in the preceding chapters that teachers in schools of different SES levels differ in many ways. Those who teach at the lowest level of School SES are, for example, on the average younger and less experienced. Although they tend to derive more satisfaction from their work, they tend to have less job satisfaction and lower morale than those who teach at the highest level. Such differences in qualifications, satisfaction, and morale, could be expected to have some effect on the job performance of teachers. Together, their effect might be considerable. We therefore hypothesized that teacher job performance would be lower in schools of lowest than in those of highest SES.

The aspects of job performance we shall consider are: professional competence, innovative behavior, interest in pupils, and cooperation with school personnel. It is our prediction that in every case, School SES will be positively related to performance. In comparison with teachers in the highest SES category, teachers in the lowest category will be less competent, will innovate less frequently, will take less interest in their pupils, and will be less cooperative with supervisors, principals, and other teachers.

Both principals and teachers were asked to estimate the percentage of teachers in their schools who displayed certain performance characteristics. If the relationship between School SES and teacher performance differed according to the two sets of observers, we would be forced to choose which to rely upon. We would have to consider that, on the one hand, the principal's longer experience in education and his supervisory role give him an advantage in observing and judging teacher behavior. He sees all the teachers, but they do not see each other in the act of teaching. On the other hand, the principal may be prone to a defensive bias in his evaluations. He is responsible for the behavior of all his teachers; they are not responsible for the behavior of each other.

As it happens, however, the reports of the two sets of observers are in agreement. According to both, the lower the School SES, the lower in general is the level of performance of the teachers. The principal questionnaire contained 33 items, all of which suggest the existence of lower performance in schools of lowest SES—22 of these trends being statistically significant.[1] The teacher questionnaire contained 13 such items, all of which also suggest the existence of lower performance in schools of lowest SES—9 of these trends being statistically significant.[2]

However, the fact that the principals and teachers are in agreement, although reassuring, does not compensate for the possibility that the reports of both groups are likely to be subjective and based more upon general impressions than upon objective samplings of teacher behavior.[3] Furthermore, the teachers and principals in the schools of lowest SES may well be using different frames of reference from those used by the teachers and principals in the schools of higher SES.[4] Although we suspect that such problems of measurement have tended to suppress rather than inflate the observed differences, we cannot be sure. However, because of the exploratory nature of this research, and because of the many problems of conducting more objective measure-

[1] Because of limitations of space only 17 of these 33 items are presented in the appendix. See Appendix Table 6A-1.

[2] Because of space limitations only 9 of these 13 items are presented in the appendix. See Appendix Table 6A-2.

[3] However, even direct observation is plagued by limitations. See, for example, Donald M. Medley and Harold E. Mitzel, "Measuring Classroom Behavior by Systematic Observation" in Nathaniel L. Gage (Editor), *Handbook of Research on Teaching* (Chicago: Rand McNally and Company, 1963), pp. 247–328. For an excellent general discussion and review of research in "teacher effectiveness" see Joseph E. Morsh and Eleanor W. Wilder, *Identifying the Effective Instructor: A Review of Quantitative Studies, 1900–1952.* Research Bulletin No. AFPTRC-TR-54-44 (San Antonio, Texas: Air Force Personnel and Training Research Center, Lackland Air Force Base, 1954).

[4] See, for example, David Gottlieb, "Teaching and Students: The Views of Negro and White Teachers," *Sociology of Education,* XXXVII (1964), pp. 345–353.

ment procedures in a large number of urban schools, we decided to pursue the question of School SES and teacher performance with the data at hand. Since the basic agreement of the principals and teachers increases our confidence in the findings, we shall present both analyses, using first the reports of principals and then those of teachers.[5]

TEACHER PERFORMANCE AS REPORTED BY THE PRINCIPAL

Professional Competence

The principals were asked to estimate the percentage of their teachers who "had mastered the skills necessary to present their subject with high competence." To the extent to which respondents focused on the part of this item referring to mastery of skills, their replies furnish us with a measure of one important qualification of teachers. But most principals may have answered in terms of the behavioral part of the item, referring to presentation of subject matter. Whatever the interpretation, there is a significant relationship between their replies and the SES of their school, since 85 per cent of the teachers in the average elementary school in the highest SES category, and 69 per cent in the average school in the lowest category are said to have this competence (Figure 6-1).[6]

Table 6-1 groups five additional aspects of teaching competence. On all five, the trend is in the same direction as that on the first item: according to their principals, teachers in the lowest SES category are more apt to waste classroom time than those in the highest category; to lack self-confidence; and to be unable to control their students. They are less apt to maintain a professional attitude

[5] It will be remembered that in Chapters 2 and 3 we used the reports of principals and teachers to describe and compare the *schools* of different SES. On the other hand, throughout Chapter 4 and the first part of Chapter 5, we compared the characteristics and attitudes of the *teachers* in four different types of schools. This seems justified because our focus was on the individual teachers in schools of different SES rather than on the schools themselves. In the latter part of Chapter 5, when we examined the morale of teachers, we used the teachers' reports to characterize the schools because, as we noted, morale is generally considered to be an attribute of a group rather than of an individual. Since in this chapter, our aim, as it was in Chapters 2 and 3 and the latter part of Chapter 5, is to characterize the schools of different SES rather than the individual teachers in them, we have again used the reports of the principals and teachers to describe each of the 187 elementary schools.

[6] See Appendix Table 6A-1 for the data on this and 16 additional items, as well as for all tests of statistical significance.

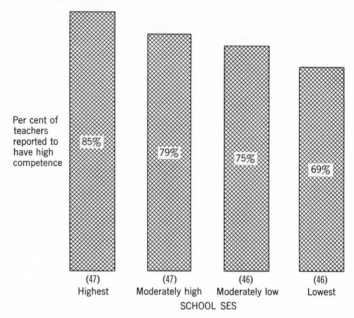

FIGURE 6-1. The lower the school SES, the lower the proportion of teachers who have mastered the skills necessary to present their subjects with high competence. (All figures and tables in this chapter present data comparing the average *elementary* school in each of the four school SES categories. Unless otherwise indicated, the reporter is the school principal.)

toward their work and to carry out their teaching assignments competently. Thus, teachers in schools for the most disadvantaged are said to display less professional competence than teachers in schools for the most advantaged. Although statistically significant, the difference for each item between the schools of highest and lowest SES is small.

Innovation and Improvement

A dominant theme in current educational literature on problems of the educationally deprived child is his need for curriculum, methods, and materials adapted to his particular requirements. The literature stresses a need for educational innovation and experiment in the slum school. However, according to our data, his teacher seems less aware of this need and less innovative than the teacher in a more privileged school where the need is perhaps less intense. Thus, according to principals in schools of the highest SES, 64 per cent of the teachers consistently try out new ideas in the classroom. However, in the average school of lowest SES, the comparable per cent is only 50 (Figure 6-2).

TABLE 6-1.   The Lower the School SES, the Smaller the Proportion of Teachers Who Are Reported as Showing Competence in a Number of Respects

	School SES			
Per cent of teachers in the average school who:	Highest $(N_m = 46)$	Moderately High $(N_m = 47)$	Moderately Low $(N_m = 45)$	Lowest $(N_m = 46)$
1. Have mastered skills necessary to present their subject matter with high competence.	85%	79%	75%	69%
2. Do not waste classroom time.	95	89	92	87
3. Have self-confidence.	96	93	90	90
4. Are able to control students.	98	95	94	93
5. Maintain a professional attitude toward work.	93	89	91	88
6. Competently carry out their teaching assignments.	91	87	88	86

The usual textbook is reputedly addressed to a middle-class or rural child; its language, illustrations, and themes bespeak a world foreign to the child in an urban slum. If this is true, and if children learn best from familiar materials, then it seems essential that teachers supplement their textbooks. A large majority of teachers apparently do so. Nevertheless, the average principal in schools of lowest as compared with highest SES reports that twice as large a percentage of his teachers (12 per cent as compared with 6 per cent) do textbook teaching only (Table 6-2).

Since, as we have seen, teachers in low SES schools have less mastery of teaching skills than those in high SES schools, they might be expected to make an extra effort to improve. However, this does not appear to be the case, since only 77 per cent in the lowest group, as compared to 88 per cent in the highest group, are said to make this effort (Table 6-2).

On the average it appears that somewhat more conventional and routine teaching is being practiced at the School SES level at which the need for changing the *status quo* may be the greatest.

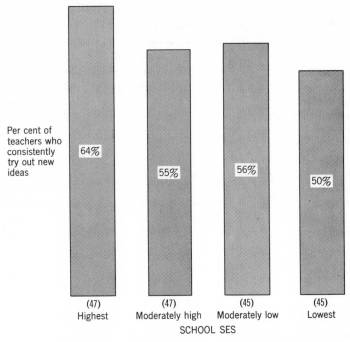

FIGURE 6-2. The lower the school SES, the smaller the proportion of teachers who consistently try out new ideas in the classroom.

TABLE 6-2. In the Average School of Lowest SES, the Proportion of Teachers Reported to Be Interested in Innovation and Improvement Is Smaller than in the Average School of Highest SES

	School SES			
Per cent of teachers in the average elementary school who:	Highest ($N_m = 47$)	Moderately High ($N_m = 47$)	Moderately Low ($N_m = 45$)	Lowest ($N_m = 46$)
1. Consistently try out new ideas in the classroom.	64%	55%	56%	50%
2. Attempt to improve their teaching skills.	88	81	87	77
3. Go beyond the textbook.	94	91	88	88

Interest in Pupils

In Chapter 1 we touched upon an issue frequently discussed in educational literature, that of the middle-class teacher's lack of understanding of, or respect for, lower-class pupils. Several of the items in the principal's questionnaire suggest that teachers in schools of lowest SES are less apt to be interested in their pupils or to make an effort to meet their individual needs than teachers in schools of highest SES. Thus, 82 per cent in the highest category, but only 70 per cent in the lowest, are reported by the principal to "make themselves available to students at some sacrifice of their own free time;" and 90 per cent in the highest category, but 79 per cent in the lowest, "plan their courses so that different types of students can benefit" (Table 6-3). The trend is the same with respect to the teachers who "get real satisfaction out of devoting their time and energy to the problems of young people." Taken together these findings suggest that in schools where pupils have greatest need for the interest and help of teachers, proportionately fewer teachers offer such interest and help.

TABLE 6-3. In the Average School of Lowest SES a Smaller Proportion of Teachers than in the Average School of Highest SES Are Reported to Take a Great Interest in Their Students

Per cent of elementary teachers in the average school who:	School SES			
	Highest $(N_m = 47)$	Moderately High $(N_m = 46)$	Moderately Low $(N_m = 43)$	Lowest $(N_m = 46)$
1. Make themselves available to students at some sacrifice of their own free time.	82%	70%	70%	70%
2. Plan their courses so that different types of students can benefit from them.	90	78	84	79
3. Get real satisfaction out of devoting their time and energy to the problems of young people.	88	78	81	79

Cooperation with School Personnel

Reports of principals indicate that teachers in urban slum schools are less cooperative with school personnel than are teachers in elementary schools of higher SES. Thus, 94 per cent in the highest category are said to "help new teachers to the school to become acclimated to the ways that things are done," whereas only 86 per cent cooperate in this respect in the lowest SES category (Table 6-4). There are

TABLE 6-4. In the Average School of Lowest SES a Smaller Proportion of Teachers than in the Average School of Highest SES Cooperate with Other Personnel

Per cent of elementary teachers in the average school who:	School SES			
	Highest ($N_m = 46$)	Moderately High ($N_m = 47$)	Moderately Low ($N_m = 45$)	Lowest ($N_m = 46$)
1. Agree with the principal's philosophy of education.	88%	84%	87%	80%
2. Would stand behind the principal if he were unfairly criticized.	94	90	94	89
3. Cooperate with the principal's efforts to improve the school program.	94	92	93	90
4. Help new teachers become acclimated.	94	91	89	86
5. Get along amicably with their supervisors.	96	94	96	92

significant differences in the same direction on items referring to cooperation with their supervisors and to cooperation with, agreement with, and loyalty to their principals (Table 6-4). Apparently, either because of lack of native talent or because of the job situation, relatively fewer teachers in the slum school are successful in human relations.

TEACHER PERFORMANCE AS REPORTED BY OTHER TEACHERS

Evidence on the relationship of School SES to teacher performance based on the teachers' observations matches very closely the evidence based on the principals' estimates.

We suggested at the beginning of the chapter that the typical principal might feel defensive about teacher performance in his school and thus might be more favorable than would teachers in his evaluation of that performance. It is also possible that teachers tend to be critical of each other. In any case, on most questions at each SES level, the percentage of teachers performing well is higher in the reports of the principals than in the reports of the teachers. The important point, however, is that regardless of who the observer is, the *relationship* of School SES to teacher performance stands.

Figures 6-3 and 6-4 illustrate the fundamental agreement between the reports of principals and teachers on the effect of School SES on teacher performance. In the case of the percentage of "teachers in your school who waste a lot of time in their classroom activities," the item

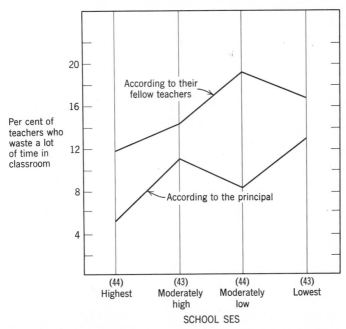

FIGURE 6-3. According to both principals and teachers, a greater proportion of teachers in the schools of lowest than of highest SES, waste time in their classroom activities.

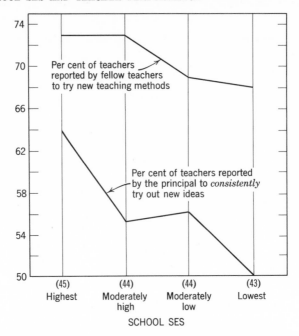

FIGURE 6-4. According to both principals and teachers, a smaller proportion of teachers in schools of lowest than of highest SES try new methods in their classrooms.

is identical in both questionnaires; the principal is, in general, more favorable; but, as we go from highest to lowest SES categories, estimates rise from 5 to 13 per cent according to the estimates of principals and from 12 to 17 per cent according to the teachers (Figure 6-3). In the question on innovation, the items are not identical, since the principal was asked to estimate the percentage "who *consistently* try out new ideas," whereas the teachers were merely asked the percentage "who try new teaching methods." The overall estimates of the principal are therefore naturally below those of teacher observers. But, according to both, the percentage declines with SES: from 64 to 50 as reported by principals, and from 73 to 68 as reported by teachers (Figure 6-4).

On all 9 items in the teacher questionnaire dealing with teachers' instructional performance, the direction of the SES differences in response are to the disadvantage of the schools of lowest SES, and on 7 items the difference is statistically significant.[7] Table 6-5 shows the

[7] See Appendix Table 6A-2 for the data on all 9 items, as well as for all tests of statistical significance.

SES response pattern on 8 items selected for illustration because of their relevance to the needs of all children, and especially to the needs of children living in city slums.

Item 1, "Are committed to doing the best job of which they are capable," refers to an attitude indispensable in the successful performance of any job, but one probably that is especially needed by the teacher in the slum schools who contends with great obstacles. We find that 87 per cent in the average school of highest SES, but 82 per cent in the school of lowest SES, are said to hold this attitude (Table 6-5).

Item 2, "Take a strong interest in the social or emotional problems of their students," measures the humanitarian interest of the teacher and his concern for the good of the "whole child." This quality seems basic to understanding and helping a pupil from a deprived background; yet it is found in a smaller percentage of those teaching the most disadvantaged than of those teaching the most advantaged (76 per cent as compared to 84 per cent, Table 6-5).

Optimism concerning student potential may be, of all the teachers' attitudes, the most difficult and yet the most important to maintain in the low SES school. The teacher who "maintains an interest in improving the educational program," "tries new teaching methods," or "provides opportunities for students to go beyond the minimum of assigned work," may be one who refuses to accept as final the evidence of low test scores, is flexible and imaginative in approach, and sets high standards for himself and his pupils. That such "optimism" is less common in elementary schools of lowest than of highest SES is suggested by the replies of the teachers. For instance, as reported by their fellow teachers, 73 per cent in the average school in the bottom SES category as compared to 81 per cent in the average top school provide opportunities for students to go beyond the minimum (Table 6-5, Item 5).

Realism and the ability to control the situation could also be basic qualifications for a successful teacher and, in the slum school, as important as humanitarian concern for the pupil's welfare or optimism as to his academic potential. Item 6 in Table 6-5, "Maintain effective discipline in their classes," shows a very small but statistically significant difference between highest and lowest SES groups (84 per cent as compared to 81 per cent).

Item 7, "Plan their classes so that different types of students can benefit from them," involves respect for the individual pupil, whatever his SES, and interest and skill in adapting instruction and curriculum to meet his needs. The difference in replies from highest to lowest

TABLE 6-5. In the Average School of Lowest SES, the Performance of Teachers, as Reported by Teacher-observers, Tends to Be Lower than in the Average School of Highest SES

Per cent of elementary teachers in the average school who:	School SES			
	Highest $(N_m = 43)$	Moderately High $(N_m = 41)$	Moderately Low $(N_m = 44)$	Lowest $(N_m = 41)$
1. Are committed to doing the best job of which they are capable.	87%	86%	85%	82%
2. Take a strong interest in the social or emotional problems of their students.	84	83	81	76
3. Maintain an interest in improving the educational program of the school.	83	83	82	79
4. Try new teaching methods in their classrooms.	73	73	69	68
5. Provide opportunities for students to go beyond the minimum demands of assigned work.	81	79	77	73
6. Maintain effective discipline in their classes.	84	86	83	81
7. Plan their classes so that different types of students can benefit from them.	84[a]	84	84	81[a]
8. Do everything possible to motivate their students.	81[a]	80	79	77[a]

[a] This highest-lowest difference is *not* significant at the .05 level.

SES levels is not significant for this item, although the direction again favors the most advantaged SES group (Table 6-5).

Item 8, "Do everything possible to motivate their students," measures acceptance on the part of the teacher of personal responsibility for academic progress. Teachers who behave in this fashion actively seek pupil cooperation through a variety of techniques and share with the underprivileged child the burden of his "lack" of motivation. According to the reports of observers, however, this behavior is less frequent (though not significantly) among teachers in schools of lowest than of highest SES (77 per cent as compared to 81 per cent, Table 6-5).

We have discussed in some detail the importance for all pupils and the special relevance for the pupil in the slum school of these eight aspects of teaching, because in Chapter 8 we shall use them as the measure of teacher performance, to be there related to the principal's performance in schools of different SES.

The prediction that the performance of teachers in schools of lowest SES would be found to be poorer than the performance of teachers in schools of highest SES is supported by the data. This conclusion is based on the evidence of two independent sets of observers—principals and teachers—and it is supported by the trend across a large number of items, and by the high proportion of statistically significant differences between schools of highest and lowest SES. Although it would seem safe to generalize this finding of a SES difference in teacher performance to the population of schools from which this sample was drawn, it should be noted that, in general, the observed differences are not very large.

Chapter 7

SCHOOL SES AND THE PRINCIPAL

In schools for disadvantaged Americans, "the role of the principal is crucial to the success of the entire staff."[1] This statement from a 1962 report of the Educational Policies Commission of the National Education Association voices the recent thinking of a number of students of the problems of slum schools. However, as we suggested in Chapter 1, little systematic research has been done to support opinion in this area.

Chapter 8 will be devoted to a discussion of the role of the principal in schools of different SES levels. On the basis of a number of theoretical considerations, we shall develop hypotheses and present evidence as to the effect of School SES on the interrelationship of the performance of a principal and that of his teachers.

However, before we consider the interrelationship of principal and teacher, we must learn something about the principal himself. We have looked at the relationship between School SES and many teacher variables: we have seen how teachers of different backgrounds, qualifications, attitudes, and behavior are distributed according to the average social and economic status of their pupils. But as yet we do not know whether School SES bears a similar relationship (or lack of relationship) to the characteristics of principals. A description of the average principal in each of the four SES categories is therefore required. Then, aware of the effect of School SES on both principals and

[1] Educational Policies Commission, *Education and the Disadvantaged American* (Washington, D. C.: National Education Association, 1962).

teachers, we can consider the interrelation of their performance in different SES contexts.

Is there any reason to suppose that a principal is entirely different from a teacher? Are his background, his upbringing, and his views distinct or akin? We suggest that three forces determine the resemblance of the average principal to the average teacher. In the first place, there is probably an identity of origin: with two exceptions, the 187 elementary principals that we studied were all at one time teachers. Since principals are, almost without exception, selected from among the ranks of former teachers, we would expect them to be similar to teachers in background. However, a different occupational role (that of "principal" rather than "teacher") demands different qualifications. The third and, from the point of view of this book, most important influence on the characteristics of both principals and teachers in the same school is the identical social context in which the role must be played. We will discuss the resemblance and dissimilarity of teachers and principals in terms of these three points.

THE ORIGINS OF PRINCIPALS
IN COMPARISON WITH TEACHERS

In Chapter 4, we presented findings on the origins of the teachers in our sample according to the SES of the schools in which they were teaching. We saw that although there seems to be a tendency for teachers in schools of lowest SES to be themselves of low SES background, this tendency is statistically significant only when the index is father's occupation and not when it is parental education or income. Teachers in schools of lowest SES are also significantly more likely to be Negro, to be Catholic, and to be of urban background. We must examine our first assumption—that principals are identical with teachers in origin, both over-all and in the different SES categories.

Figure 7-1 shows on a single graph the percentage of elementary principals and of teachers who grew up in a large city. The differences between the two groups are negligible.[2] Overall and within School SES

---

[2] In this chapter (unless especially noted) we will not examine the relationship of the characteristics of the principals to the SES of their school for statistical significance. Our interest is instead primarily one of comparison between teachers and principals. Therefore, our focus will be on the differences between the relationship of many variables with School SES for teachers and principals.

Ideally in examining these differences one would want to test the null hypothesis that there is no interaction between the scores of principals and teachers

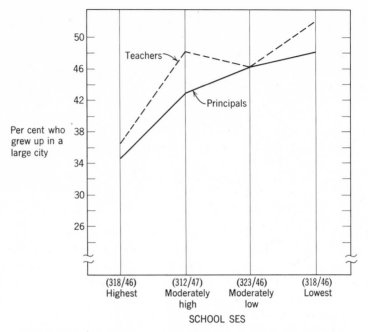

FIGURE 7-1. In schools of lowest SES, as compared with those of highest SES, a greater proportion of both teachers and principals are urban in background. (All figures and tables in this chapter refer to *elementary* schools.)

categories, a highly similar proportion of principals and teachers are urban in background (35 per cent and 36 per cent, respectively, in the highest, and 48 per cent and 52 per cent, respectively, in the lowest SES group).

In socioeconomic origin, also, principals resemble teachers. Figure 7-2 shows only part of the data on the occupation of fathers, namely, the percentage who were classified in Chapter 4 as blue collar. There we see that whereas the fathers of 30 per cent of teachers and 32 per cent of principals in the highest SES category were skilled or unskilled laborers, 43 per cent of the teachers and 39 per cent of the principals in the lowest category are in this group. In other words,

---

on each dependent variable. However, appropriate statistical tests (for example, a two-way analysis of variance with an unbalanced design) are very difficult to perform, and given the apparent similarity of the two groups, seem unnecessary.

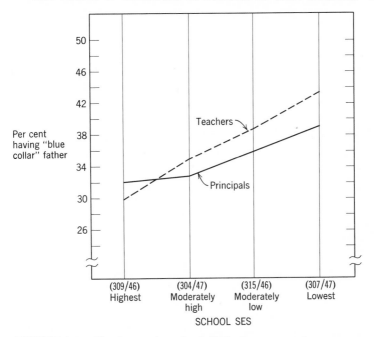

FIGURE 7-2. The lower the school SES, the greater the proportion of both teachers and principals who report a blue collar occupation for their fathers.

not only are principals and teachers very alike in this respect in each
School SES category, but also the slight difference by School SES in
the case of teachers seems to persist in the case of principals.

The line graph showing the percentage of teachers and principals
who reported that their families had incomes above the average in
their communities at the time of their high school graduation is interesting, for the overall percentages are very close, and they follow the
same pattern as we go from highest to lowest School SES (Figure
7-3). For principals, the percentage drops from 45 to 43; for teachers,
from 50 to 43; but for both, those in schools of moderately high SES
are least apt to have enjoyed above-average parental income (30 per
cent in the case of principals and 39 per cent in the case of teachers).
Reports of principals as to the educational level of their parents led
to the same conclusion as to socioeconomic origin as did the data on
father's occupation and parental income. However, space limitations
prevent graphic presentation of the percentage of mothers and fathers
of principals at each educational and School SES level.

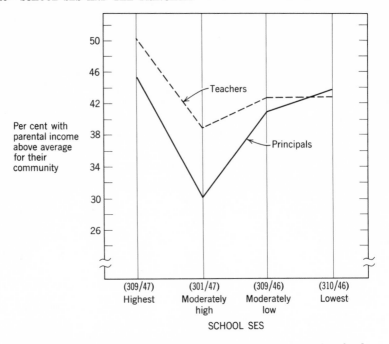

FIGURE 7-3. The parental income (at the time of high school graduation) of teachers and principals varies in a similar fashion by school SES.

In sum, principals and teachers are similar in socioeconomic origin, over-all, and at each School SES level. At no SES level is a difference between principals and teachers very noticeable, although the tendency for the SES of teachers to decline with School SES seems weaker in the case of the principals.

The religious affiliation of principals and teachers shown in Figure 7-4 is nearly identical at the moderately high and lowest School SES levels, where almost two-thirds of the staff are Protestant, about a quarter Catholic, and the rest Jewish. In schools of highest and moderately low SES, there seem to be proportionately fewer Jewish and more Protestant principals than teachers. At these two SES levels also are the smallest proportion of principals and teachers who are Jewish or Catholic, and the greatest proportion who are Protestant.

The final background characteristic examined in order to establish the identity, in respect to origin, of principals and teachers is race. We have already reported that schools of lowest SES, as compared to those of highest SES, have (1) more nonwhite pupils (73 per cent as compared to 2 per cent, Figure 4-13), (2) more nonwhite teachers (41 per cent as compared to 1 per cent, Figure 4-13), but (3) a smaller ratio of nonwhite teachers to nonwhite pupils (Figure 4-15). Now we will add the race of the principal to this picture of the racial composition of elementary schools at each SES level.

However, before considering the racial congruency of principals and teachers in each School SES category, we will follow the procedure of Chapter 4 and examine first the over-all racial congruency. Table 7-1, like Table 4-3, shows the proportion of teachers who are nonwhite according to the proportion of pupils who are nonwhite. However, Table 7-1 also shows the proportion of principals in each cell who are nonwhite.

If the reader looks first at the bottom line of Table 7-1, which gives the percentage of nonwhite principals and teachers in all schools

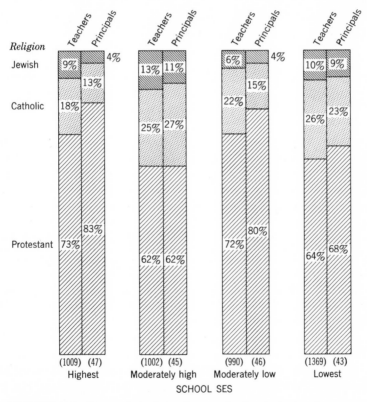

FIGURE 7-4. Proportion of teachers and of principals who are Jewish, Catholic, or Protestant, by school SES.

(regardless of the race of pupils), he will note that the proportion of nonwhite principals rises with the proportion of nonwhite teachers, but less rapidly for principals than for teachers. None of the principals is nonwhite in the 121 schools in which none of the teachers is non-

TABLE 7-1. Proportion of Principals Who Are Nonwhite, According to the Proportion of Teachers and the Proportion of Pupils Who Are Nonwhite, for 185 Schools

Per Cent of Pupils Who Are Nonwhite	Per Cent of Teachers Who Are Nonwhite												
	0	1 to 9	10—19	20—29	30—39	40—49	50—59	60—69	70—79	80—89	90 to 99	100	All Schools
100						0/1		0/1		0/1	1/2	6/6	7/11
90–99	0/3	0/1	0/2	0/2	0/1	1/1		0/2		1/2	2/2	2/2	6/18
80–89		0/3	0/1	0/1	0/1								0/6
70–79			0/1	0/1									0/2
60–69	0/1			0/1									0/2
50–59	0/2		1/1	0/1			0/1						1/5
40–49	0/1	0/1											0/2
30–39	0/2			0/3	0/1								0/6
20–29	0/2	0/4											0/6
10–19	0/10	0/2	0/1										0/13
1–9	0/56	0/7	0/2	0/1									0/66
0	0/44	0/4											0/48
All schools	0/121	0/22	1/11	0/8	0/2	1/2	0/1	0/3	—	1/3	3/4	8/8	14/185[a]

[a] Data on race of teachers unknown for two of the 187 elementary schools.

Note. For each cell the denominator of the proportion represents the total number of principals and the numerator represents the number of those principals who are nonwhite.

white, and all principals are nonwhite in the 8 schools in which all teachers are nonwhite. But although there is one nonwhite principal in a school in which 10 to 19 per cent of the teachers are nonwhite, and one in a school in which 40 to 49 per cent of the teachers are nonwhite, in general, the nonwhite principals are located in schools where over 80 per cent of the teachers are nonwhite.

The rest of the table shows the location of nonwhite principals in relation to the race of pupils as well as teachers. Of the 14 nonwhite principals in the sample, all except one are in schools in which over 90 per cent of the student body is nonwhite.

We are now in a position to understand the relation of School SES to the racial background of principals in comparison with that of teachers. Figure 7-5 shows that the percentage of nonwhite principals rises as SES falls, from zero in schools of highest or moderately high SES to 17 per cent in schools of lowest SES. However, there are nonwhite teachers even in schools of highest SES, and the proportion rises much more rapidly for teachers than for principals until, in the lowest category, it is 41 per cent or twice that of principals. From the evidence of Table 7-1 it seems safe to infer that in this lowest SES category there are many white principals in schools in which almost all pupils and a large number of teachers are nonwhite.

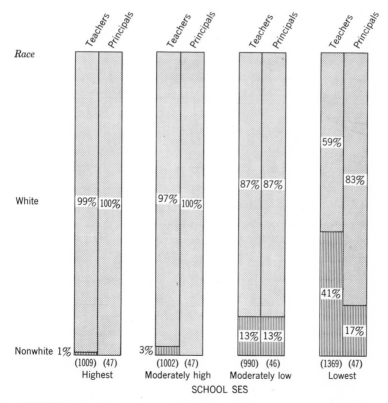

FIGURE 7-5. Proportion of teachers and of principals who are white or nonwhite, by school SES.

It therefore appears that our assumption of identity of origin of principals and teachers, supported by the evidence in respect to urban background, socioeconomic origin, and religion, is not supported in regard to race. In comparison with teachers, the proportion of principals who are nonwhite is smaller and more thoroughly confined to low SES schools and to schools attended predominantly by nonwhite pupils. With this exception, however, we can say that principals and teachers appear to be alike in background, over-all, and also in each School SES category.

CAREER CHARACTERISTICS OF PRINCIPALS IN COMPARISON WITH TEACHERS

The job of a principal demands different qualifications than does that of a teacher. There are a number of characteristics on which we would expect principals, in general, to differ from teachers in general. But we have no reason to expect these characteristics to bear a different relation to School SES in the case of principals than in the case of teachers. In the case of the background characteristics of principals and teachers we predicted identity, both over-all, and in relation to School SES. In the case of career characteristics, we expect that teachers and principals will differ, but that the relation to School SES will be the same for both groups.

Table 7-2 summarizes the data necessary to examine this general expectation.[3] In Chapter 4, we reported the percentage of teachers who had been teaching less than 5 years, from 5 to 10 years, and over 10 years, and we concluded that the teaching experience of those in schools of highest SES was significantly longer than the experience of those in the lowest category (Figure 4-2). Table 7-2 focuses on the average experience, rather than on the percentage in each of several experience categories, of teachers and principals in schools of highest and lowest SES.

Quite naturally, the average experience in education of principals is much longer than that of teachers, since it usually includes a number of years as teacher and in a quasiadministrative position as well as in the principalship. However, the average experience in education for principals in the lowest School SES category (25 years) is 5 years shorter than that for principals in the highest category. This matches

[3] For the number of cases on which each summary statistic presented in Table 7-2 was based, see Appendix Table 7A-1.

our previous finding that the average experience of teachers in schools of lowest SES (11 years) is 4 years shorter than that of teachers in schools of highest SES. There is also a drop in average experience in present school for both principals and teachers as we go from schools of highest to those of lowest SES. Whether, for staff as experienced as principals, such small differences have any practical significance is debatable. Our purpose at this point is merely to note the trends.

TABLE 7-2. Summary Table of Career Characteristics of the Teachers and the Principals in Schools of Highest and Lowest SES

	Teacher		Principal	
	Highest SES $(N_m = 1009)$	Lowest SES $(N_m = 1369)$	Highest SES $(N_m = 47)$	Lowest SES $(N_m = 47)$
Mean experience				
As teacher	15 years	11 years	11 years	12 years
As administrator			6	3
As principal			13	10
In education	15	11	30	25
In school	7	6	8	6
Mean age	42	39	55	50
Mean per cent				
Above average quality college work	68%	60%	81%	72%
MA or doctorate	23	25	92	94
Male	11	19	47	58
Mean salary	$5711	$5854	$9032	$9202

Just as we expect the average principal to be more experienced than his teachers, so too we expect him to be older. He is, as a matter of fact, more than 10 years older. But average age for both principal and teacher drops as SES drops, so that whereas the average principal in schools of highest SES is 55 years old, he is only 50 years old in schools of lowest SES.

Quality of college work is a variable that behaves in the same fashion as do experience, tenure, and age, when the role of the staff member is considered. Not only does a greater proportion of principals

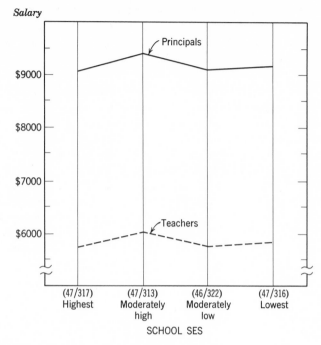

FIGURE 7-6. The salary of both principals and teachers varies by school SES in a similar manner.

than teachers report that their college work was above average, but also in the case of both, the proportion falls with School SES. In the case of teachers, 68 per cent in the highest category and 60 per cent in the lowest report that their college work was above average. In the case of principals, the corresponding percentages are 81 and 72 (Table 7-2).

The last three items in Table 7-2 show further the type of difference that we expected between all principals and all teachers. However, the effect of School SES is in a different direction from that in the case of experience, age, or quality of college work. Thus, the proportion of principals who are men, or who hold a degree above that of bachelor, is several times as great as the proportion of teachers who are men, or who hold higher degrees; in addition, the mean salary of principals is comparably higher than that of teachers. In each case, however, the percentage rises between highest and lowest SES. This SES difference seems negligible in the case of higher degrees and not great in the case of salary or per cent male although, as reported in

Chapter 4, the difference in the percentage of male teachers between schools of highest and lowest SES reaches the level of statistical significance.

In order to illustrate the interrole difference, but similar SES pattern, of the career characteristics of principals and teachers, we have graphed their salaries in the four SES categories in Figure 7-6. It is evident that role produces a large difference, but that SES produces extremely little difference in salary. The reader may also want to compare this figure with Figure 7-3. The comparison reveals that members of both staff positions in schools of moderately high SES had relatively less family income in their childhood, but have a relatively higher income at present. These teachers and principals appear to be the most socially mobile group.

All in all, with respect to career qualifications such as those summarized in Table 7-2, the principal is on the average above his teachers. However, School SES seems to bear the same relation to the characteristics of both principal and teacher. For incumbents of both staff positions it appears to be age, experience, and sex that are related to School SES: on the average those in schools at the bottom of the SES ladder are younger, less experienced, and more apt to be male than those in schools at the top of the ladder.

THE ATTITUDES OF PRINCIPALS
IN COMPARISON WITH TEACHERS

In origin, as we have seen, principals are similar to teachers, both over-all and in relation to School SES. In role qualifications, principals differ from teachers, but are affected in the same manner by School SES. Do we expect the satisfactions and aspirations of principals and teachers to be alike because of common origin, or different because of different role, and do we expect School SES to have a similar influence on the attitudes of both? Since they are "drawn from the same pool," we might expect principals and teachers to have similar attitudes. But, since their different roles demand different socialization, give different vantage points from which to view the problems of education, and expose them to different pressures and rewards, we might expect their attitudes to differ. However, since we found the different social contexts of schools in high and low SES neighborhoods related to the attitudes of teachers (Chapter 5), we expect the same relation for the attitudes of principals, except in those areas in which role differences may be paramount. As a test of this prediction, let us examine the replies of principals to two sets of questions similar to those already presented for teachers.

Chapter 5 was devoted to the satisfaction of teachers with their job, their career, and their work. In the case of job satisfaction, we found an especially clear positive relation with School SES. Principals too are much more apt to be satisfied with various aspects of their jobs in schools of high rather than low SES. On 14 out of 19 items the tendency is in this direction. For instance, 100 per cent of the principals in schools of highest SES report some measure of satisfaction with the teaching effectiveness of their faculty, whereas only 89 per cent of those in schools of lowest SES are thus satisfied (Figure 7-7).

Figure 7-8 graphs on the same scale the satisfaction of teachers and principals with teacher-administration cooperation in their schools. Although the role of the principal may make him more favorable on the average than the teacher, for both, the lower the School

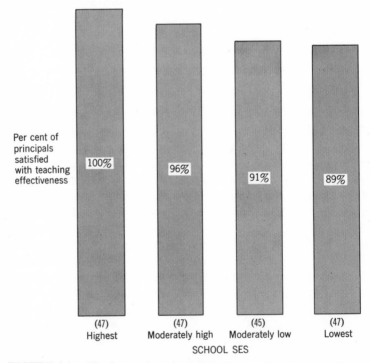

FIGURE 7-7. The lower the school SES, the smaller the proportion of principals who are satisfied with the teaching effectiveness of their faculty.

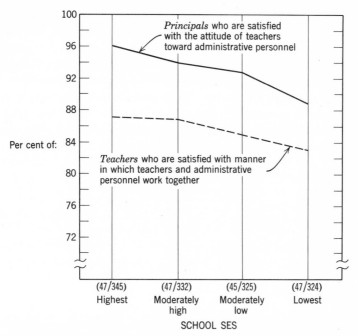

FIGURE 7-8. The lower the school SES, the less satisfied are both principals and teachers with teacher-administrator cooperation.

SES, the lower the satisfaction. If two parties are dissatisfied with the cooperation between them, one might expect them to act to improve cooperation and thus increase their satisfaction. However, the unfavorable context in which the principals and teachers of slum elementary schools work apparently affects even their ability to achieve the cooperation desired by both groups (Figure 7-8).

Teachers in low as compared with high SES schools were found in Chapter 5 to be more often eager to leave for a new position. Although the principals are often thought to be more interested in vertical mobility than teachers, our data find them just as interested in horizontal mobility (Table 7-3). Thus, the percentage who say they are anxious for a "principalship of greater responsibility" rises from 17 in the highest SES category to 43 in the lowest one (Figure 7-9).

"A principalship of greater responsibility" might be interpreted by some as a principalship in a school where the needs of pupils are greater or where low achievement of pupils and morale of teachers is a greater challenge to the administrator—in other words, in a school of low SES. But since Figure 7-9 shows a relatively strong inclination on the part of principals in the lowest category to seek "greater responsibility," this is apparently not their interpretation of the meaning of the item.

We suggest that the phrase is for many principals a euphemism referring to nonaltruistic goals. Table 7-3 supports this assertion. The percentage of those who want a "principalship of more prestige" is exactly the same as the percentage who want "more responsibility" in both the highest SES category (17 per cent) and the lowest (43 per

TABLE 7-3. Principals in Schools of Lowest SES Have a Higher Level of Aspiration than Principals in Schools of Highest SES

Per cent of principals who "have some desire to," "would very much like to," or "are extremely anxious to":	School SES			
	Highest $(N_m = 47)$	Moderately High $(N_m = 47)$	Moderately Low $(N_m = 46)$	Lowest $(N_m = 47)$
1. Obtain a principalship of greater responsibility.	17%	28%	30%	43%
2. Obtain a principalship of more prestige.	17	13	30	43
3. Obtain a principalship paying more money.	40	47	41	55
4. Take a more important role in professional educational organizations.	34	51	48	55
5. Obtain a higher administrative position in this school system.	40	36	46	51

cent). A cross-tabulation of the replies of principals to these two items reveals that 71 per cent of the principals who desire greater responsibility also desire greater prestige (Table 7-4). On the other hand, only 7 per cent of those *not* desirous of greater responsibility desire greater prestige. Moreover, the correlation between the two replies increases as School SES falls, since only 63 per cent of those wanting responsibility in the highest SES category, but 90 per cent of the comparable group in the lowest category also want prestige. Our guess that the phrase "greater responsibility" refers to "nonaltruistic goals," especially at the lowest School SES level, therefore seems justified.

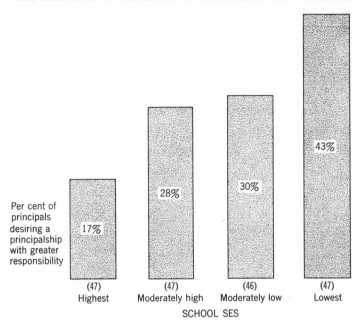

FIGURE 7-9. The lower the school SES, the greater the proportion of principals who desire a principalship with greater responsibility.

TABLE 7-4. Most Principals Who Desire a "Principalship of Greater Responsibility" also Desire a "Principalship of Greater Prestige," and Especially in Schools of Lowest SES

Principal's Desire for Greater Responsibility	Per Cent of Principals Who Desire Greater Prestige				
	School SES				
	Highest	Moderately High	Moderately Low	Lowest	All Schools
Desirous	63%(8)a	46%(13)	71%(14)	90%(20)	71%(55)
Not desirous	8 (39)	0 (34)	13 (32)	7 (27)	7 (132)
All principals	17 (47)	13 (47)	30 (46)	44 (47)	26 (187)

a Figures in parentheses refer to the number of cases upon which the associated percentage was based.

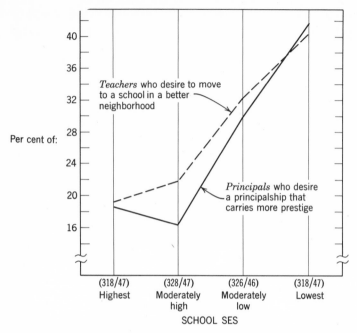

FIGURE 7-10. In schools of lowest SES, as compared with those of highest SES, both teachers and principals desire to move to a "better" school.

Although there is less difference between schools of different SES levels in the desire for a "principalship paying more money," the trend is clearly in the same direction as on the two previous items (Table 7-3). It is therefore probable that such financial considerations also played a part in the response to the first item.

We reported in Chapter 5 that the lower the School SES, the more the teacher wants to leave for a new position. This tendency was especially strong in response to the item "move to a school in a better neighborhood" (Figure 5-2). In order to show that the aspirations of principals and teachers are similar in this respect, we have graphed together in Figure 7-10 the percentage of teachers who want a better neighborhood and the percentage of principals who want more prestige. The curves are very close indeed, although teachers are, in general, more anxious than principals to move for this reason.

The fourth item in Table 7-3, "Take a more important role in professional educational organizations," is a measure of the emphasis placed on support of the profession. A greater percentage of principals in schools of moderately high and lowest SES (51 per cent and 55 per cent) desire greater involvement in professional organizations than in schools of high or moderately low SES (34 per cent and 48 per cent).

The satisfactions and aspirations of principals and teachers are, as predicted, very similar, particularly in areas like those we have discussed, where role differences are unlikely to produce conflicting outlooks. Moreover, the effect of School SES on the occupants of both staff positions seems the same: the lower the SES, the greater the emphasis placed on the profession itself, the lower the job satisfaction, and the greater the desire to move to a different assignment.

PRINCIPAL PERFORMANCE

The performance of teachers was found in Chapter 6 to be significantly related to School SES. On the basis of reports from both principals and teachers, the higher the SES of the school, the more likely are its teachers to perform well. Our list of items indexing such behavior was long, comprehensive, and varied—in wording and context. We pointed out at the end of the chapter, however, that the positive relation between School SES and teacher performance revealed by our data is nevertheless not as strong as might be expected, given the still stronger relation between School SES and pupil performance. We shall now consider the performance of the principal and ask whether this, too, may be influenced by the social context of the school.

It can be argued that the performance of the average principal might be affected by School SES either as much as or less than that of the average teacher. On the one hand, principals in general have a common background (except with respect to race) with teachers, and the satisfaction they feel toward many aspects of their job is held in common with teachers. These considerations suggest that the performance of the principal, like that of his teachers, may decline with the SES of his school.

On the other hand, the career qualifications of principals are much greater than those of teachers over-all, and they reveal SES differences whose direction may not necessarily be to the advantage of the privileged school. Thus, as we saw in Table 7-2, principals are apt to be older and more experienced than teachers. Moreover, the lower the School SES, the lower the age and experience of both. It is to be noted, however, that although comparative youth and inexperience for the teacher might mean poorer performance, lower age and less experience for principals (who are in general much older) might mean more vigorous administrative performance on the part of the younger ones. On three other characteristics reported in Table 7-2—salary, per cent male, and proportion who hold a higher degree—the general tendency is to the advantage of the underprivileged school. In general, the relation of SES to career characteristics suggests that we might find less difference by SES in the performance of principals than in that of teachers.

There is another reason why low School SES may not depress the performance of the principal to the extent that it appears to depress that of the teacher. We showed that a considerable proportion of both principals and teachers in the low SES school is eager to move to another position. Would not either principals or teachers who are eager for such a move attempt to earn a transfer by keeping up the level of their job performance? We suggest that such considerations are more likely to seem important to the principal than to the teacher. Of the two, the position of principal is much more visible to those in the higher administration who control transfers. Moreover, a comparison of Table 5-1 and item 5 in Table 7-3 reveals that by and large, principals are more desirous for vertical mobility than are teachers. These considerations add weight to the arguments based on the different career characteristics of principals and teachers and lead us to predict that the job performance of principals is likely to be *less* affected by School SES than is that of the teachers.

The data which we shall use to measure the performance of principals in schools of different SES levels are the evaluations of 4 to 10 teacher observers in each school. As was reported in Chapter 2, a questionnaire was mailed to a random sample of 10 teachers in each of 476 of the 501 schools participating in the National Principalship Study, 71 per cent of whom replied. One section of the questionnaire listed 23 aspects of the job of principal and asked respondents to indicate for each whether they viewed the performance of their principal as "outstanding," "excellent," "good," "fair," "poor," or "very poor." Although individual replies ranged from very poor to outstanding, the average on all items falls at various points between good (scored 4) and excellent (scored 5).

The fact that, over-all, the evaluations are so favorable is not surprising. It is usual for people to distinguish among categories of "good," rather than between categories of "good" and "bad" when rating others. It is more surprising, in view of the other findings of the School SES Study, to discover that on only three items are SES differences between the schools of highest and lowest SES large enough to be statistically significant: Item 5, referring to "obtaining parental cooperation with the school"; Item **27**, "Publicizing the work of the school"; and Item **22**, "Attracting able people to the school staff." The data presented in Chapter 3 concerning the relation of SES to parental visits to and cooperation with the school may in part explain why principals in slum schools are considered relatively unsuccessful in parental relations. Their relative lack of attention to publicity may be caused by the poorer achievement and behavior of pupils and lower social prestige of parents in these neighborhoods, while their relative lack of success in staff recruitment may be explained by the preference of teachers for schools of higher SES.

Figure **7-11** contrasts the effect of School SES on the principal's success in obtaining parental cooperation with the effect on his success in getting experienced teachers to improve their performance. On the first item there is a sharp drop as School SES falls; on the second, there is almost no difference between the schools of highest and lowest SES.

Table **7-5** shows the mean (average) rating on each of the 23 items for all principals in each School SES category as well as the

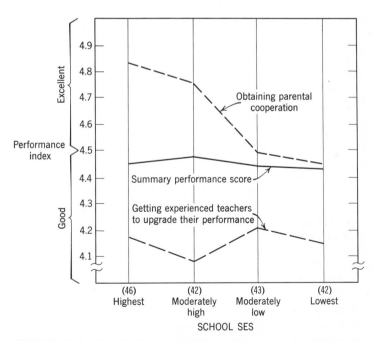

FIGURE 7-11. Teachers' ratings of the performance of principals in schools of different SES with respect to two aspects of their work, as well as a summary score based upon 23 aspects of their work.

TABLE 7-5. Mean Score on 23 Aspects of the Principals' Performance by School SES, According to the Reports of Teacher Observers

How do you view the performance of your principal [outstanding (6), excellent (5), good (4), fair (3), poor (2), very poor (1)] in each of the following areas?	School SES				Lowest–Highest SES Difference
	Highest (N = 46)	Moderately High (N = 42)	Moderately Low (N = 43)	Lowest (N = 42)	
1. Running meetings or conferences.	4.46	4.39	4.55	4.41	−.05
2. Handling delicate interpersonal situations.	4.43	4.43	4.40	4.33	−.10
3. Working with community agencies.	4.65	4.66	4.69	4.60	−.05
4. Getting teachers to use new educational methods.	4.23	4.29	4.31	4.29	+.06
5. Obtaining parental cooperation with the school.	4.83	4.76	4.49	4.45	−.38*
6. Resolving student discipline problems.	4.16	4.26	4.20	4.14	−.02
7. Directing the work of administrative assistants.	4.39	4.53	4.49	4.49	+.10
8. Cutting red tape when fast action is needed.	4.37	4.36	4.37	4.43	+.06
9. Maximizing the different skills found in the faculty.	4.35	4.42	4.34	4.39	+.04

TABLE 7-5 (Continued)

How do you view the performance of your principal [outstanding (6), excellent (5), good (4), fair (3), poor (2), very poor (1)] in each of the following areas?	School SES				Lowest–Highest SES Difference
	Highest (N = 46)	Moderately High (N = 42)	Moderately Low (N = 43)	Lowest (N = 42)	
10. Communicating the objectives of the school program to the faculty.	4.56	4.63	4.63	4.64	+.08
11. Improving the performance of *inexperienced* teachers.	4.09	4.17	4.21	4.17	+.08
12. Getting *experienced* teachers to upgrade their performance.	4.17	4.18	4.21	4.15	−.02
13. Giving leadership to the instructional program.	4.34	4.38	4.46	4.36	+.02
14. Developing *esprit de corps* among teachers.	4.22	4.37	4.27	4.23	+.01
15. Revising school procedures in the light of modern educational practices.	4.38	4.43	4.38	4.47	+.09
16. Handling parental complaints.	4.78	4.79	4.65	4.69	−.09
17. Publicizing the work of the school.	4.62	4.43	4.52	4.40	−.22*

(*Continued*)

TABLE 7-5 (Concluded)

How do you view the performance of your principal [outstanding (6), excellent (5), good (4), fair (3), poor (2), very poor (1)] in each of the following areas?	School SES				Lowest–Highest SES Difference
	Highest (N = 46)	Moderately High (N = 42)	Moderately Low (N = 43)	Lowest (N = 42)	
18. Keeping the school office running smoothly.	4.68	4.85	4.70	4.74	+.06
19. Planning generally for the school.	4.73	4.81	4.75	4.78	+.05
20. Knowing about the strengths and weaknesses of teachers.	4.49	4.55	4.51	4.53	+.04
21. Getting teachers to coordinate their activities.	4.27	4.30	4.32	4.33	+.06
22. Attracting able people to the school staff.	4.43	4.37	4.27	4.22	−.21*
23. Knowing about the strengths and weaknesses of the school program.	4.62	4.61	4.58	4.70	+.08
Total mean score	4.45	4.48	4.45	4.43	−.02

* Lowest–highest difference statistically significant at the .05 level.

difference between the two extreme categories. The difference between highest and lowest SES is positive on some items and negative on others but, for the most part, it is negligible. The average mean score for all items, shown at the bottom of the table, (as well as in Figure 7-11) varies only slightly from one SES category to another.

Although the SES differences in principal performance are thus

TABLE 7-6. Rank Order of 23 Aspects of the Performance of Principals, According to the Magnitude of the Difference between the Mean Score of Principals in the Highest and Lowest SES Categories

Aspect of the Performance of Principals	L-H SES Difference
5. Obtaining parental cooperation with the school.	−.38*
17. Publicizing the work of the school.	−.22*
22. Attracting able people to the school staff.	−.21*
2. Handling delicate interpersonal situations.	−.10
16. Handling parental complaints.	−.09
3. Working with community agencies.	−.05
1. Running meetings or conferences.	−.05
12. Getting *experienced* teachers to upgrade their performance.	−.02
6. Resolving student discipline problems.	−.02
14. Developing *esprit de corps* among teachers.	+.01
13. Giving leadership to the instructional program.	+.02
20. Knowing about the strengths and weaknesses of teachers.	+.04
9. Maximizing the different skills found in the faculty.	+.04
19. Planning generally for the school.	+.05
8. Cutting red tape when fast action is needed.	+.06
18. Keeping the school office running smoothly.	+.06
4. Getting teachers to use new educational methods.	+.06
21. Getting teachers to coordinate their activities.	+.06
11. Improving the performance of *inexperienced* teachers.	+.08
10. Communicating the objectives of the school program to the faculty.	+.08
23. Knowing about the strengths and weaknesses of the school program.	+.08
15. Revising school procedures in the light of modern educational practices.	+.09
7. Directing the work of administrative assistants.	+.10

* Lowest–highest difference statistically significant at the .05 level.

generally very slight, it is still instructive to group the items according to the size and direction of the difference between schools of highest and lowest SES. Table 7-6 does this, and an examination of the order of the items suggest that teachers in schools of lowest SES tend to report that their principals are weaker in public and human relations than teachers in schools of highest SES. On the other hand, principals in the lowest category are viewed as relatively strong in comparison with those in the highest category in all matters relating to the instructural program of the school. However, since these small differences are positive for some of the items and negative for others, the over-all difference for all items together is negligible.

This chapter has described the average elementary school principal in each of the four School SES categories. In order to capitalize on the more detailed descriptions in the preceding three chapters of the effect of School SES on teachers, we have, in this chapter, compared principals with teachers in this regard. We have shown that, except in respect to race, the background of principals is like that of teachers in each School SES category, with little variation from one category to another. Although the career qualifications of principals are necessarily higher than those of teachers, School SES bears the same relation to the qualfication of the occupants of both positions. The role of the principal and his greater age and longer experience may influence his *attitudes,* and cause them to diverge from those of his teachers. But School SES has a similar effect on those attitudes of teachers and principals which were tested in this study. Finally, it would seem that the *performance* of the principal differs from the performance of the teacher in being less associated, on the average, with the SES of the school in which it takes place. We now turn to a consideration of the interrelationship of the performance of principals and teachers in schools of different SES levels.

Chapter 8

THE ROLE OF THE PRINCIPAL IN SCHOOLS OF DIFFERENT SES

In the preceding five chapters we have focused in turn upon the pupils, their parents, teachers, and principals in urban elementary schools of different socioeconomic composition. The performance of pupils, although associated with School SES, seems to be less so than our data on parental reinforcement of the school might lead us to predict; the performance of teachers, also associated with School SES, seems to be less so than that of their pupils; and the performance of principals is likely to be still less closely associated with School SES. Figure 8-1 presents a rough representation of these apparent trends.[1] It suggests that as we move from parental behavior to the performance of pupils, teachers, and principals, the slope of the difference between schools of highest and lowest SES diminishes.

Why might School SES have less effect on teachers than on pupils and less effect on principals than on teachers? In order to answer this question we shall frame a general picture of schools of different SES based upon some of our other data. Our formulation will have to be an oversimplification, but consideration of the effects of School

[1] Figure 8-1 is intended to be suggestive rather than authoritative. It represents a rough estimation of the trends noted in Figure 3-4, Figure 3-8, Table 6-5, and Table 7-5. A more careful representation of these trends would require the measurement of the behavior of parents and the performance of pupils, teachers, and principals in far greater detail than was possible in this research. Once measured, these indices could be related to School SES in such a manner that standardized slope coefficients could be computed and compared.

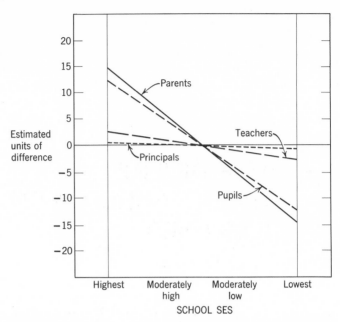

FIGURE 8-1. Slope of the estimated difference between the average school of highest and lowest SES on rough indices of parental support, and of pupil, teacher, and principal performance. (Data not plotted for the average school of moderately high or moderately low SES. All figures and tables in this chapter refer to *elementary* schools only.)

SES in the abstract may help us to understand its very complicated nature.

A CONCEPTUAL FRAMEWORK

We assume, to begin with, that social forces are operating to mediate the effect of social class upon the performance of individuals in schools of different SES. For example, if the performance of pupils is not as highly related to School SES as might be expected, given a knowledge of the behavior of their parents, this may be due to the mediating effect of the performance of teachers. In other words, the performance of teachers may affect that of pupils differently in schools of different SES.

Similarly, if the performance of teachers is not as closely related to School SES as might be predicted from a knowledge of the performance of pupils, this may be due to the mediating effect of the performance of principals. To put it another way, the performance of principals may affect that of teachers differently in schools of different SES.

Both hypotheses can be investigated empirically, but within this study of principals and teachers, only the second hypothesis (that the performance of principals affects that of teachers differently in schools of different SES) will be considered. Before doing so, it is important to review some of the phenomena which distinguish schools of high and low SES. In this way we can make explicit the assumptions which permit us to specify the manner in which the relationship between a principal's performance and that of his teachers will differ between schools of high and low SES. Further assumptions again oversimplify the complex phenomena under study, and many of them will not hold in all schools and under all conditions. However, abstraction is a necessary part of scientific inquiry.

The Phenomenon of Urban Change

Urban change in the 1960's, as noted in Chapter 1, is affecting schools of different SES in different ways. The socioeconomic level of a few schools on the periphery or in redeveloped sections of some cities may be rising. The socioeconomic level of many more central city school districts in all regions of the United States is falling, often very rapidly. Associated with low SES is an increase in its many correlates considered in Chapter 3: social and emotional problems, deprivation, home instability, and parental disinterest, to name but a few. In many schools of low SES there is also an increase in the proportion of pupils who are nonwhite.

If the objectives of urban education are to reflect the needs of the pupils, then a changing school neighborhood demands a changing school. Under such circumstances the principal occupies a key position for affecting this change, since he is the official primarily responsible for the direction of the school. When the school population is changing rapidly, traditional methods and procedures no longer suffice, and although revisions in instructional materials, in course offerings, and in teacher-pupil ratios are generally determined at administrative levels above that of the school, it is the principal who must fight for them and direct their implementation. It is he who must plan for the school, must chair the many meetings and conferences necessary to interpret the changing needs of pupils, and must encourage teachers to adopt new techniques.

The picture for the urban school of high SES is quite different. Initially higher property values, unwritten restrictive real estate covenants, and a higher degree of community activity serve to buffer the more prosperous school district from many of the effects of urban decline. Under less turbulent conditions in the immediate social world outside the school there is less need for adaptation in the educational world inside. With the same type of pupils from one year to the next, the need for curriculum modification and new instructional materials, as well as for leading a faculty to understand and accept a changing work environment, is minimal. With less turnover in staff as well as pupils, the demand for the orientation and training of teachers is also less than it is in the school of lower SES.

These assumptions with respect to the phenomenon of urban change lead us to predict that the quality of the principal's performance is more crucial to the performance of his teachers in the schools of *low* SES than it is in those of high SES.

The Phenomenon of Pupil Unreadiness

One consequence of urban decline is that the school in areas of low SES, if it is to carry out its chief task of intellectual training, must more and more assume responsibility for something which a decade ago had generally been assumed—that its pupils would be ready and willing to learn. Lack of readiness and motivation on the part of pupils along with a changing social conscience has led many schools to concern themselves with the health of pupils, their moral training, their cultural stimulation, and their basic vocabulary—all of which have traditionally been considered to be the responsibility of the home.[2] Faced with pupils from "deprived" backgrounds, schools must, it is argued, take on new roles if they are to succeed in their traditional one. They have had to become concerned with the well-being of the "whole child," not just his intellect, and for teachers this means that they must reformulate both their objectives and their methods. Again, the principal is the key to this reformulation. It is he who must lead his teachers to accept a new interpretation of their role, must attract able teachers to the low SES school and hold them once they are there. In addition, he must establish and maintain a liaison between teacher and parent which is quite different from that to which many teachers are accustomed.

In the school of high SES, where this revolution of changing pupil needs has taken place to a lesser degree (if it has taken place at

[2] For an excellent review of some of the literature in this area, see Benjamin S. Bloom, Allison Davis, and Robert Hess, *Compensatory Education for Cultural Deprivation* (New York: Holt, Rinehart and Winston, 1965), pp. 12–19.

all), where traditional conceptions of the role of teacher are not challenged, and where parental interest is found rather than sought, the principal's role can remain one of routine administrator rather than of staff leader.

Each of the assumptions above as to the consequences of the phenomenon of pupil unreadiness leads us to predict again that the principal's performance is more crucial to that of his teachers in slum schools than it is in privileged ones.

The Phenomenon of Teacher Restlessness

In view of the many problems of the schools of low SES, it is not surprising that their teachers have relatively low morale, are less satisfied with their jobs, and aspire to move to a "better" situation. Again, the principal plays a crucial role. Much of the dissatisfaction expressed by teachers may be due to their inability to find ways to cope with the pressing demands of their pupils. The teacher in schools of low SES may need to learn how to appreciate improvements in student performance which can at best be measured in negative terms, such as *less dis*interest in learning or in *fewer* years *below* grade level in achievement. In addition, able teachers must be found, trained, and held. The rewards of the educational system must encourage teachers not to work to get *out* of schools of low SES but to work to stay *in* them, and here too the principal plays an important part. He is the major link between the teachers and the central office personnel whose function is to assist the teachers.

The school of highest SES is one that teachers seek to enter rather than escape. Teachers in schools of lowest SES may leave if they do not get effective leadership from the principal to help them cope with the environment pressing so dramatically upon them, but teachers in schools of high SES perform so that they can stay where they are. Clearly, these are two different forms of motivation. In the schools of highest SES the teachers do not need the principal to raise their morale or to sharpen their performance; in fact he may even suppress it. (For example, if the principal is very capable in handling parental complaints, he may reduce one source of pressure conducive to high teacher performance.) In many respects the teachers in schools of high SES can perform at a high level, irrespective of the performance of the principal; whereas in schools of lowest SES, their performance may depend on his.

Again, as with the other two phenomena, assumptions about teacher restlessness lead us to predict that the principal's performance is more crucial to his teachers in the schools of low SES than it is in those of high SES.

Our arguments concerning each of the three phenomena known to affect the urban school of the 1960's all assume that the principal can act as a buffer between the social class composition of the school and the performance of its teachers, moderating (and possibly redirecting) the influence of the former on the latter. Since these arguments assume a more positive role for the principal in schools of low SES than in those of high SES, we propose the following hypothesis: *that the performance of the principal is more closely related to that of his teachers in schools of low SES than it is in those of high SES.*

TESTING THE HYPOTHESIS

In order to test the above hypothesis we shall examine data from the elementary schools of the School SES Study, utilizing statistical models proposed by Lazarsfeld and extended by Blalock.[3] We cannot establish beyond any shadow of doubt the validity of the reasoning presented above, for such certainty is unfortunately beyond the limits of our data, but we can begin to accumulate evidence in support of it. The data which we shall use do not permit us the luxury of "proof," but they do enable us to ascertain whether or not the reasoning which we have introduced *could* be true.

Before testing the hypothesis let us review briefly the relationship of School SES, teacher performance, and principal performance. We saw in Chapter 6 that the performance of teachers is significantly related to the SES of the schools in which they teach. In general, the lower the SES of elementary schools, the smaller the proportion of teachers who were reported to be performing in several desirable ways. In Chapter 7 it was shown that the performance of principals was *not* significantly related to the SES of the schools which they administer. In general, elementary schools of different SES contain about the same proportion of principals rated as being "poor," "fair," "good," etc. in many aspects of administrative behavior. Since School SES is related to teacher performance in elementary schools but is not related to that of the principal, we have within our data

---

[3] The reader not familiar with the logic or method used in making causal inferences from nonexperimental data is referred to: Herbert H. Hyman, *Survey Design and Analysis: Principles, Cases, and Procedures* (Glencoe, Illinois: The Free Press, 1955) or Hubert M. Blalock, *Causal Inferences in Nonexperimental Research* (Chapel Hill: The University of North Carolina Press, 1964).

the two characteristics necessary for discovering the conditional relationship we seek.[4]

Measurement of Key Variables

Before we can relate the principals' performance to that of their teachers in schools of different SES, it is necessary to consider ways of defining each variable (School SES, Principal Performance, and Teacher Performance) in a manner which will make their measurement independent. In measuring teacher performance in Chapter 6, both the report of the school principal and the average report of from four to ten "teacher-observers" were used. In measuring the performance of the principals only the average report of the teacher-observers was used, while the measure of School SES was based upon the reports of the principals alone. Since the principals had been used to observe School SES we decided to use only the reports of the teacher-observers in measuring principal and teacher performance. However, to avoid using the same teachers as observers of both variables we split at random into two groups the four to ten teachers who served as our observers in each of the 158 elementary schools where complete data were available for all relevant variables. Group A, containing from two to five teachers from each school, was used as the observers of the principal's performance. Group B, containing the other two to five teachers from each school, was used as the observers of the performance of their fellow teachers. The principals' reports continued to serve as our measure of School SES.

To obtain a "best estimate" of the performance of the *principal* of each school, the reports of the teachers in Group A as to his performance in each of 23 aspects of his role were averaged for each aspect.[5] For illustrative purposes, we summarized in Figure 8-2 the teachers' reports about their principals' performance in "giving leadership to the instructional program" (one of 23 aspects of administrative behavior to be considered). It will be noted there that in four of the 158 schools the average teacher in Group A considers his principal to be "poor" in this respect. Similarly, in six of the schools he is considered to be "outstanding." In general, however, the teachers have a moderate evaluation of their principals: in 69 schools he is con-

---

[4] For a more detailed discussion of this point, see Hyman, *op. cit.*, Chapter VII.

[5] For the means and standard deviations of the reports of the average teachers to each of the 23 questions as well as their intercorrelations, see Appendix Table 8A-1.

sidered by the average teacher to be "good," and in 61 others to be "excellent" (Figure 8-2).

A "best estimate" of the performance of the *teachers* in each of the 158 elementary schools was obtained by averaging within each school the reports of the two to five teachers in Group B for each of eight indices of teacher performance.[6] The variability of these aver-

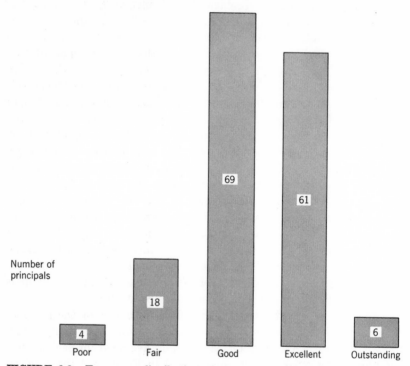

FIGURE 8-2. Frequency distribution of the performance of 158 school principals in "giving leadership to the instructional program," as reported by the average teacher-observer in Group A.

age scores as to the teachers' performance in "doing everything possible to motivate their students" (one of the eight indices of teacher performance) is shown in Figure 8-3. Although, in general, more than 75 per cent of the teachers perform in this manner, in four schools the proportion is less than 50 per cent, while in 10 others it is more than 95 per cent (Figure 8-3).

[6] For the means and standard deviations of the reports of the average teachers to each of the eight questions, as well as their intercorrelations, see Appendix Table 8A-2.

Principal and Teacher Performance

To demonstrate the relationship of these measures of principal and teacher performance for elementary schools in general, we computed the average proportion of teachers who are "doing everything possible to motivate their students" separately for schools where the

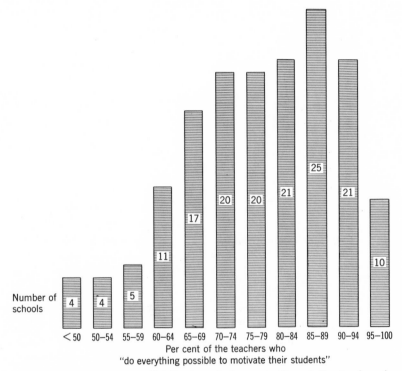

FIGURE 8-3. Frequency distribution of the proportion of the teachers in each of 158 schools who "do everything possible to motivate their students," as reported by the average teacher-observer in Group B.

principal's performance in "giving leadership to the instructional program" is rated as "poor or fair," "good," or "excellent or outstanding."[7] Whereas in schools where the principal's performance is rated

[7] In order to make the computation of mean teacher performance scores more reliable, the four schools in which the principal was rated as "poor" were combined with the 18 in which he was rated "good." Similarly, the six schools in which he was rated as "outstanding" were pooled with the 61 in which he was rated "excellent."

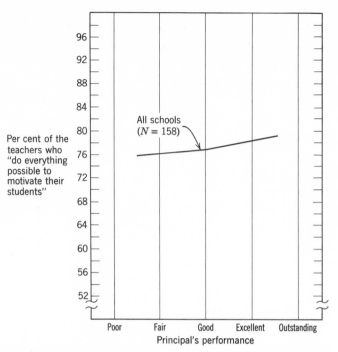

FIGURE 8-4. Relationship, within 158 schools, of the average proportion of the teachers who "do everything possible to motivate their students" to the principal's performance in "giving leadership to the instructional program."

as "poor or fair" 76 per cent of the teachers, on the average, are reported to be "doing everything possible to motivate their students"; in schools where he is rated "good" or "excellent or outstanding" it is 77 and 79 per cent respectively (Figure 8-4). Thus a slight positive relationship is seen to exist between these aspects of principal and teacher performance, irrespective of the SES of the school to which they have been assigned. The product-moment correlation coefficient representing this trend is .19, which is statistically significant. Similar coefficients were computed between the principals' performance in "giving leadership to the instructional program" and the seven other indices of teacher performance discussed in Chapter 6. Five of the seven are also statistically significant (Table 8-1).

In order to summarize the eight indices of teacher performance into a single stable summary score, a "factor analysis" was performed.[8] As we expected, the resulting Teacher Performance Score

[8] See Appendix Tables 8A-2 and 8A-3 for the details of the principal components factor analysis.

TABLE 8-1. Correlation Coefficients for the Relationship of the Performance of 158 Principals in "Giving Leadership to the Instructional Program" with Eight Indices of Teacher Performance and a Teacher Performance Score

Index of Teacher Performance The per cent of teachers who are reported to:	Coefficient of Correlation
1. Do everything possible to motivate their students.	.19*
2. Are committed to doing the best job of which they are capable.	.12
3. Take a strong interest in the social or emotional problems of their students.	.20*
4. Plan their classes so that different types of students can benefit from them.	.09
5. Maintain an interest in improving the educational program of the school.	.20*
6. Try new teaching methods in their classrooms.	.19*
7. Provide opportunities for students to go beyond the minimum demands of assigned work.	.18*
8. Maintain effective discipline in their classes.	.18*
Teacher performance score[a]	.18*

* $p < .05$.

[a] The teacher performance score is a weighted average of the eight indices of teacher performance given above. For the details of its operational definition, see Appendix Tables 8A-2 and 8A-3.

is also significantly related to the principals' performance in "giving leadership to the instructional program" (Table 8-1).

Each of the 22 additional indices of the principals' performance considered in Chapter 7 was also related to the Teacher Performance Score and for 15 the correlation was statistically significant. Table 8-2 reveals, for example, that the performance of the principal in "planning generally for the school," "keeping the school office running smoothly," and "attracting able people to the staff" is positively related to the Teacher Performance Score. On the other hand, his performance in "working with community agencies," "directing the work of administrative assistants," and "cutting red tape when fast action is needed" appears to be unrelated.[9]

[9] A more comprehensive test of the relationship between principal and teacher performance can be made by examining the multiple correlation of the 23 aspects of principal performance with the Teacher Performance Score. The resulting coefficient is .47 which, with 23 and 134 degrees of freedom, is statistically significant at below the .05 level.

TABLE 8-2.   Correlation Coefficients for the Relationship of 23 Aspects of the Performance of 158 Principals with the Teacher Performance Score

Aspect of the Principal's Performance	Coefficient of Correlation
1. Running meetings or conferences.	.16*
2. Handling delicate interpersonal situations.	.12
3. Working with community agencies.	.04
4. Getting teachers to use new educational methods.	.20*
5. Obtaining parental cooperation with the school.	.14*
6. Resolving student discipline problems.	.20*
7. Directing the work of administrative assistants.	.09
8. Cutting "red-tape" when fast action is needed.	.08
9. Maximizing the different skills found in the faculty.	.10
10. Communicating the objectives of the school program to the faculty.	.10
11. Improving the performance of *inexperienced* teachers.	.18*
12. Getting *experienced* teachers to upgrade their performance.	.11
13. Giving leadership to the instructional program.	.18*
14. Developing *esprit de corps* among teachers.	.16*
15. Revising school procedures in the light of modern educational practices.	.17*
16. Handling parental complaints.	.17*
17. Publicizing the work of the school.	.16*
18. Keeping the school office running smoothly.	.27*
19. Planning generally for the school.	.27*
20. Knowing about the strengths and weaknesses of teachers.	.17*
21. Getting teachers to coordinate their activities.	.22*
22. Attracting able people to the school staff.	.24*
23. Knowing about the strengths and weaknesses of the school program.	.15*

* $p < .05$.

Principal and Teacher Performance, by School SES

The major focus of this chapter, however, is not upon the performance of teachers and principals in general, but rather upon them in schools of different SES. To consider this question the 158 elementary schools were divided into two groups—those of highest or moderately high SES (hereafter referred to as high SES) and those of lowest or moderately low SES (hereafter referred to as low SES).[10]

[10] It was necessary to deviate from our earlier policy of comparing primarily the schools of highest and lowest SES in order to obtain more reliable correlation

A correlation analysis similar to that presented in Table 8-2 was then conducted separately within the 79 schools of high SES and the 79 of low SES.[11]

For the schools of high SES, none of the 23 indices of the principal's administrative performance is significantly related to the Teacher Performance Score (Table 8-3). On the other hand, within those of low SES 19 of the 23 coefficients are statistically significant.[12] In addition, for all 23 indices of the principals' performance, the correlation coefficient for the low SES schools is greater than that for the high SES schools. *The hypothesis that the performance of principals is more closely related to that of their teachers in schools of low SES than of high SES is supported.*

We can gain some insight into what is behind these coefficients of correlation by considering within schools of high and low SES the relationship discussed earlier between the principal's performance in "giving leadership to the instructional program" and the percentage of his teachers who "do everything possible to motivate their students." In Figure 8-5 the mean percentage of the teachers who are reported to "do everything possible to motivate their students" in schools where the principal's performance in "giving leadership to the instructional program" is rated as "poor or fair," "good," or "excellent or outstanding" are presented and graphed separately for the two types of schools.[13] It can be seen that whereas in elementary schools of high SES the percentage of teachers who so perform *falls* slightly from 80 to 78 to 76 as the principal's performance rises, in the schools of low SES the corresponding percentages *rise* from 72 to 76 to 82 as the principal's performance rises. Clearly, the relationship between

---

coefficients. The same general differences in the relationships presented in Table 8-3 between principal and teacher performance in schools of high and low SES can be shown between schools of highest and lowest SES, but the reduced number of degrees of freedom makes interpretation more difficult.

[11] For the means and standard deviations of the report of the average teachers in the schools of high and low SES to each of the 23 questions, see Appendix Table 8A-4.

[12] Within the schools of high SES the multiple correlation of the 23 aspects of principal performance with the Teacher Performance Score is .41 which, with 23 and 55 degrees of freedom, is *not* statistically significant at below the .05 level. Within the schools of low SES the corresponding coefficient is .69 which is statistically significant.

[13] Again, for greater reliability of mean teacher performance scores, the categories of "poor" and "fair" as well as of "excellent" and "outstanding" were combined.

TABLE 8-3. Correlation Coefficients for the Relationship of 23 Aspects of the Performance of Principals with the Teacher Performance Score in Schools of High and Low SES

Aspect of the Principal's Performance	Coefficient of Correlation	
	High SES Schools $(N = 79)$	Low SES Schools $(N = 79)$
1. Running meetings or conferences.	$-.04$	.34*
2. Handling delicate interpersonal situations.	$-.03$	.22*
3. Working with community agencies.	$-.03$	.08
4. Getting teachers to use new educational methods.	.04	.35*
5. Obtaining parental cooperation with the school.	$-.08$	.25*
6. Resolving student discipline problems.	$-.04$	.37*
7. Directing the work of administrative assistants.	$-.01$	.17
8. Cutting "red-tape" when fast action is needed.	.00	.16
9. Maximizing the different skills found in the faculty.	$-.02$	.19
10. Communicating the objectives of the school program to the faculty.	$-.03$	.21*
11. Improving the performance of *inexperienced* teachers.	$-.02$	.35*
12. Getting *experienced* teachers to upgrade their performance.	$-.05$	.25*
13. Giving leadership to the instructional program	$-.03$	.31*
14. Developing *esprit de corps* among teachers.	$-.06$	.23*
15. Revising school procedures in the light of modern educational practices.	.05	.31*
16. Handling parental complaints.	$-.09$	.33*
17. Publicizing the work of the school.	$-.04$	.30*
18. Keeping the school office running smoothly.	.08	.40*
19. Planning generally for the school.	.02	.45*
20. Knowing about the strengths and weaknesses of teachers.	$-.07$	.34*
21. Getting teachers to coordinate their activities.	.04	.35*
22. Attracting able people to the school staff.	.07	.34*
23. Knowing about the strengths and weaknesses of the school program.	$-.06$	.32*

*$p < .05$.

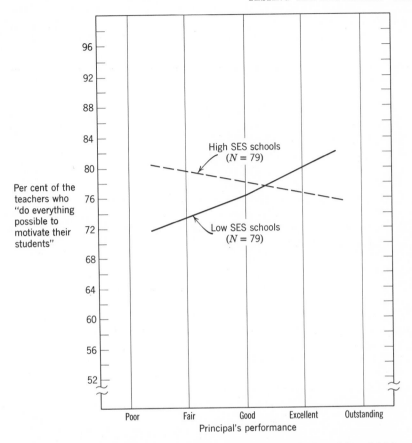

FIGURE 8-5. Relationship, within 79 schools of low SES and 79 of high SES, of the average proportion of the teachers who "do everything possible to motivate their students" to the principal's performance in "giving leadership to the instructional program."

the principals' performance in "giving leadership to the instructional program" and that of their teachers in "doing everything possible to motivate their students" is different in these two types of elementary schools. In those of high SES it is slightly negative (but not significantly) while in those of low SES it is moderately positive (and statistically significant).

In Table 8-4 the 23 areas of administrative behavior presented earlier have been ordered in terms of the relative magnitude of the 23 correlations within the schools of low SES. Thus it can be seen that in schools of low SES the impact of the principal's performance

TABLE 8-4.   Rank Order of 23 Aspects of the Performance of 79 Principals in Schools of Low SES, According to the Magnitude of Their Relationship with the Teacher Performance Score

Aspect of the Principal's Performance	Coefficient of Correlation
19. Planning generally for the school.	.45*
18. Keeping the school office running smoothly.	.40*
6. Resolving student discipline problems.	.37*
4. Getting teachers to use new educational methods.	.35*
11. Improving the performance of inexperienced teachers.	.35*
21. Getting teachers to coordinate their activities.	.35*
20. Knowing about the strengths and weaknesses of teachers.	.34*
22. Attracting able people to the school staff.	.34*
1. Running meetings or conferences.	.34*
16. Handling parental complaints.	.33*
23. Knowing about the strengths and weaknesses of the school program.	.32*
13. Giving leadership to the instructional program.	.31*
15. Revising school procedures in the light of modern educational practices.	.31*
17. Publicizing the work of the school.	.30*
12. Getting *experienced* teachers to upgrade their performance.	.25*
5. Obtaining parental cooperation with the school.	.25*
14. Developing *esprit de corps* among teachers.	.23*
2. Handling delicate interpersonal situations.	.22*
10. Communicating the objectives of the school program to the faculty.	.21*
9. Maximizing the different skills found in the faculty.	.19
7. Directing the work of administrative assistants.	.17
8. Cutting red tape when fast action is needed.	.16
3. Working with community agencies.	.08

*$p < .05$.

on that of his teachers is likely to be most pronounced with respect to his ability to "plan generally for the school," "keep the school office running smoothly," "resolve student discipline problems," and "get teachers to use new educational methods." In contrast, his ability to "work with community agencies," "cut red tape," "develop *esprit de corps* among teachers," and "direct the work of administrative assistants," apparently has little effect on teacher performance in schools of low SES.

We have offered empirical evidence to test the hypothesis that the performance of the principal is more closely related to that of his teachers in schools of low than of high SES. We have seen that although 16 of 23 indicators of the administrative performance of principals are significantly related to teacher performance in general, when the schools are separated according to their SES, significant relationships are found for 19 of the indicators in schools of low SES, but for none in those of high SES. Although, as we mentioned earlier, causation cannot be demonstrated through the use of a cross-sectional analysis such as that presented above, the results of this analysis lend support to the proposition that the performance of the principal is more crucial to that of his teachers in schools of low than in those of high SES. Some of the implications of these findings for further research will be presented in Chapter 11.

Chapter 9

THE EFFECT OF SCHOOL LEVEL ON THE RELATIONSHIP OF SCHOOL SES TO THE CHARACTERISTICS OF PUPILS AND STAFF

All the findings presented up to this point have concerned the elementary school alone. We have occasionally referred the reader to appendix tables showing comparable data for secondary schools, but the discussion in the text has made no reference to the effect of whether a school is classified as "elementary," "junior high," or "senior high" (hereafter referred to as School Level) on the relationship of School SES to characteristics of pupils, parents, teachers, and principals.

Since School Level is associated with both the educational tasks of the school and the socioeconomic status of its clientele, we chose to consider schools at the three levels separately. The data presented in Chapters 3 through 7 supported the expectation that *at the elementary level,* the SES of the school is related to certain important client and staff characteristics. In this chapter we ask the question: Do similar relationships exist within the other school levels? In Chapter 2 we described the method used to divide the 490 schools in our sample into four categories of School SES. At each level, schools were arranged according to their summary SES score (based on the socioeconomic characteristics of parents) and partitioned into four SES groups. Figure 9-1 shows (as did Figure 2-3) the range of scores for each level and also the cutting points used to secure equal numbers in the respective categories of highest, moderately high, moderately low, and lowest SES.

Since secondary schools are larger and draw students from a wider

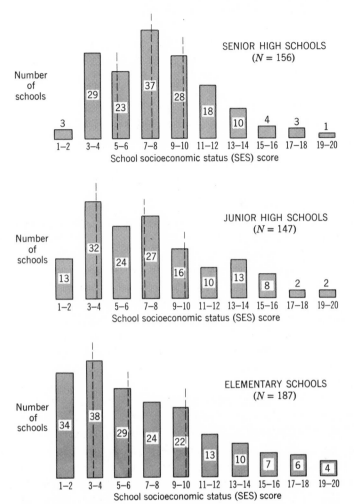

FIGURE 9-1. Frequency distribution of **156** senior high, **147** junior high, and **187** elementary schools, according to the value of their school socioeconomic status (SES) score.

geographic and socioeconomic area than do elementary schools, the cutting points are not identical at the three levels. The difference does not affect the highest SES category, but does affect the others. The average SES of the lowest category of elementary schools is somewhat lower than at the junior high level; and again at the junior high than at the senior high level. In other words, the SES difference between highest and lowest categories decreases somewhat as School Level rises (Figure 9-1).

The differences in School SES from level to level are slight, but they make it inappropriate to compare across levels the *magnitude* of differences by School SES with respect to other school characteristics. Instead, we shall ask whether the *conclusions* concerning the relationship of School SES and pupil and staff characteristics on the basis of the data for junior high or senior high schools differ in any way from those based on the data for elementary schools already presented.

FUNDAMENTAL DIFFERENCES AMONG SCHOOL LEVELS

Many important differences in pupil, staff, and organization characteristics are known to be associated with differences in School Level. In general, the secondary school is a larger and more complex organization than the elementary school. It has more of an administrative hierarchy and more staff members who are not directly involved in teaching. Secondary school teachers are specialized; they teach the same subject to different groups of pupils in the course of the day, while elementary teachers generally teach different subjects to a single group of children. Most elementary teachers are women; secondary teachers are more evenly divided as to sex. The elementary principal may be either a man or a woman; the secondary principal is most commonly a man.

In a study of School SES, the crucial difference between elementary, junior or senior high schools, however, is not in the characteristics of their staffs but in the age of the pupils. Each stage in child development has its attendant problems, but the precise nature of these problems varies according to social class background. It is not possible to review here all the differences in the needs of pupils according to their age and social class. But as we turn from the effect of School SES on the elementary school to its effect on the junior and senior high schools, certain points should be borne in mind.

In the first place, academic retardation is cumulative, and slight differences (by School SES or other background variables) in the early grades become large differences in the higher grades. The pressure of imminent decisions as to college or vocation separates secondary school students into diverse curricula and graded sections, and this separation accentuates original differences in academic and social behavior. Extracurricular activities become a very important part of school life, and the claims of the peer culture become stronger than those of the home and often vie with those of the school.[1] Since the reactions of students to these pressures vary with SES background, we expect greater differences by School SES in student behavior, and so in the task of teachers, at the secondary than at the elementary school level.

On the other hand, dropping out at school-leaving age is much more common in low SES than in high SES schools. The academically deficient or rebellious students are usually the ones who withdraw, and their departure raises the average achievement and behavior level of their school, thus reducing the difference between schools of low and high SES. A second factor which could reduce the association of School SES with student behavior at the secondary level was mentioned above: the average SES of the lowest category of senior high schools is somewhat higher than at the junior high level, and at the junior high than at the elementary level.

The junior high school occupies a position midway between elementary and senior high school in many organizational and staff characteristics as well as in level. Young adolescents are restless and their transition from one form of school to another poses special problems for staff at this level, whatever the SES of the school. However, we would expect the contradictory trends we have just discussed to make the problems especially acute for junior high schools of lowest SES, and to magnify the differences between them and junior high schools of highest SES. On the one hand, the compounding of academic and social problems through the grades results in serious deficiencies for many students in the junior high of lowest SES. On the other hand, not many students reach school-leaving age during their junior high years and so the lowest achievers are still in school. Moreover, the average SES background of pupils in the lowest category of junior high schools is only very slightly higher than at the lowest category of elementary schools.

We have reason, therefore, to expect School SES to exert both a greater and a lesser effect on secondary than on elementary schools, and to expect the differences between schools of highest and lowest SES to be greatest in the junior high schools.

We turn now to an examination of the actual data. Our aim is to be selective rather than exhaustive, and the curious reader is referred

[1] James S. Coleman, *The Adolescent Society* (Glencoe, Illinois: The Free Press, 1961); Herbert J. Gans, *The Urban Villagers* (Glencoe, Illinois: The Free Press, 1962); and Hylan Lewis, "The Changing Negro Family," in Eli Ginzberg (Editor), *The Nation's Children* (New York: Columbia University Press, 1960).

to the tables in Appendix A for the more complete data on junior and senior high schools.

SCHOOL LEVEL, SCHOOL SES, AND PUPIL CHARACTERISTICS

Regardless of School Level, characteristics of pupils and their parents are significantly related to School SES. Out of 55 items referring to pupil background, parental reinforcement, or school performance, all except 2 show significant differences between the highest and lowest SES categories at the junior high level and all except 11 at the senior high level.[2]

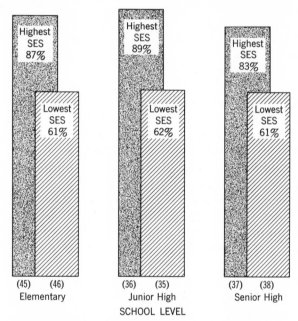

(45)   (46)   (36)   (35)   (37)   (38)
Elementary   Junior High   Senior High
SCHOOL LEVEL

FIGURE 9-2. Proportion of parents of pupils who are interested in the academic achievement of their children, by school level and school SES. (Unless otherwise stated, all figures in this chapter are based on the reports of principals.)

Figures 9-2, 9-3, and 9-4 illustrate three recurring patterns. At each level the percentage of parents in the lowest SES category reported by principals to be interested in the academic achievement of their children

[2] For the complete data on which this section is based, see Appendix Tables 3A-1 through 3A-4.

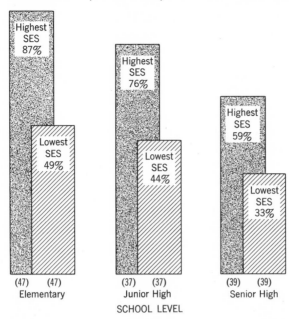

FIGURE 9-3. Proportion of parents of pupils who visit school at least once a year, by school level and school SES.

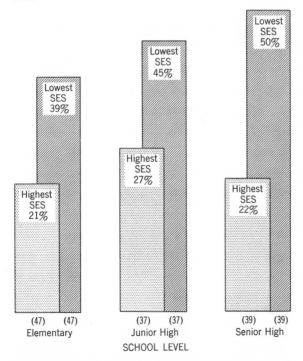

FIGURE 9-4. Proportion of mothers who are employed full time, by school level and school SES.

is the same (61 per cent). Although the percentage in the highest SES group fluctuates somewhat, the SES difference is large at all three levels (Figure 9-2). On the other hand, the percentage of parents who visit the school at least once a year decreases with School Level for both highest and lowest School SES, but the difference between SES categories is great at all levels (Figure 9-3). One reason for the decrease may be that the percentage of mothers with full-time jobs rises from elementary to senior high school in the case of schools of lowest SES but not in those of highest SES. As a result, the percentage difference between the average school in the highest and lowest category is only 18 at the elementary level but 28 at the senior high level (Figure 9-4).

Our prediction that the junior high school would be the level at which academic deficiency and discipline problems would be greatest is supported by the findings expressed in Figures 9-5 and 9-6. The percentage of pupils who are over a year behind their grade in reading is greatest at that level for the highest SES (15 per cent) as well as the lowest (52 per cent). Regardless of level, however, the magnitude of the difference by School SES in reading deficiency is very great (Figure 9-5).

Even one or two disrespectful pupils can cause a great deal of disturbance for a teacher. Although the percentage of pupils who behave in this fashion is not great in any category of School SES or School Level, it can be seen that such conduct is reported by the principals to be a problem especially at the junior high level (Figure 9-6). Most important, there is a consistent SES difference on this item at each school level.

Figures 9-2 through 9-6 serve to illustrate the large and consistent differences by School SES in pupil and parental characteristics at all three school levels. The replies of principals and teachers to the many other questions about the behavior of pupils and parents would, if graphed, corroborate the conclusion that, whatever the effect of School Level on such behavior, the additional effect of School SES is great.

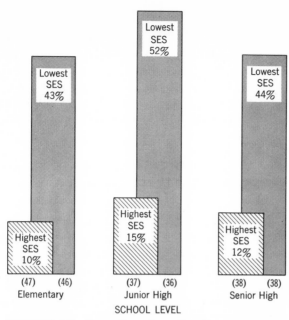

FIGURE 9-5. Proportion of pupils who are one year or more below grade level in reading, by school level and school SES.

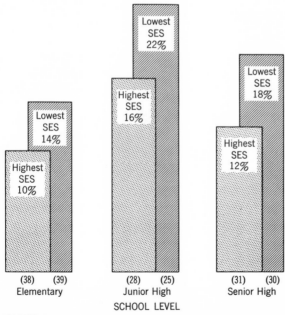

FIGURE 9-6. Proportion of pupils who (according to the average teacher-observer) show disrespect for teachers, by school level and school SES.

165

SCHOOL LEVEL, SCHOOL SES,
AND TEACHER CHARACTERISTICS

In order to present for the secondary levels the relationship between School SES and the many teacher background characteristics discussed for the elementary level in Chapter 4, we have prepared a table summarizing the direction and level of statistical significance of differences between variables for the highest and lowest SES categories on 16 characteristics within each of the three levels.[3]

TABLE 9-1. Summary Table of Differences in Teachers' Characteristics in Elementary, Junior, and Senior High Schools of Highest and Lowest SES

Characteristic of the Teachers	School Level		
	Elementary	Junior High	Senior High
Years of teaching experience	$H > L^*$	$H > L^*$	$H > L^*$
Age	$H > L^*$	$H > L^*$	$H > L^*$
Years of teaching experience in current school	$H > L^*$	$L > H^*$	$H > L^*$
Highest academic degree	$H = L$	$H = L$	$H > L^*$
Quality of college work	$H > L$	$H = L$	$H > L$
Salary	$L = H$	$L > H$	$L > H$
Per cent male	$L > H^*$	$L > H^*$	$H = L$
Per cent white	$H > L^*$	$H > L^*$	$H > L^*$
Per cent Protestant	$H > L^*$	$L > H$	$H > L^*$
Per cent Catholic	$L > H^*$	$L > H^*$	$L > H^*$
Per cent Jewish	$L > H$	$H > L^*$	$L = H$
Per cent nonurban	$H > L^*$	$H > L^*$	$H > L$
Level of father's occupation	$H > L^*$	$H > L^*$	$H > L^*$
Level of father's education	$H = L$	$H > L$	$H > L^*$
Level of mother's education	$H = L$	$H > L$	$H > L$
Income position of family	$H = L$	$H = L$	$H > L^*$

Key:

$L > H$: Mean for lowest school SES quarter greater than mean for highest quarter ($p < .33$).

$H > L$: Mean for highest school SES quarter greater than mean for lowest quarter ($p < .33$).

$L = H$: Difference between means for highest and lowest school SES quarters "negligible" ($p \geq .33$).

* Difference between means for highest and lowest school SES quarters statistically significant ($p < .05$).

[3] For the complete data on which this section is based, see Appendix Tables 4A-1 through 4A-15.

On most items the pattern by School SES is the same at each level: if the direction of the difference is positive for elementary schools, it is positive for junior and senior high schools; if it is negative for elementary, then it is negative for secondary schools. The exact size of the difference by SES, and whether or not it reaches statistical significance on a particular item, seems to be less important than the direction of the differences, which seldom change from level to level. In addition, over-all, there are roughly the same number of significant differences at each level (Table 9-1). Figure 9-7 illustrates this point by showing that the average years of experience in education of teachers in schools of lowest SES is below that of teachers in schools of highest SES in junior and senior high schools as well as in elementary schools.

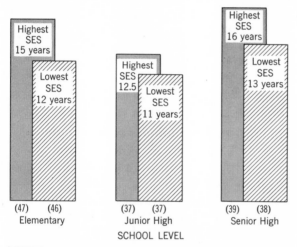

FIGURE 9-7. Average number of years of teaching experience of teachers, by school level and school SES.

The percentage of white elementary teachers in each School SES category, both over-all and in relation to the race of their pupils, was presented in some detail in Chapter 4. The over-all difference between the highest and lowest SES categories as to the percentage of teachers in our sample who are white is roughly the same at each level of school, as Figure 9-8 shows. It is also true that teachers in schools of lowest, as compared with highest, SES are at all three levels more apt to be Catholic and more apt to be urban in their background (Table 9-1).

Particularly pertinent to a study of social class is the distribution of teachers of various socioeconomic backgrounds among schools of different SES levels. In Chapter 4, we considered four measures

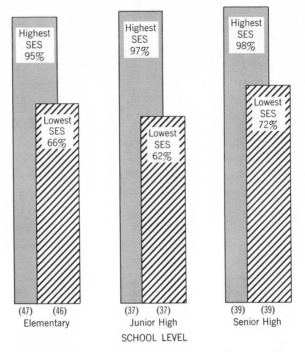

FIGURE 9-8. Proportion of teachers who are white,
by school level and school SES.

of socioeconomic background: father's occupation, father's education,
mother's education, and family income. There we reported that at the
elementary level there is a nonsignificant tendency for teachers in
schools of lowest SES to come from families of relatively less education and lower income. However, this association of lower socioeconomic background and lower School SES was significant only when
the index of the SES of the teacher was father's occupation.

As we consider junior and senior high school teachers, a relationship between lower socioeconomic background and lower School SES
becomes more noticeable. Thus the difference in parental income between teachers in the lowest and highest SES categories, which was
7 percentage points at the elementary level, is 9 percentage points
at the junior high level, and 13 percentage points at the senior high
level (Figure 9-9). Furthermore, as School Level rises from elementary
and junior high to senior high, the number of indices on which differences in socioeconomic background are significant increases from one
to three (Table 9-1).

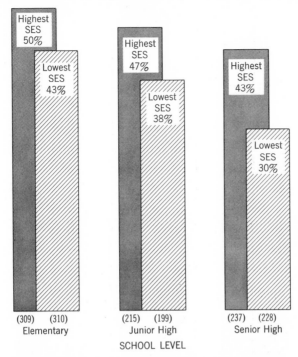

FIGURE 9-9. Proportion of teachers who (according to their self-reports) had parental income above the average of their high school community, by school level and school SES.

SCHOOL LEVEL, SCHOOL SES, AND TEACHER ATTITUDES

We reported in Chapter 5 on the relationship revealed by our data between School SES and the satisfactions of elementary school teachers. By and large, teachers in low SES elementary schools are relatively eager for new assignments. However, they are not less satisfied with their careers than are teachers in high SES schools, and they actually report greater enjoyment with most aspects of the work of teachers. The data in Table 9-2 provide an answer to the question: Would our conclusions as to the satisfaction of teachers have been the same if we had considered in detail the staff of junior or senior high schools?

Looking at the evidence from the work satisfaction questions first (Table 9-2), we find that, just as in the case of teachers in elementary schools, those in junior and senior high schools are more apt to enjoy

TABLE 9-2. Summary Table of Differences in the Replies of Teachers in Elementary, Junior, and Senior High Schools of Highest and Lowest SES on Items in Four Instruments Measuring Their Attitudes

	Num-ber of Items	School Level								
		Elementary			Junior High			Senior High		
Instrument		$L > H$	$H > L$	$L = H$	$L > H$	$H > L$	$L = H$	$L > H$	$H > L$	$L = H$
Work satisfaction	26	5/13	2/3	0/10	4/14	3/4	0/8	10/17	1/6	0/3
Career satisfaction	13	1/5	1/4	0/4	3/6	1/4	0/3	7/13	0/0	0/0
Job satisfaction	14	0/0	7/9	0/5	0/1	11/13	0/0	1/6	1/3	0/5
Job aspiration	10	8/10	0/0	0/0	5/10	0/0	0/0	8/10	0/0	0/0

Key:

$L > H$: Mean for lowest school SES quarter greater than mean for highest quarter ($p < .33$).

$H > L$: Mean for highest school SES quarter greater than mean for lowest quarter ($p < .33$).

$L = H$: Difference between means for highest and lowest school SES quarters "negligible" ($p \geq .33$).

Note. Digit to right of slash represents number of items. Digit to left of slash represents number of items on which difference is statistically significant ($p < .05$).

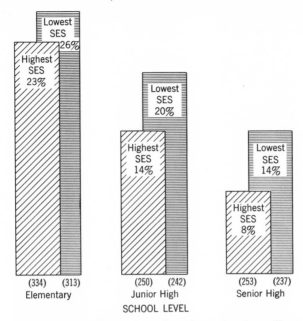

FIGURE 9-10. Proportion of teachers who (according to their self-reports) enjoy correcting papers, by school level and school SES.

many aspects of the teacher's job if they are located in the lowest rather than in the highest SES category.[4] Figure 9-10 illustrates one of a number of items for which the SES difference is most pronounced at the senior high level. Few teachers enjoy correcting papers; as School Level rises and the number and length of student papers increase, teachers apparently find the job increasingly burdensome. But the difference between the replies of the teachers in our sample in the highest and lowest SES categories becomes greater on this item as School Level rises. In view of the over-all differences by School Level with respect to such teacher characteristics as sex, age, training, and specialization, the relation of work satisfaction to School SES, regardless of level, is noteworthy.

Although low SES was associated with greater work satisfaction, it was *not* associated with greater career satisfaction in the case of elementary teachers. The data in Table 9-2 show that our conclusion would not vary much if we had studied in detail junior high school

[4] For the complete data on which this section is based, see Appendix Tables 5A-1 through 5A-4.

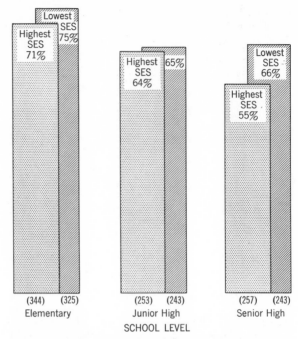

FIGURE 9-11. Proportion of teachers who (according to their self-reports) are satisfied with the state of teaching as a profession, by school level and school SES.

teachers only. However, a stronger relationship appears between School SES and career satisfaction at the senior high than at the other levels. With respect to every one of 14 aspects of the career, senior high school teachers in schools of lowest SES are *more* satisfied than teachers in schools of highest SES, and over half of these differences are statistically significant.[5] Figure 9-11 shows the greater satisfaction of teachers in senior high schools of lowest SES with the "state of teaching as a profession." One possible interpretation of the relatively high career satisfaction of senior high teachers in slum schools is that their professional status represents greater achievement relative to their own parents than is the case for teachers in schools of highest SES. Such an interpretation is supported by our data on the socioeconomic background of teachers at the three levels (Table 9-1). Other interpretations could probably also be made.

Teachers in senior high schools of low SES are as satisfied with many aspects of their current jobs as are teachers in schools of higher

[5] For the specific items, see Appendix Table 5A-3.

SES. This is definitely not the case at the elementary level, as was shown in Chapter 5; nor is it the case at the junior high level (Table 9-2). In fact, SES differences in teachers' job satisfaction occur on more items at the junior high level than at any other level. Thus, 37 per cent of junior high teachers at the lowest SES level (as compared with 18 per cent at the highest level) express dissatisfaction with "the attitude of the students toward the faculty" in their schools (Figure 9-12). At the elementary level there was a similarly significant SES difference on this item. However, senior high teachers in the lowest as compared with the highest category express themselves as more, rather than less, satisfied with student attitudes. We suggest that the converging trends with respect to School SES and School Level discussed at the beginning of this chapter explain such differences by level in the relation of School SES and job satisfaction. On the one hand, the greater socioeconomic heterogeneity and percentage of dropouts at the high school level reduces the differences between School SES categories. On the other hand, differences by School SES in academic

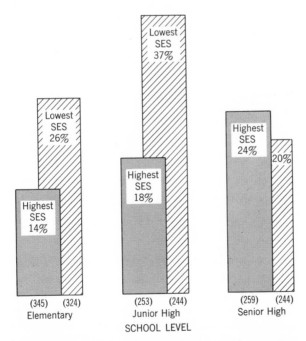

FIGURE 9-12. Proportion of teachers who (according to their self-reports) are dissatisfied with the attitudes of students toward faculty, by school level and school SES.

achievement and pupil behavior become greater in the higher grades. These opposite trends meet at the junior high level, the very stage at which adolescents of any social class may be most rebellious. It is not surprising that the SES differences in job satisfaction are especially great for junior high teachers.

Given these differences in job satisfaction, what differences in job *aspiration* can we expect? In view of our interpretation of the findings on job satisfaction, we expect *junior high* teachers in slum schools to be especially eager for a change. Since senior high teachers in such

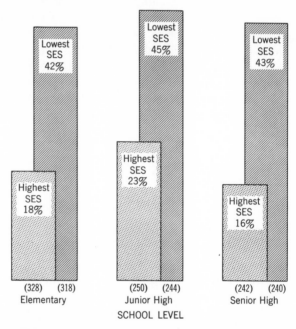

FIGURE 9-13. Proportion of teachers who (according to their self-reports) desire to move to a school in a "better neighborhood," by school level and school SES.

schools are more satisfied with their work situation, they should be less desirous of a change.

The data in Table 9-2 do not support the prediction of an *especially* strong desire to change jobs on the part of junior high teachers or of no desire to do so on the part of senior high teachers. As a matter of fact, at each level there are large differences by School SES in the job aspirations of teachers.

We find in fact that, irrespective of School Level, teachers in schools of lowest as compared with highest SES are more eager for both vertical and horizontal mobility. The proportion of teachers in schools of highest SES who say they desire a school in a "better neighborhood" is roughly one-fifth within each of the three kinds of schools. The corresponding proportion is roughly two-fifths for schools of lowest SES (Figure 9-13). The desire for vertical mobility from a teacher's job to one in the higher administration increases with School Level. However, at each level a greater proportion of teachers in the lowest than in the highest School SES category have this ambition (Figure 9-14).

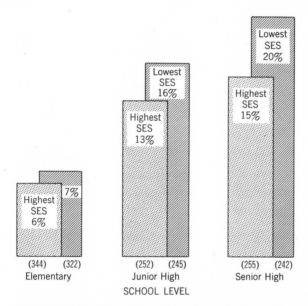

FIGURE 9-14. Proportion of teachers who (according to their self-reports) have some desire to become an assistant superintendent, by school level and school SES.

The summary of the response pattern by School SES and School Level on all items measuring job aspiration (Table 9-2) shows that at each level the job aspiration of teachers in the lowest group is much stronger than that of teachers in the highest. The prediction of especially strong desire on the part of junior high teachers to change jobs, or of less desire on the part of senior high teachers to do so is not supported.

Thus, the effect of School SES on the satisfaction of teachers is found to be roughly the same at the three school levels in the case of work satisfaction and job aspiration, but different in the case of job satisfaction and career satisfaction. In the latter areas the relation of School SES to the responses of junior high teachers is similar to that of elementary teachers. Senior high teachers, however, are much more satisfied with their careers and somewhat more satisfied with their jobs if they teach in schools of very low rather than very high SES.

SCHOOL LEVEL, SCHOOL SES, AND THE CHARACTERISTICS OF PRINCIPALS

In Chapter 7 we presented evidence in support of the prediction that within each School SES category the elementary principal has the same general background as his teachers, although he is more apt than they to be white. His career qualifications are higher than

TABLE 9-3. Summary Table of Differences in Principals' Characteristics in Elementary, Junior, and Senior High Schools of Highest and Lowest SES

	School Level		
Characteristic of the Principal	Elementary	Junior High	Senior High
Years of experience			
In education	$H > L$	$H > L$	$H > L$
As principal	$H > L$	$H > L$	$H > L$
In school	$H > L$	$H > L$	$H > L$
Age	$H > L$	$H > L$	$H > L$
Per cent with M.A. or doctorate	$L > H$	$L > H$	$L > H$
Salary	$L > H$	$L = H$	$L > H$
Per cent male	$L > H$	$L > H$	$L > H$
Per cent white	$H > L$	$H > L$	$H > L$
Per cent Protestant	$H > L$	$H > L$	$H > L$
Per cent nonurban	$H > L$	$H > L$	$H > L$
Per cent white-collar father	$H > L$	$H > L$	$H > L$
Per cent above average in parental income	$H > L$	$H > L$	$H > L$

Key:
    $L > H$: Mean for lowest school SES quarter greater than mean for highest quarter ($p < .33$).
    $H > L$: Mean for highest school SES quarter greater than mean for lowest quarter ($p < .33$).
    $L = H$: Difference between means for highest and lowest school SES quarters "negligible" ($p \geq .33$).
    Note. Relationships not tested for statistical significance at the .05 level.

those of his teachers, but are as affected by School SES as are theirs. Moreover, like his teachers, the lower the SES of his school, the greater his dissatisfaction with many aspects of his present job, and the greater his desire for a new situation. In this chapter we have seen that (with the exception of job and career satisfaction at the senior high level) all teacher variables we have considered bear a similar relation to School SES at the secondary level as at the elementary school level. It therefore seems logical to predict that the relation of School SES to the characteristics of secondary school principals will be the same as it was to those of elementary school principals and to those of teachers at all levels.

The summary presentation in Table 9-3 of the direction of differences in 12 characteristics of principals from highest to lowest SES categories across the three school levels confirms the above prediction.[6] For every background and career characteristic the *direction* of the difference is the same at the junior and senior high levels as at the elementary level (Table 9-3). Moreover, in each case, except the salary of junior high school principals, the probability that the difference could have occurred by chance is less than 1 in 3.[7]

The association of School SES with the attitudes of principals at the three levels is shown in Table 9-4. In general, at each level, principals in the lowest category are more often dissatisfied with aspects of their jobs than principals in the highest category, but the number of items that show a difference in this direction diminishes as School Level rises. At the senior high level, principals of slum schools are more satisfied in respect to four aspects of their jobs and less satisfied in respect to six aspects than principals in schools most favored in SES. Senior high principals in slum schools thus do not completely match their teachers, who were more apt to be satisfied than teachers in high SES schools.

The job aspiration of principals is greater at every level for those who are in schools of lowest rather than highest SES. For junior and senior high as well as elementary school principals there are differences on items referring to *horizontal* mobility to other principalships, as

[6] Due to space limitations we have been unable to present the complete data on which this section is based. Readers interested in greater detail than that provided are invited to correspond with the authors directly.

[7] Consistent with our practice in Chapter 7 of comparing principals to teachers rather than to each other, relationships for principals presented in this section were not tested for statistical significance. We present the .33 level merely for illustrative purposes.

TABLE 9-4. Summary Table of Differences in the Replies of Principals in Elementary, Junior, and Senior High Schools of Highest and Lowest SES on Items in Two Instruments Measuring Their Attitudes

Instrument	Number of Items	School Level								
		Elementary			Junior High			Senior High		
		$L > H$	$H > L$	$L = H$	$L > H$	$H > L$	$L = H$	$L > H$	$H > L$	$L = H$
Job satisfaction	18	1	11	6	2	8	8	4	6	8
Job aspiration	16	7	0	9	7	1	8	8	3	5

Key:

$L > H$: Mean for lowest school SES quarter greater than mean for highest quarter ($p < .33$).

$H > L$: Mean for highest school SES quarter greater than mean for lowest quarter ($p < .33$).

$L = H$: Difference between means for highest and lowest school SES quarters "negligible" ($p \geq .33$).

Note. Relationships not tested for statistical significance at .05 level.

well as on items referring to *vertical* mobility into higher administration. The principal of the slum secondary school, like the principal of the slum elementary school, and like teachers at all three levels in these schools, is very apt to look forward to a transfer to another position. All in all, the data presented in very summary fashion in this chapter support the generalization that the relationship between School SES and the characteristics of school staff, documented in detail in Chapters 4 through 7, holds for junior and senior high schools as well as for elementary schools.

Chapter 10

THE EFFECT OF SCHOOL RACE ON THE RELATIONSHIP OF SCHOOL SES TO THE CHARACTERISTICS OF PUPILS AND STAFF

We reported in Chapter 2 that the racial and socioeconomic compositions of the schools in the sample of the School SES Study are correlated. The 47 elementary schools of highest SES, for example, have a predominance of white pupils, whereas those of lowest SES are predominantly nonwhite (Figure 2-8). In this chapter we shall try to find out whether this correlation has led us into a spurious interpretation of the relationship between School SES and the many characteristics of pupils, teachers, and principals which we have found to be related to it. If the racial composition of a school is thought to produce both its socioeconomic composition and the characteristics and behavior of the school's pupils and staff, then the relationships between School SES and the many dependent variables may be simply artifacts. In such a case the "true" relationship would be between the racial composition of a school (rather than its socioeconomic composition) and the characteristics of its pupils, teachers, and principal. We do not believe this to be the case, but such an important assumption warrants investigation.

OTHER STUDIES OF RACE AND
SOCIOECONOMIC STATUS

To explore the possibility of a spurious effect of race on the relationship between socioeconomic status and any variable influenced by it, we must study the three variables simultaneously.[1] Compared to the attention given race and socioeconomic status separately, such a simultaneous consideration is infrequent in the literature of both sociology and education; when these two variables are considered together, it is usually for a purpose quite unlike our own.

Studies of Individuals

One of the few studies explicitly designed to consider within different racial groups the effect of socioeconomic status on attitudes and behavior was reported in 1946 by Davis and Havighurst.[2] After examining extensive data on the child-rearing practices of fifty Chicago mothers in each of four groups (white middle class, white lower class, Negro middle class, and Negro lower class) they reported "considerable social class differences in child-rearing practices," and further that "these differences are greater than the differences between Negroes and whites of the same social class."[3] Of particular interest is their report of "more class differences than color differences," and that "the class differences occurred approximately equally often in Negro and white groups."[4]

Aside from this study there has been relatively little systematic inquiry specifically directed at the question of the differential effect of racial and socioeconomic characteristics. However, it is sometimes possible to recast analyses of different questions to see whether they support hypotheses beyond those they were designed to test. Stephenson, for example, in a study of the occupational plans and aspirations of ninth-grade pupils, reports that within a sample of 567 white and 88 Negro pupils, the occupational aspirations of both groups are related positively to the class position of their fathers.[5] Holloway and Berreman, in a replication of this study, considered the occupational and educational plans and aspirations of 182 white and 118 Negro pupils in the sixth, seventh, and eighth grades. Within their data it

---

[1] See, for example, Herbert H. Hyman, *Survey Design and Analysis: Principles, Cases, and Procedures* (Glencoe, Illinois: The Free Press, 1955), Chapter VI; or Hubert M. Blalock, *Social Statistics* (New York: McGraw-Hill Book Company, 1960), pp. 337–343.

[2] Allison Davis and Robert J. Havighurst, "Social Class and Color Differences in Child-Rearing," *American Sociological Review,* XI (1946), pp. 698–710.

[3] *Op. cit.,* p. 707.

[4] *Op. cit.,* p. 705.

[5] Richard M. Stephenson, "Mobility Orientation and Stratification of 1,000 Ninth Graders," *American Sociological Review,* XXII (1957), pp. 204–212. See especially Table 6.

can be observed that for each of these four dependent variables both white and Negro pupils from "lower class" homes score *lower* than those from "middle class" homes.[6]

In a study of the achievement motivation of boys, Rosen reports data for 122 white Protestants and 65 Negroes. Although, as might be expected, the motivation scores for the white Protestants were in general higher than those for the Negroes, the mean scores for both groups fall consistently across four levels of decreasing social class placement.[7]

Killian and Grigg report data on the anomia of 190 white and 436 Negro urban adults. With respect to each of three indices of social class (amount of formal education, occupation, and self-placement in social class), the lower the social class of both whites and Negroes, the higher their anomia.[8]

These five studies of the relationship of indices of social class to such class-related phenomena as child-rearing practices, aspiration, motivation, and anomia all present data which lead us to conclude that such relationships are unlikely to be produced exclusively by racial differences among the subjects. Other studies within samples of both white and Negroes point to a similar conclusion,[9] as do studies conducted within samples of Negro subjects alone.[10]

[6] Robert G. Holloway and Joel V. Berreman, "The Educational and Occupational Aspirations and Plans of Negro and White Male Elementary School Students," *Pacific Sociological Review*, II (1959), pp. 56–60. See especially Table 3.

[7] Bernard C. Rosen, "Race, Ethnicity, and the Achievement Syndrome," *American Sociological Review*, XXIV (1959), pp. 47–60. See especially Table 2.

[8] Lewis M. Killian and Charles M. Grigg, "Urbanism, Race, and Anomia," *American Journal of Sociology*, LXVII (1962), pp. 661–665. See especially Tables 2 through 4.

[9] Georges Sabagh, *et al.*, "Social Class and Ethnic Status of Patients Admitted to a State Hospital for the Retarded," *Pacific Sociological Review*, II (1959), pp. 76–80; Joel B. Montague and Edgar G. Epps, "Attitudes Toward Social Mobility as Revealed by Samples of Negro and White Boys," *Pacific Sociological Review*, I (1958), pp. 81–84; Sanford M. Dornbusch, "Correlations Between Income and Labor Force Participation by Race," *American Journal of Sociology*, LXI (1956), pp. 340–344; Aaron Antonovsky and Melvin J. Lerner, "Occupational Aspirations of Lower Class Negro and White Youth," *Social Problems*, VII (1959), pp. 132–138; Albert J. Reiss, Jr. and Albert L. Rhodes, *A Socio-Psychological Study of Conforming and Deviating Behavior Among Adolescents*, Final Report, Cooperative Research Project No. 507, (Iowa City: The State University of Iowa, 1959), especially Tables III-5, V-3, V-13, and VI-4; Alan B. Wilson, "Social Stratification and Academic Achievement," in A. Harry Passow (Editor), *Education in Depressed Areas* (New York: Bureau of Publications, Teachers College, Columbia University, 1963), pp. 217–235, espe-

Studies of Census Tracts

These studies focus on selected class-related phenomena of *individuals;* they merely suggest what we might expect to find with respect to *schools.* However, before we turn to the data from the School SES Study, we ought to consider two studies of census tracts, a unit of analysis rather similar to the school attendance districts in which we are primarily interested.

In a well-designed study of the relationship of juvenile delinquency, race, and economic status, Blue analyzed 1940 data from 363 Detroit census tracts.[11] Using the average rent of household units in the tracts as his measure of "economic status," percentage of dwellings in a tract that were occupied by nonwhite persons as a measure of "race," and the average number of court-defined delinquents aged 10 to 17 per 100 children of school age (over a four year period) as a measure of "delinquency," Blue conducted a series of partial correlation analyses to test the hypothesis "that economic status is more closely related to juvenile delinquency than [is] race."[12] Although in the School SES Study we have not attempted to state which of these two potentially causal variables is the *more related* to school effects,[13] Blue's analysis can be addressed to our concern as well as its own. The fact that the correlation between economic status and delinquency ($r = -.62$) experienced only a negligible reduction when the linear effects of race were removed (partial $r = -.59$) suggests that it is most unlikely that the variable of race produces the observed relationship between economic status and delinquency.[14]

In a similar study Lander reports 1940 data for 155 Baltimore

---

cially Tables 6, 9, and 11; and Martin Deutsch and Bert Brown, "Social Influences in Negro-White Intelligence Differences," *The Journal of Social Issues,* XX (1964), pp. 24–35, especially Tables 1 and 2.

[10] Herman G. Canady, "The Intelligence of Negro College Students and Parental Occupation," *American Journal of Sociology,* XLII (1936), pp. 388–389; Mary L. Robinson and Max Meenes, "The Relation Between Test Intelligence of Third Grade Negro Children and the Occupations of Their Parents," *Journal of Negro Education,* XVI (1947), pp. 136–141; O. Uzell, "Occupational Aspirations of Negro Male High School Students," *Sociology and Social Research,* XLV (1961), pp. 202–204.

[11] John T. Blue, Jr., "The Relationship of Juvenile Delinquency, Race, and Economic Status," *Journal of Negro Education,* XVII (1948), pp. 469–477.

[12] *Op. cit.,* p. 477.

[13] The rationale for this decision is presented in Chapter 11.

[14] *Op. cit.,* pp. 476–477.

census tracts.[15] One of his measures of socioeconomic status was the median years of school completed by all persons in the tract 25 years of age or over. His measure of "race" was similar to that of Blue: the percentage of nonwhites residing in the census tract. As his measure of delinquency Lander computed an average (across four years) of the ratio of the number of court-defined delinquents to the total tract population of the ages of 6 to 17 inclusive. Although Lander was interested in the relative contribution of many correlates to the prediction of delinquency rates, his data also shed light on the question raised by the School SES Study.

Lander reports a moderate correlation between education and delinquency ($r = -.51$).[16] From his other data we can compute the coefficient of partial correlation of education and deliquency with the linear effects of race removed.[17] This coefficient (partial $r = -.34$), although it represents a greater reduction in the primary relationship than that reported by Blue, also lends credence to our assumption that, among schools, variation in the racial composition of the enrolled pupils will not "explain away" the observed relationship between socioeconomic composition and the many phenomena found to vary with it.

RESEARCH DESIGN

To determine whether the data of the School SES Study are consistent with the above findings, the School SES Score was related to some of the dependent variables presented in Chapters 3 through 7. This association was examined twice; first in zero-order form and then with the linear effects of the varying racial composition of the different schools (hereafter referred to as "School Race") removed through partial correlation.[18]

[15] Bernard Lander, *Towards an Understanding of Juvenile Delinquency* (New York: Columbia University Press, 1954).

[16] *Op. cit.*, Table 5.

[17] *Ibid.*

[18] The reader familiar with the several assumptions of the partial correlation model (see, for example, Blalock, *op. cit.*, Chapter 19) may in the light of the joint distribution of School Race and School SES presented in Table 10-1 question the appropriateness of using partial correlation to remove the effects of the different racial characteristics of the schools. Such a question is certainly in order, but the use of any one of several alternatives (e.g., Kendall's partial rank correlation, a two-way analysis of variance, a one-way analysis of variance with covariance adjustments) can also be questioned. The consequences of using partial correlation when the joint distributions are not multivariate normal are

Our choice of dependent variables to be considered in this way was deliberate rather than random. From among the many variables presented in earlier chapters we chose 20 which: (1) were representative, (2) bore a statistically significant relationship with School SES, and (3) bore a statistically significant relationship with School Race. We reasoned that the relationship between School SES and, for example, the average IQ of the pupils, would not be entirely explained by the relationship between it and School Race, and would thus persist in the form of a statistically significant coefficient of first-order partial correlation.[19] However, before examining the results of our correlational analyses, it may be helpful to consider a few of the dependent variables, using rough categories of School SES and School Race, rather than their full variation.

The definition of rough categories of School SES was made in a manner similar to that described in Chapter 2. Because, as was noted in Figure 2-8, there are few elementary schools of moderately

---

not known, but the advantage of parsimony gained from using the model in the present context appears to outweigh the disadvantage of uncertainty.

However, we have attempted to reduce some of this uncertainty by considering whether the computation of product moment correlations between School Race and a chosen dependent variable as well as between School Race and School SES has tended to underestimate the "true" strengths of these relationships. If this were the case we would, in partialling out School Race, be removing too little variance from the relationship of School SES and the chosen dependent variable. Our exploration of this question with the alternate statistical models mentioned above suggests that we have not done so. Furthermore, a comparison of the correlation of School SES and School Race for the 490 schools ($r = .55$) with that reported by Lander ($r = .41$) and Blue ($r = .29$) for the relationship of indices of the socioeconomic and racial charac̈ṫ̇istics of census tracts suggests that, if anything, we have overestimated ratḣr than underestimated this relationship, removing *too much* variance. If this is the case, then our test of the independent effects of School SES is a conservative one.

[19] This is only one of the many "three variable models" which could be applied to study the effects of School Race on the relationship between School SES and a selected dependent variable. However, it is the one most crucial to the problem under consideration. We shall have to leave to future research the fascinating problem of determining the conditions of School Race under which expected relationships between School SES and the characteristics and behavior of teachers and principals which we have failed to find may appear, as well as the conditions under which existing relationships might be stronger or weaker. For a discussion of the general model for introducing a third variable to "elaborate" the relationship between two others, see Herbert H. Hyman, *Survey Design and Analysis: Principles, Cases and Procedures* (Glencoe, Illinois: The Free Press, 1955), Chapter 7.

high or highest SES which contain many nonwhite pupils, we decided to combine the data from the 187 elementary schools, the 147 junior high schools, and the 156 senior high schools into one test using all 490 schools, instead of making three separate tests with more limited samples. That this "pooling" is in general appropriate was seen in Chapter 9, where, in spite of the association between School SES and School Level (Figure 9-1), the relationships reported in Chapters 3 through 7 for elementary schools seem to apply (with only a few exceptions) to junior and senior high schools as well. Therefore, the 490 elementary, junior and senior high schools were pooled and reassigned to four categories of School SES in terms of their position on the over-all distribution of the School SES Score reported in Figure 2-2. This classification produced a distribution of 123 schools of highest SES, and 123, 122, and 122 schools of moderately high, moderately low, and lowest SES, respectively.[20]

Even after combining the elementary, junior and senior high schools, the distribution of the schools according to School Race is clearly nonrandom across the four categories of School SES. It can be seen in Table 10-1 that in the category of highest SES, schools of predominantly white enrollments are overrepresented, whereas in the category of lowest SES, schools of predominantly nonwhite enrollments are overrepresented. By inspecting Table 10-1 it can be noted further that the tighter the control on School Race (that is, the shorter the range assigned to each category), the fewer the number of predominantly nonwhite schools of highest, moderately high, and even moderately low SES. On the other hand, if in assigning the 490 schools to categories of School Race the range of the predominantly nonwhite category is made great, much of the desired control is sacrificed.

Since our use of categories is primarily illustrative, we decided to limit the presentation of data to three categories of School Race as follows: (1) Predominantly White Schools (those with a student body 96 to 100 per cent white), (2) Mixed Schools (those with a student body from 5 to 95 per cent white), and (3) Predominantly Non-

---

[20] It should be noted that this SES assignment of the 490 schools, although similar, is not identical to that which resulted from the definition of highest, moderately high, moderately low, and lowest SES *within* each of the three categories of School Level (elementary, junior high, and senior high school) discussed in Chapter 2. There, it will be remembered, that since separate analyses were to be conducted for each school level, we established different cutting points for each level according to the distribution shown in Figure 9-1. Here, where no distinction as to level is to be made, it is essential to use the same cutting point for all schools, and this was done.

TABLE 10-1.   Distribution of School Race by Four Categories of School SES

School Race (Per Cent of Pupil Enrollment that is White)	School SES				
	Highest	Moderately High	Moderately Low	Lowest	All Schools
100	42	22	16	7	87
96–99	58	36	35	9	138
91–95	7	16	10	3	36
86–90	5	14	7	8	34
81–85	4	8	2	2	16
76–80	2	4	6	4	16
71–75	2	6	4	2	14
66–70	1	3	3	3	10
61–65		2	1	4	7
56–60		4		1	5
51–55	1			3	4
45–50	1		6	4	11
40–44				1	1
35–39		1		1	2
30–34			2	2	4
25–29		1	2	2	5
20–24			2	2	4
15–19			1	7	8
10–14			2	5	7
5–9			6	4	10
1–4		2	10	22	34
0		4	7	26	37
All schools	123	123	122	122	490

white Schools (those with a student body from 0 to 4 per cent white). Thus it is only in the two extreme categories of School Race that variation in the racial composition of the schools is in any sense "controlled." For this illustration almost one-half (225) of the 490 schools of the School SES Study were classified as predominantly white, whereas about one-seventh (71) were classified as predominantly nonwhite (Table 10-2).

Table 10-2 also reports the joint distribution resulting when the 490 schools are classified simultaneously according to the three categories of School Race and the four categories of School SES. The fact that the 12 cells of Table 10-2 differ dramatically in the number of

TABLE 10-2. Joint Frequency Distribution of 490 Elementary, Junior and Senior High Schools, by School Race and School SES

	School SES				
School Race	Highest	Moderately High	Moderately Low	Lowest	All Schools
Predominantly white (96–100% white)	100	58	51	16	225
Mixed (5–95% white)	23	59	54	58	194
Predominantly nonwhite (0–4% white)	0	6	17	48	71
All schools	123	123	122	122	490

schools represented therein (100 of the 225 predominantly white schools are of highest SES, whereas none of the 71 predominantly non-white schools is of highest SES) reflects the high correlation of School SES and School Race.[21]

SCHOOL SES AND SELECTED DEPENDENT VARIABLES BY SCHOOL RACE

In this section the association of School SES with each of 20 variables is considered both before and after the effects of School Race are held constant. Although, as was discussed in Chapters 1 and 3, the effects of the social class composition of schools on pupils and their parents is well known, it is not as well established whether these effects exist irrespective of the racial composition of the schools. After considering 10 variables indicative of the characteristics, attitudes, and behavior of pupils and their parents, we shall focus on ten additional variables indicative of the characteristics, attitudes, and behavior of teachers and principals.

[21] The product moment correlation for the relationship between the un-grouped School SES Score and the percentage of white pupil enrollment (i.e., School Race) across the full sample of 490 schools is .55. For analyses based upon a more limited number of schools, or upon the teachers as subjects, the observed coefficient is slightly weaker (see Tables 10-4 and 10-6).

Characteristics, Attitudes, and Behavior of Pupils and Parents

It was reported in Chapter 3 (Figure 3-8) that the lower the School SES of elementary schools, the greater the proportion of pupils who were reported by their teachers to be one year or more below grade level in reading. That this is so irrespective of School Level can be seen in Table 10-3. In the schools of highest SES 19 per cent of the pupils are said to be so retarded, whereas in those of moderately high, moderately low, and lowest SES the percentages are 28, 33, and 44, respectively. (The Pearsonian product moment correlation coefficient for the underlying continuous variables is —.53.)

It can be further seen that, as expected, school retardation in reading is associated with School Race, with 23 per cent of the pupils in the predominantly white schools being retarded at least one year, while in the mixed and predominantly nonwhite schools the percentages are 35 and 47, respectively ($r = $ —.58). Of particular interest in the present context is the relationship of School SES and reading retardation within the predominantly white and predominantly nonwhite schools. A further inspection of Table 10-3 shows that within each category of School Race, retardation generally rises as School SES falls.

TABLE 10-3. Mean Proportion of Pupils Who Are One Year or More Below Grade Level in Reading by School Race and School SES

School Race	Highest	Moderately High	Moderately Low	Lowest	All schools
Predominantly white (96–100% white)	19%(80)a	24%(46)	24%(48)	39%(14)	23%(188)
Mixed (5–95% white)	21 (17)	30 (42)	39 (38)	43 (41)	35 (138)
Predominantly nonwhite (0–4% white)	— (0)	39 (6)	48 (13)	48 (87)	47 (56)
All schools	19 (97)	28 (94)	33 (99)	44 (92)	31 (382)

a Figures in parentheses indicate the number of cases upon which each percentage is based.

TABLE 10-4.   Zero-Order and First-Order Partial Correlation and Regression Coefficients (Holding Constant School Race) for the Relationship of School SES with Each of 10 Dependent Variables Measuring Pupil Characteristics, Attitudes, or Behavior

Dependent Variable		Coefficient[a]				
		XY_i	ZY_i	XZ	$XY_i \cdot Z$	N[b]
1. Mean IQ of the Pupils, i.e., "School IQ" (as reported by the principal).	r	.73*	.70*	.55*	.58*	489
	b	1.42*	0.16*	4.81*	.96*	489
2. Per cent of pupils with parents interested in their academic achievement (as reported by the principal).	r	.41*	.20*	.55*	.37*	465
	b	2.23*	0.12*	4.74*	2.34*	465
3. Per cent of pupils with emotional or social problems (as reported by the principal).	r	−.36*	−.33*	.54*	−.23*	485
	b	−1.56*	−0.16*	4.75*	−1.12*	485
4. Per cent of pupils one year or more below grade level in reading (as reported by the teachers).	r	−.53*	−.58*	.52*	−.32*	382
	b	−2.18*	−0.27*	4.63*	−1.27*	382
5. Per cent of pupils one year or more below grade level in reading (as reported by the principal).	r	−.55*	−.67*	.54*	−.30*	483
	b	−2.79*	−0.39*	4.77*	−1.35*	483
6. Per cent of pupils one year or more below grade level in arithmetic (as reported by the principal).	r	−.53*	−.65*	.54*	−.27*	481
	b	−2.52*	−0.35*	4.77*	−1.16*	481
7. Per cent of pupils who have stayed back one year or more (as reported by the principal).	r	−.45*	−.43*	.54*	−.28	481
	b	−1.19*	−0.13*	4.75*	−0.80*	481
8. Per cent of pupils not interested in academic achievement (as reported by the teachers).	r	−.38*	−.39*	.52*	−.22*	382
	b	−1.26*	−0.15*	4.63*	−0.79*	382
9. Per cent of pupils not interested in academic achievement (as reported by the principal).	r	−.35*	−.36*	.54*	−.19*	481
	b	−1.27*	−0.15*	4.79*	−0.77*	481

TABLE 10-4 (Continued)

Dependent Variable		Coefficient[a]				
		XY_i	ZY_i	XZ	$XY_i \cdot Z$	N[b]
10. Per cent of pupils who were discipline problems during past year (as reported by the principal).	r	−.28*	−.33*	.54*	−.12*	487
	b	−0.47*	−0.06*	4.78*	−0.23*	487

[a] Key:
  r = Correlation coefficient.
  b = Regression coefficient.
  X = School SES.
  Y_i = Dependent variables 1 to 10.
  Z = School Race.
[b] Difference in Ns due to unavailability of data from some schools.
* $p < .05$.

To estimate the average relationship of School SES and reading retardation within a large number of relatively homogeneous categories of School Race (as opposed to just the two extremes which have been illustrated), the linear effects of School Race were removed from the product moment correlation of School SES and retardation ($r = -.53$). The resulting coefficient of first-order partial correlation (partial $r = -.32$) is statistically significant. Although School Race affects the relationship between School SES and reading retardation, it does not explain it away. School SES appears to bear a relationship to school retardation in reading, independent of that associated with School Race.[22]

Zero- and first-order partial *correlation* coefficients were computed for nine additional dependent variables focusing on the principals' or teachers' reports of pupil or parental attitudes and behavior. In addition, zero- and first-order partial *regression* coefficients were computed for all ten dependent variables.[23] These coefficients, and those for the

[22] For a discussion of the possibility that this relationship might be conditional, see Chapter 11.

[23] Technically, slope (regression) coefficients are the appropriate statistics to use in exploring the possible spurious effects of a third variable on the relationship between two other variables. (See, for example, Hubert M. Blalock, "Controlling for Background Factors: Spuriousness Versus Developmental Sequences," *Sociological Inquiry*, XXXIV (1964), pp. 28–40.) However, since the interpretation of correlation coefficients is more widely understood, they have been presented also. As can be seen in Table 10-4 and Table 10-6, in these 20 cases the interpretation of both statistics generally leads to the same conclusion.

variable already discussed, are presented in Table 10-4. There it can be seen that regardless of the reporter (the principals or the teachers) there is a statistically significant relationship between School SES and measures of the motivation, achievement, and behavior of pupils and the attitudes of their parents. Furthermore, as expected, when the linear effects of School Race are removed, through either partial correlation or partial regression, all relationships, although reduced, are still statistically significant.

Characteristics, Attitudes, and Behavior of Teachers and Principals

One of the most striking relationships reported in Chapters 4 through 7 between School SES and the characteristics, attitudes, and behavior of school staff was that concerning the proportion of elementary school teachers who would like to move to a school in a "better neighborhood." Whereas only 18 per cent of the sample of teachers in the elementary schools of highest SES reported a desire to move, the percentage rose steadily to a high of 42 per cent for those in the schools of lowest SES (Figure 5-2). This relationship is also apparent, as expected, for all 490 elementary, junior and senior high schools: 19 per cent of the 815 teachers sampled in the 123

TABLE 10-5. Proportion of Teachers Who Desire to Move to a School in a "Better Neighborhood," by School Race and School SES

		School SES			
School Race	Highest	Moder-ately High	Moder-ately Low	Lowest	All Schools
Predominantly white (96–100% white)	19%(662)a	20%(380)	26%(382)	31%(104)	22%(1528)
Mixed (5–95% white)	21 (153)	30 (356)	36 (337)	45 (386)	35 (1232)
Predominantly nonwhite (0–4% white)	— (0)	33 (36)	45 (104)	45 (300)	44 (440)
All schools	19 (815)	25 (772)	33 (823)	43 (790)	30 (3200)

a Figures in parentheses refer to the number of cases upon which the associated percentage was based.

schools of highest SES desire to move to a school in a "better neighborhood," while the percentages for the schools of moderately high, moderately low, and lowest SES are 25, 33, and 43, respectively (Table 10-5).

Similarly, the percentage of teachers who desire to move varies with School Race: only 22 per cent of the 1528 teachers sampled in the 225 predominantly white schools desire to move, whereas the percentages for the mixed and predominantly nonwhite schools are 35 and 44, respectively (Table 10-5). When we examine the relationship between School SES and desire to move within categories of School Race, we find that, in general, the lower the School SES, the greater the percentage of teachers who desire to move to a school in a "better neighborhood" (Table 10-5).

In order to use all the variation in the variables involved in this partial relationship (instead of just that represented by the categories discussed), zero-order and first-order partial correlation and regression coefficients were computed relating School SES, School Race, and "desire to move" for the 3200 teachers for whom complete data were available. Table 10-6 presents the results of this analysis, as well as those of similar analyses for each of 9 additional dependent variables found earlier to be related to School SES: the race, age, experience, job aspiration, satisfaction, and performance of teachers and the desire of principals for a position of greater responsibility. For each of these 10 staff variables the zero-order correlation and regression coefficients are statistically significant, and for 7 the coefficients of first-order partial correlation and regression are also significant.[24] As in the case of the pupil and parent variables, in general the association of School SES and School Race does not "explain away" the relationships reported between School SES and the characteristics, attitudes, and behavior of teachers and principals. Although teachers and principals are affected by the racial composition of the pupil population, they also appear to be affected by the socioeconomic composition of their pupil populations regardless of their racial compositions.

---

[24] An interesting anomaly occurs in the case of the sixth dependent variable presented in Table 10-6. Although in zero-order form School SES is related positively to the percentage of teachers who are white ($r = .36$), when the linear effects of School Race are removed the observed relationship becomes negative ($r = -.11$). Perhaps because the proportion of teachers who are white differs so greatly between schools of different pupil racial compositions ($r = .77$), the possibility that the higher the School SES the *smaller* the proportion of teachers who are white (within both the predominantly white and the predominantly nonwhite schools) is being masked.

TABLE 10-6. Zero-Order and First-Order Partial Correlation and Regression Coefficients (Holding Constant School Race) for the Relationship of School SES with Each of 10 Dependent Variables Measuring Staff Characteristics, Attitudes, or Behavior

Dependent Variable		Coefficient[a]				
		XY_i	ZY_i	XZ	$XY_i \cdot Z$	N^b
1. Desire of teacher to move to a school in a "better neighborhood" (self-report: extremely anxious = 5, would very much like to = 4, some desire to = 3, not especially anxious to = 2, would not want to = 1).	r	$-.20*$	$-.22*$	$.54*$	$-.10*$	3200
	b	$-0.05*$	$-0.01*$	$4.61*$	$-0.03*$	3200
2. Desire of teacher to remain in current school for the remainder of his educational career (self-report: extremely anxious = 5, would very much like to = 4, some desire to = 3, not especially anxious to = 2, would not want to = 1).	r	$.14*$	$.17*$	$.53*$	$.06*$	3265
	b	$0.04*$	$0.01*$	$4.57*$	$0.02*$	3265
3. Satisfaction of the teacher with the academic performance of the students in his school (self-report: very satisfied = 6, moderately satisfied = 5, slightly satisfied = 4, slightly dissatisfied = 3, moderately dissatisfied = 2, very dissatisfied = 1).	r	$.39*$	$.37*$	$.54*$	$.24*$	3260
	b	$0.13*$	$0.01*$	$4.59*$	$0.09*$	3260
4. Desire of the principal to obtain a principalship that has greater responsibility than his present one (self-report: extremely anxious = 5, would very much like to = 4, some desire to = 3, not especially anxious to = 2, would not want to = 1).	r	$-.14*$	$-.12*$	$.55*$	$-.10*$	489
	b	$-0.04*$	$-0.00*$	$4.81*$	$-0.03*$	489

TABLE 10-6 (Continued)

Dependent Variable		XY_i	ZY_i	XZ	$XY_i.Z$	N[b]
		Coefficient[a]				
5. Average age of teachers in the school (computed from the report of the principal).	r	.13*	.13*	.55*	.07*	486
	b	0.14*	0.02*	4.84*	0.09	486
6. Per cent of teachers who are white (as reported by the principal).	r	.36*	.77*	.55*	−.11	483
	b	2.41*	0.59*	4.74*	−0.60	483
7. Average number of years of teaching experience of the teachers (computed from the reports of the principal).	r	.20*	.24*	.54*	.08*	484
	b	0.20*	0.03*	4.84*	0.10*	484
8. Per cent of teachers who consistently try out new ideas in their classrooms (as reported by the principal).	r	.12*	.09*	.55*	.09*	484
	b	0.78*	0.09*	4.76*	0.67*	484
9. Per cent of teachers who make themselves available to students at some sacrifice of their own free time (as reported by the principal).	r	.13*	.12*	.55*	.08*	482
	b	0.83*	0.08*	4.81*	0.60*	482
10. Per cent of teachers who have mastered the skills necessary to present their subject matter with high competence (as reported by the principal).	r	.15*	.21*	.54*	.05	486
	b	0.73*	0.11*	4.78*	0.26	486

[a] Key:
  r = Correlation coefficient.
  b = Regression coefficient.
  X = School SES.
  Y_i = Dependent variables 1 through 10.
  Z = School Race.
[b] Difference in Ns due to unavailability of data from some schools.
* $p < .05$.

In this chapter we have addressed ourselves to the perplexing question of whether known relationships between socioeconomic status and the characteristics, attitudes, and behavior of individuals are independent of considerations of racial status. We have seen from the literature of both sociology and education that there is evidence that such a relationship exists, both for individuals and for collectivities such as residents of census tracts. The results of the School SES Study reveal that regardless of whether our source of data is teachers or principals, or whether it focuses on pupils, their parents, their teachers, or their principals, School SES is apparently related to many dependent variables when School Race is controlled. In the next chapter, when discussing the implications of the major findings of the School SES Study, we shall return to some of the limitations of our consideration of this question and some ways in which it could be extended through further research.

Chapter 11

CONCLUSIONS

In Chapter 1 we stated two major objectives for the School SES Study: (1) to examine a set of available nationwide data for insight into the impact of the socioeconomic context of urban schools on teachers and principals, and (2) to establish guidelines for further research. In this chapter we shall attempt to pull together some of the findings and methodological discussions presented in Chapters 2 through 10. After reviewing selected limitations of our data and methods we shall summarize our major findings in terms of the issues raised in Chapter 1. We shall conclude with a discussion of how research in this area might be extended.

LIMITATIONS OF DATA AND METHODS

Many of the important questions raised in Chapter 1 have not been answered by this research, and others have been considered only indirectly. To a large extent this neglect is due to the limitations of the data available to us and the methods we chose to apply to them. Our methodological problems arose particularly in the following areas: sampling, tests of statistical significance, measurement procedures, and control for extraneous variation.[1]

[1] It should be noted that these are primarily the limitations of our inquiry and not necessarily those of the National Principalship Study, the major focus of which was on other questions.

Sampling

One of the major limitations of this inquiry lies in the sample of schools and school personnel used. Although the universe of cities defined by the National Principalship Study was a national one, and was stratified on such important variables as region, size of city, and per-pupil expenditure for public education, it was restricted to cities with populations of 50,000 or more. This restriction excluded from the sample many of the homogeneous suburbs of high SES which ring most major cities and form an important part of the "urban complex." Conant has dramatized the range in the social class composition of American public schools with the phrase "slums and suburbs."[2] The schools of "lowest SES" considered in this study may accurately represent the urban slum to which Conant referred, but those of "highest SES" probably are not as high in average social class as many suburban schools. Therefore, our estimates of differences by School SES are likely to be conservative. Undoubtedly, a more adequate consideration of the effects of variation in the social class composition of schools could be made if the full range of American communities was sampled.

Within cities, the National Principalship Study sampled schools in terms of their level and of an estimate of the socioeconomic composition of their student bodies. These are important variables, but, as was seen in Chapter 10, the high correlation between School SES and School Race made it very difficult for us to interpret SES differences apart from racial differences. Ideally, a study of the effects of School SES in urban settings would provide for the random sampling of a sufficient number of predominantly white and nonwhite schools of different SES, to permit an adequate assessment of SES differences within homogeneous racial categories. In that way, important questions of the relative effects of racial and socioeconomic compositions could be considered. However, before such sampling can be conducted, accurate classifications of schools in terms of both racial and social class compositions must be obtained and made available to researchers by school officials.

Not only were there limitations in our sample of cities and schools, but also in the sample of teachers within each school. The National Principalship Study used teachers as observers of their principals. Teachers were not the focus of that study; therefore, the sam-

[2] James B. Conant, *Slums and Suburbs* (New York: McGraw-Hill Book Company, Inc., 1961).

ple was restricted to ten teachers in each school, regardless of its size. Although we have reason to believe that the resulting sample of teachers was *not* biased because of this restriction (for evidence, see Appendix Table 4A-16), a more desirable procedure for studying the teachers themselves would be to sample the teachers in proportion to the size of each school.

Tests of Statistical Significance

One limitation imposed by the multistage cluster sampling procedure of the National Principalship Study affects tests of statistical significance. In studying teachers we are dealing with a sample of clusters within clusters (that is, teachers within schools within school systems), and estimates of the standard error of conventional statistics become extremely complex. However, as noted in Chapter 2, we need some means of assessing variation *among* schools in terms of variation *within* them. Therefore we have computed estimates of error, using conventional formulas for simple random samples, and have treated them as "rules of thumb" instead of absolute standards. To decide on the "statistical significance" of a relationship we have chosen the .05 level; but, realizing that others may prefer a different level, we have tried to provide *estimates* of the exact chance probability for our statistics.

Whether a given difference between schools of highest and lowest SES achieves "statistical significance" is partly a function of the number of cases on which the difference was computed. Since for the elementary schools (within the schools of highest and lowest SES) there were approximately 100 principals and 2400 teachers, 700 of whom completed the teacher questionnaire, an identical difference is frequently statistically significant for the larger group and not for the smaller one. In making tests of statistical significance we have in general used as many cases as the available data provided. However, in assessing the background characteristics of principals, it did not seem appropriate to use the same procedures as were used with the much larger number of teachers. Thus we chose to compare the principals' curves with those of the teachers rather than with a curve of zero slope. Since we could find no generally appropriate test for this comparison, we made it informally. Future investigators of the effects of School SES on principals will no doubt want to provide for larger samples than were possible in this case.

One effect of measurement error, as noted earlier, is to cause relationships to appear weaker than might be "true." This has not been a severe handicap in the present study, for in general our interest has been in ascertaining the *presence* of a relationship, rather than its *strength*. Future investigators, interested in the strengths of these relationships, may (assuming more reliable measures or more sensitive statistical tests) find their differences to be larger than here reported.

Measurement Procedures

The major sources of data for this research have been the reports of the principals and teachers in the schools. When, as in Chapter 3, our focus was on the *perceptions* by school personnel of pupils and their parents, our procedure seems to be not only defensible but essential. However, in other cases more objective data would have been preferable had they been available.

To measure School SES we asked the principals six questions about the educational, occupational, and income characteristics of the parents of the pupils in their schools and summarized their answers through the statistical technique of factor analysis. Although we feel that this procedure is sufficiently valid for the purposes of the current study (for evidence, see Chapter 2, footnote 8), a major improvement might be made by summarizing the reports of the parents themselves. However, the advantages in validity would have to be weighed against the expense of data collection and the possibility of bias due to class-related nonresponse or distortion. It is highly questionable whether the use of pupils as reporters of their parents' SES is preferable to the use of principals or teachers, since the pupils' replies might be more inaccurate than those of their principal. Extensive research is needed to establish the most efficient and effective means of measuring School SES.

Our use of teachers as observers of the principal (and vice versa), although within the tradition of sociological research in educational settings,[3] has many drawbacks. In the first place the school staff was not trained as observers, and probably utilized varying criteria in as-

[3] See, for example, Andrew W. Halpin, "The Leader Behavior and Leadership Ideology of Educational Administrators and Aircraft Commanders," *Harvard Educational Review*, XXV (Winter, 1955), pp. 18–32; Andrew W. Halpin, *The Leadership Behavior of School Superintendents* (Chicago: The Midwest Administration Center, University of Chicago, 1956); Andrew W. Halpin and Don B. Croft, *The Organizational Climate of Schools* (Chicago: The Midwest Administration Center, University of Chicago, 1963); or Neal Gross and Robert E. Herriott, *Staff Leadership in Public Schools: A Sociological Inquiry* (New York: John Wiley and Sons, 1965).

sessing the performance of each other. However, such "unreliability" is likely to weaken rather than accentuate relationships with School SES. If this is the case, then the "true" relationships—those that could be observed between variables of perfect reliability—are most likely stronger than those observed within our data.[4] Our approach seemed adequate for an exploratory study. However, in future efforts to extend our understanding of such relationships, we shall need to improve our measurement techniques. Participant observers trained in the observation and recording of behavior in school settings will be required, as will techniques for making observations with limited distortion of the phenomena being observed.[5]

Control for Extraneous Variation

One of the limitations of a "survey" such as this, in comparison with an "experiment," is the fact that it makes particularly difficult the establishment of causal relationships. Nevertheless, we have tried to go beyond the level of description typical of social surveys. We have reasoned that the social class composition of schools influences teachers and principals—it affects their selection as well as their attitudes and behavior—and we have assembled our data in such a way as to determine whether this *could* be true.[6] However, we have on occasion been plagued by the possibility that variables extraneous to those considered in a particular analysis are affecting the relationships under study.

Our major concern in this respect was the extent to which School Race affects the relationship of School SES to the many dependent variables. Although we were limited by the distribution of School Race in our sample and its joint distribution with School SES (see Table 10-1), it seems safe to conclude that the major findings of this study

[4] For a more detailed discussion of this point, see Jay P. Guilford, *Fundamental Statistics in Psychology and Education* (Fourth Edition), (New York: McGraw-Hill Book Company, Inc., 1965), pp. 486–487.

[5] For an excellent discussion of research designs for the measurement of teacher classroom behavior, see Donald M. Medley and Harold E. Mitzel, "Measuring Classroom Behavior by Systematic Observation," in Nathaniel L. Gage (Editor), *Handbook of Research on Teaching* (Chicago: Rand McNally and Company, 1963), pp. 247–328.

[6] For a discussion of the rationale underpinning our approach, see, for example, Paul F. Lazarsfeld, "Evidence and Inference in Social Research," *Daedalus*, LXXXVII (1958), pp. 99–130; and Paul F. Lazarsfeld, "The Algebra of Dichotomous Systems," in Herbert Solomon (Editor), *Studies in Item Analysis and Prediction* (Stanford: Stanford University Press, 1961), pp. 111–157.

cannot be "explained away" by variation in School Race. Somewhat neglected, however, is the possibility that School Race "specifies" the relationship between School SES and selected dependent variables. For example, although retardation in reading is related to School SES within both the predominantly white and the predominantly nonwhite schools (Table 10-3), it appears on close examination that this relationship may be stronger in the predominantly white schools than it is in the predominantly nonwhite ones. This possibility could not be adequately explored with our sample.

One instance in which we were able to "specify" a relationship occurred in Chapter 8. There we predicted and found the performance of principals to be more closely related to that of teachers in schools of low SES than in those of high SES. Since our data were nonexperimental, we could not demonstrate conditional causation. However, we did show that it *could* be taking place. Because of the limited number of teacher-observers in the junior and senior high schools, we did not attempt to replicate this particular relationship at those levels.

On the other hand, in Chapter 9 we did introduce the "third variable" of School Level to replicate within junior and senior high schools many of the bivariate relationships noted earlier within elementary schools. In general, we found such replication to exist. However, in several instances the *difference* on a dependent variable between schools of highest and lowest SES seemed itself to be related to School Level (see, for example, Figures 9-3, 9-9, 9-10, and 9-14). If this is the case, then School Level sometimes specifies the relationship between School SES and the dependent variable, and deserves further consideration.

The characteristics and origins of the teachers discussed in Chapter 4 also deserve careful scrutiny as third variables in any consideration of the relationship of School SES and teacher attitudes and behavior. However, before instituting such controls, one must think through the causal sequence of such variables. For example, it could be argued that the variable of age rather than School SES produces the high mobility aspirations of teachers in the schools of low SES; for age was shown to be related to School SES (Figure 4-4) and is likely to be related to mobility—young people generally are more eager to move. However, it seems more plausible to argue that the low SES of a school is responsible for the fact that its teachers are young, since such a school is avoided by older teachers. This produces a vacuum which under current conditions is filled by younger teachers with low seniority and limited choice of jobs. It would thus be inappropriate to use teacher age as evidence of spuriousness in the relationship between School SES and teacher mobility aspirations. Under such conditions, teacher age is an intervening variable and should be used to interpret the relationship rather than explain it away.[7]

There is one area in which greater control over extraneous variation would have been particularly desirable. That is in studying the source of teacher restlessness in schools of low SES. We have related this to their dissatisfaction with the low academic performance of their pupils (Table 5-3), but our lack of adequate data prevented any control for such alternate explanations as their dissatisfaction with: the manners and morals of the pupils, the lack of parental interest, the rate of pupil turnover, the condition of the school plant, the physical dangers of the school neighborhood, or even the amount of parking space. Until proper consideration of each of these alternatives (as well as their relationship to each other) can be given, our inference that teachers desire to move on to escape from pupils who exhibit low academic performance must remain tentative.

MAJOR FINDINGS

Our investigation of the impact of the socioeconomic composition of urban elementary schools[8] on teachers and principals was based on the way in which these school personnel viewed the pupils and parents with whom they interact. We classified four categories of schools in terms of the educational, occupational, and income characteristics of the pupils' parents, and found great variation between the resulting groups of schools. In schools of highest SES, only 13 per cent come from homes where the total income is $5000 or less, 17 per cent from homes where fathers are in unskilled or semiskilled oc-

[7] For a more detailed discussion of this point, see Herbert H. Hyman, *Survey Design and Analysis: Principles, Cases, and Procedures* (Glencoe, Illinois: The Free Press, 1955), pp. 254–274; or Hubert M. Blalock, Jr., "Controlling for Background Factors: Spuriousness Versus Developmental Sequences," *Sociological Inquiry*, XXXIV (1964), pp. 28–40.

[8] Since the major focus of this monograph has been on the elementary school, the summary and implications presented here will be based primarily on these data. However, many of these findings apply to junior and senior high schools as well. The reader interested particularly in secondary schools will want to check carefully Chapter 9 and the many relevant tables in Appendix A.

cupations, and 20 per cent from homes where neither parent has gone beyond high school. In schools of lowest SES these comparable percentages are 85, 89, and 94.

School SES and The Pupil

We then considered some of the attitudes and behavior of pupils and their parents found by previous research to be highly correlated with SES. We did not attempt to measure these correlates "objectively," but rather to understand how the teachers and principals view the "clients" with whom they must interact in attempting to accomplish the objectives of the school. The reports of the two sets of observers are consistent with each other and with the results of previous investigations, which led us to believe that, although affected by perception, these reports may also be fairly realistic. A very large percentage of a long list of characteristics of parents and pupils were found to vary significantly and, for the most part, monotonically by School SES, while the direction of the variation is without exception to the disadvantage of pupils in schools of low SES.

Schools of lowest and highest SES were found to differ significantly in indices of home stability and of parental support of the school. The lower the School SES, the smaller the percentage of parents reported to attend school events, to initiate talks with teachers, or to give their children adequate supervision. Principals and teachers believe that the attitudes of parents match their behavior, for the lower the School SES, the smaller the percentage of parents said to be interested in the school work of their children.

Achievement in reading dramatically differentiates pupils in schools of different SES levels. In schools of lowest SES, 43 per cent of the pupils are reported to be one or more years retarded in this skill, as compared to 10 per cent in schools of highest SES. Similar, if less striking, differences in other measures of academic achievement appeared in the reports of staff in schools of different SES levels. Further, according to both principals and teachers, the lower the School SES, the greater the percentage of pupils who are uninterested in academic achievement and who present discipline problems. Given such differences in school motivation and success, the very different prognoses of elementary staffs at the various SES levels as to the future school careers of their pupils are understandable. In schools of lowest SES, 7 per cent are expected to go to college and 44 per cent to drop out. In schools of highest SES, 64 per cent are expected to go to college and 7 per cent to drop out.

School SES and the Teacher

Quite clearly, the role of teachers and principals, as defined by their views of the needs of pupils, is very different in schools of different socioeconomic composition. In Chapter 1 we discussed three themes that have guided research on the relation between pupil social class and the public school teacher. We called these themes "the culture gap hypothesis," "the horizontal mobility hypothesis," and "the hypothesis of inequality." Let us summarize our findings on the impact of School SES on its staff in terms of these hypotheses.

The culture gap hypothesis assumes that teachers are middle-class in origin, status, and values and are therefore very different from their lower-class pupils. In view of the responsibility of the occupation and the professional skill and level of education required, the present status of teachers clearly seems middle class. We had no evidence as to the values of pupils or teachers and therefore could not test that part of the hypothesis. However, we did compare the origin of teachers with that of their pupils in several respects.

In the first place, at all School SES levels there appears to be a gap between teachers and their pupils in respect to the size of their community of origin. This is partly a function of the increasing urbanization of the nation: adults are more apt than children to have been raised on the farm or in a small town. For our sample this gap is greatest in schools of highest SES. There two-thirds of the teachers grew up in communities smaller than the city in which they teach. In schools of lowest SES, less than one-half of the teachers came from a smaller community.

With respect to socioeconomic level, it appears that there is as much of a discrepancy between the status of a teacher's own parents and the status of his pupils' parents in schools of highest as in schools of lowest SES. However, the discrepancy is in the opposite direction in the two categories of schools. The teachers in our sample are not, by and large, from either very high or very low SES backgrounds. Therefore, those who teach in schools of highest SES are apt to be of *lower* SES than their pupils, and teachers in schools of lowest SES (although of somewhat lower origins than teachers in highest SES schools) are nevertheless of *higher* status than their pupils. Pupil-teacher congruency in respect to SES is fairly close in schools of moderately high or moderately low SES.

Our study of the racial congruency of pupils and teachers indicates that at all levels there exists a gap between the percentage of nonwhite teachers and the percentage of nonwhite pupils, but that the tendency for the percentage of nonwhite pupils to exceed the percentage of nonwhite teachers is greatest at the lowest SES level. Pupil-teacher congruency on religion is generally closer than pupil-teacher congruency on race. In schools of highest SES there are proportionately fewer Jewish teachers than Jewish pupils; in schools of lowest SES, the opposite is true.

The hypothesis of a *greater* gap in schools of low than of high SES between pupils and teachers in respect to various social and economic characteristics has thus not been supported by our findings. With respect to size of community of origin, there is a decreasing gap as School SES falls. With respect to parental SES, pupils are as far above teachers in schools of highest SES as they are below them in schools of lowest SES. A small difference in the percentage of Jewish teachers and pupils is in different directions at the highest and lowest School SES levels. In respect to race only, the gap is greater in schools of lowest SES.

The hypothesis of horizontal mobility has received considerable indirect support from our data. The fact that elementary schools of low SES have proportionately more young and inexperienced teachers than do those of higher SES suggests that the career patterns of many teachers must be away from low SES and toward high SES schools. Further evidence in support of the hypothesis comes from the replies to the job aspiration and job satisfaction questionnaires. Teachers in schools of lowest SES are, of all teachers, the least satisfied with various aspects of their teaching situation. Moreover, 42 per cent of the teachers in these schools, as compared with 18 per cent in schools of highest SES, aspire to a school "in a better neighborhood." Thus, although it would take longitudinal data to prove that horizontal mobility is as dominant a career pattern in city schools across the nation today as Becker[9] found it to be in 1952 in Chicago, nevertheless our findings indicate that it is highly possible that this is the case.

Evidence in support of the hypothesis of inequality is less clear. Are schools of lowest SES "discriminated against" with respect to the staff assigned to them? If the fact that teachers in these schools are on the average significantly younger, less experienced, newer to the school, and receiving lower salaries within each age bracket than teachers in schools of highest SES is conclusive evidence, the answer is "yes." But it is possible to argue that superior teaching is a function

[9] Howard S. Becker, "The Career of the Chicago Public Schoolteacher," *American Journal of Sociology*, LVII (1952), pp. 470–477.

of youth and inexperience rather than of age and experience.[10] More-over, if teaching competence is a function of formal academic training (and it may not be), then the lack of significant differences in highest academic degree held by teachers in schools of different SES levels or in their self-reports as to the quality of their college work argues against the hypothesis of inequality.

Differences in job satisfaction cited above, as well as the fact that principals and teachers both report lower teacher morale in schools of low SES, indicate at least that pupils in these schools have less contented teachers. If such dissatisfaction encouraged a teacher to work harder to improve the status quo for pupils, then it might produce better teaching. But in view of the desire of teachers to leave such schools and of the reports of principals and teachers as to teacher performance, it seems probable that teacher dissatisfaction should be considered a handicap to a school. Teaching performance, whether in respect to competence in subject matter, innovation, interest in pupils, cooperation with school personnel, teaching methods, or the mainte-nance of discipline, was found to be somewhat poorer in schools of lowest than of highest SES. On the other hand, although this trend was consistent over a large number of items, none of the differences was very large.

All in all, the hypothesis of inequality has not been very clearly supported by findings of this study, although there is some indication that the weight of evidence is on the side of inequality rather than of equality.

School SES and the Principal

The findings of this study in relation to the background and career characteristics of principals can be related to the same three hypotheses to which we related the characteristics of teachers, and, in general, the conclusions are similar. In most background character-istics the culture gap between principals and pupils is not especially great in schools of lowest SES. In socioeconomic origin, principals re-semble teachers. They come from a lower background than their pupils if they are located in schools of highest SES and from a higher back-ground than their pupils (but a lower background than principals in other school SES categories) if they are located in schools of lowest SES. Like teachers, principals are more rural in background than

[10] For a provocative discussion of the difference in teaching styles of old and young teachers, see Margaret Mead, *The School in American Culture* (Cam-bridge, Massachusetts: Harvard University Press, 1951).

their pupils, especially in high SES schools. In race only is the origin of a principal unlike that of his teachers. In all schools there are fewer nonwhite teachers than nonwhite pupils and fewer non-white principals than nonwhite teachers. As School SES falls, the proportion of nonwhite pupils, teachers, and principals rises, but the proportion of pupils rises more rapidly than that of teachers, and the proportion of teachers rises much more rapidly than that of principals. The relatively few nonwhite principals are generally located in low SES schools, in which over 80 per cent of the teachers and 100 per cent of the pupils are nonwhite. These findings with respect to the lack of close pupil-teacher-principal racial congruency suggest that staff is not randomly distributed among schools irrespective of race, and that racial discrimination probably affects the promotion of teachers to the principalship.[11]

Both horizontal and vertical mobility appear to characterize the career of the public school principal. In career characteristics we found the principal to be more experienced than his teachers. However, as in the case of teachers, as School SES declines, principals are younger and less experienced, and more apt to be male. Like their teachers, principals in low SES schools express dissatisfaction with many aspects of the job and indicate a desire for a position of greater "responsibility" or "prestige." But unlike their teachers, they also look forward to vertical mobility into higher administration.

The hypothesis of inequality apparently receives less support from the data about the principals than from the data on teachers. Although, like his teachers, the principal tends to be younger and less experienced in schools of lowest SES, it seems that for staff as experienced as principals this fact can hardly be taken as evidence of incompetence. It could even be that relative youth (50 instead of 55 years, on the average) means a more vigorous administration in schools of lowest SES than in schools of highest SES. It is also true that the greater dissatisfaction of principals at the bottom of the SES ladder might be less depressing in its effect on the school as a whole, since the principal can initiate changes more easily than can the teacher. Fi-

---

[11] No doubt there are many other variables on which the distribution of principals is nonrandom. One note-worthy example is the characteristic of sex. For the nation as a whole, at all school levels the proportion of *principals* who are female appears to be less than the proportion of *teachers* who are female. For an extensive study of men and women as elementary school principals, see Neal Gross and Anne E. Trask, *The Sex Factor and the Administration of Schools* (New York: John Wiley and Sons, forthcoming, title tentative).

nally, we must remember that no over-all difference in the level of performance of principals between schools at the different SES levels was found.

The hypothesis that the performance of the principal is more closely related to that of his teachers in schools of low than of high SES received support from the data. In schools of low SES a significant relationship with a Teacher Performance Score was found for 19 out of 23 indices of the administrative performance of principals. The impact of the principal of low SES schools on his teachers is apparently most pronounced in such areas as planning for the school, smoothing office routine, handling students, and upgrading the performance of teachers, especially those who are inexperienced. Such underscoring of the role of the principal in the low SES school should be evaluated in the context of the methodological limitations discussed at the beginning of this chapter and of the apparent necessity for further research.

NEED FOR FURTHER RESEARCH

Most research studies can be characterized by what they fail to consider as well as by what they study. We have neglected many important questions which others will want to explore. However, we do have some observations on the directions in which such research might go.

This study has found great differences among urban schools in the average SES level of their pupils. Our focus on this phenomenon and its correlates does not imply that we consider existing school districting policies and techniques either necessarily good or necessarily inevitable. Instead, we suggest that one variable particularly worthy of detailed consideration in future research is the socioeconomic homogeneity of schools. In schools of either very high or very low SES there can be relatively little variation in the socioeconomic background of the pupils. But in schools that are on the average of moderately high or moderately low SES, our School SES Score could represent either the actual SES of almost all the pupils, or merely the average of pupils from very different SES levels. Havighurst has suggested that *homogeneity* of SES might be as important in its effect on pupils as its modal tendency.[12] Research is needed which focuses

[12] Robert J. Havighurst, "Urban Development and the Educational System," in A. Harry Passow (Editor), *Education in Depressed Areas* (New York: Bureau of Publications, Teachers College, Columbia University, 1963), pp. 24–45.

simultaneously on both the mean and variance in the SES of pupils attending urban schools.

To the extent that schools of highest and lowest SES are homogeneous they could be considered as examples of *de facto* social class segregation. It would be enlightening to compare the results of the School SES Study with a study of the effects of *de facto* racial segregation. To do so, one would want to focus on School Race as the independent variable rather than as a variable to be controlled for, as was the case in this study. If possible, the independent and joint effects of social class and racial segregation should be considered.

Future research should consider not only the modal tendency and variation in the social class and racial composition of schools, but also the change in such measures over time. For some urban schools, the *change* in pupil composition may be more crucial to the understanding of teacher attitudes and behavior than its current state.

Such longitudinal studies could serve many purposes. After all, the data upon which the School SES Study was based were collected during the 1960–1961 school year. Since that time many urban school systems have instituted extensive programs for the improvement of education in general, but in the more culturally deprived areas in particular. Systematic longitudinal research is needed to evaluate the extent to which changes in school plant and size as well as in personnel policies, salary schedules, and curriculum materials have resulted in changes in the attitudes and behavior of teachers noted here. The data presented in this book might serve as a base line for such comparisons.

Research is also needed on the training of teachers. More information is needed about the distinguishing characteristics of teachers who are most effective with different types of pupils in schools of different levels of SES. Our findings suggest that in addition to differentiating the preparation of teachers in terms of the grade level for which they are preparing or the type of subjects they will teach, a further differentiation should perhaps be made in terms of the type of pupils whom they will teach.[18]

Future researchers might consider in greater detail than was possible in this study the culture-gap hypothesis. To what extent do teachers stress such "middle-class values" as: achievement, upward

[18] For a discussion of a teacher training program designed to prepare teachers for schools of low SES, that at Hunter College in New York, see Vernon F. Haubrich, "Teachers for Big-City Schools," in Passow, *op. cit.*, pp. 243–261; and Vernon F. Haubrich, "The Culturally Different: New Context for Teacher Education," *The Journal of Teacher Education*, XIV (1963), pp. 163–167.

mobility, respectability, promptness, and hard work, irrespective of the SES of the pupil and the SES composition of the school. Do these "values" differ with School SES? In schools of different SES, how do teachers' values differ from those of the pupils?

There is a need for further research focused on the principal. We have seen that the principal may exert a different effect upon teachers in schools of different SES levels. What are the distinguishing characteristics of those principals who are most effective in the schools of highest SES? of lowest SES? How do they influence both teachers and pupils, thus mediating the negative effects which the environment can have on the school? As the chief administrative officer, the principal is in a key position to act as a mediating agent, but we need to know more about how this can be done.

However, as a practical matter, such variables as the values, attitudes, and performance of teachers and principals, as interesting as they may be, are important primarily because of their assumed relationship with measures of pupil learning. The comprehensive understanding of schools of different socioeconomic composition requires that this assumed linkage be studied and demonstrated. This will not be easy, for there are many obstacles to systematic research on teacher-pupil interaction. Essential to overcoming some of these obstacles is a more careful statement of the objectives for urban education in general, and for the school and pupil of low SES in particular.

Throughout this book we have considered questions of importance to those whose major concern is the practice of education or the study of social phenomena. We have applied the methods of social research to the study of urban schools in order to consider the impact of their social class composition on teachers and principals. We trust that through our efforts, others can begin to see more clearly some of the problems and prospects of research in this important area of modern social concern.

Appendix A
SUPPLEMENTARY TABLES

In this appendix are presented many of the summary tables and technical details which may be of interest to other research workers studying schools of different socioeconomic composition. Included with the summary tables are the specific results of all tests of statistical significance referred to in the text or in the footnotes. Since the statistical test used may vary from table to table some rationale for the different tests is in order.

In general when the dependent variable is of interval measurement (or when it seemed to us reasonable to assume an interval) we have performed the conventional t-test (indicated on the tables by the symbol "t") on the difference between the means of the schools of highest and lowest SES. When the dependent variable is of ordinal measurement (or when we have been particularly skeptical of the ability of our data to meet the assumptions of the t-test) we have performed the Kolmogorov-Smirnov test on the maximum difference (indicated by the symbol "d") in the cummulative frequency distributions of the schools of highest and lowest SES. When the measurement of a dependent variable for schools of highest and lowest SES is nominal we have used a test of the difference between two proportions (indicated by the symbol "z") if the dependent variable consists of two categories, and the conventional chi-square test (indicated by the symbol "χ^2") if it consists of more.

All probability statements are for an *estimate* of the exact probability of an outcome as rare as that observed occurring purely by chance from random sampling from a common population in which there is no difference between the schools of highest and lowest SES on the variable under consideration. Unless noted by the subscript "2" all probability statements refer to only *one* tail of the sampling distribution of the statistic involved.

TABLE 2A-1. Means, Standard Deviations, and Correlation Coefficients for the Six Indices of School Socioeconomic Status (SES), $N = 490$

Index of School SES								
The per cent of students who come from homes where:	1	2	3	4	5	6	Mean	S.D.
1. The father is an unskilled or semi-skilled worker.		$-.61$	$.65$	$-.63$	$.66$	$-.56$	48.0	30.1
2. The father is a professional person, business executive, or manager.			$-.64$	$.86$	$-.54$	$.76$	17.9	21.1
3. Neither parent has gone to school beyond high school.				$-.72$	$.55$	$-.59$	57.9	30.4
4. At least one parent is a college graduate.					$-.56$	$.73$	19.5	21.4
5. The combined family income is less than $5000.						$-.61$	40.3	30.0
6. The combined family income is $10,000 or more.							16.6	20.1

TABLE 2A-2. Factor Weights Resulting from the Principal Components Analysis of the Correlation Matrix of the Six Indices of School Socioeconomic Status (SES), N = 490

Index of School SES	FACTOR					
The per cent of students who come from homes where:	I (School SES Factor)	II	III	IV	V	VI
1. The father is an unskilled or semiskilled worker.	−.81	.38	−.20	−.37	.14	−.02
2. The father is a professional person, business executive, or manager.	.88	.33	−.06	.16	.15	−.25
3. Neither parent has gone to school beyond high school.	−.82	.02	−.44	.34	.07	.06
4. At least one parent is a college graduate.	.90	.27	.07	.05	.21	.26
5. The combined family income is less than $5000.	−.77	.49	.33	.17	−.19	.02
6. The combined family income is $10,000 or more.	.85	.21	−.34	−.08	−.34	.04
Latent root	4.23[a]	0.62	0.47	0.31	0.24	0.13
Cumulation per cent of trace.	70.5	80.8	88.6	93.8	97.8	100.0

[a] $p < .05$.

TABLE 2A-3. Summary of the Socioeconomic, Ethnic, and Religious Background of the Pupils in Elementary, Junior, and Senior High Schools of Highest and Lowest SES (as Reported by Principals)

What per cent of the pupils in your school:		Highest SES			Lowest SES			$t_{(H-L)}$	p
		Mean	S.D.	N	Mean	S.D.	N		
1. Come from homes where at least one parent is a college graduate?	E	50.2	21.8	47	1.5	2.0	47	15.25	.001
	J	51.3	18.2	37	2.1	1.9	36	16.13	.001
	S	46.5	18.8	39	4.2	3.8	39	13.77	.001
2. Come from homes where neither parent has gone beyond high school?	E	19.6	17.8	47	93.6	7.0	47	−26.52	.001
	J	24.3	15.4	37	84.4	17.4	37	−15.73	.001
	S	28.3	18.9	39	84.9	12.3	39	−15.67	.001
3. Come from homes where the father is a professional person, business executive, or manager?	E	46.3	25.8	47	1.5	2.2	47	11.86	.001
	J	50.0	17.3	37	2.1	2.2	36	16.48	.001
	S	44.0	19.3	39	4.0	4.4	39	12.62	.001
4. Come from homes where the father is an unskilled or semiskilled worker?	E	16.6	15.0	47	89.3	12.7	47	−25.36	.001
	J	18.9	12.6	36	84.5	13.4	37	−21.54	.001
	S	19.3	11.5	39	73.6	16.0	39	−17.21	.001
5. Come from homes where the combined family income is $10,000 or more?	E	45.2	23.6	47	0.5	1.2	46	12.83	.001
	J	40.2	20.9	37	1.7	2.5	34	10.67	.001
	S	39.5	19.8	39	3.3	4.9	37	10.81	.001
6. Come from homes where the combined family income is less than $5000?	E	13.2	9.3	45	85.0	15.5	47	−26.79	.001
	J	12.4	9.7	37	79.6	17.5	37	−20.43	.001
	S	15.2	12.5	39	64.1	20.5	39	−12.72	.001
7. Are Puerto Rican?	E	0.36	1.13	45	1.85	6.59	47	−1.50	.067
	J	0.19	0.58	36	3.81	11.0	36	−1.97	.024
	S	0.08	0.27	38	3.64	11.5	39	−1.91	.028
8. Are Oriental?	E	0.47	1.04	45	0.57	1.68	46	−0.33	.371
	J	0.87	2.11	37	1.09	2.80	33	−0.38	.352
	S	1.16	3.37	38	3.63	14.4	38	−1.03	.152

TABLE 2A-3 (Continued)

What per cent of the pupils in your school:		Highest SES			Lowest SES			$t_{(H-L)}$	p
		Mean	S.D.	N	Mean	S.D.	N		
9. Are Negro?	E	0.54	2.13	46	54.2	42.5	47	−8.56	.001
	J	3.49	8.85	37	49.2	42.7	37	−6.38	.001
	S	3.23	6.79	39	50.1	39.3	38	−7.35	.001
10. Are Mexican?	E	0.67	2.79	42	5.67	20.2	45	−1.59	.056
	J	0.77	2.22	35	9.81	26.6	31	−2.01	.022
	S	1.08	2.63	39	8.08	21.7	37	−2.00	.023
11. Are White?	E	97.7	3.37	47	36.7	40.2	46	10.4	.001
	J	94.1	10.7	37	36.7	39.2	36	8.59	.001
	S	94.6	9.59	39	36.8	36.7	39	9.53	.001
12. Are Catholic?	E	17.3	18.3	47	19.1	23.9	47	−0.41	.341
	J	16.7	11.5	37	31.1	28.7	37	−2.83	.002
	S	19.1	14.8	39	24.3	20.6	37	−1.27	.102
13. Are Protestant?	E	66.5	29.8	47	79.1	24.5	46	−2.22	.013
	J	55.4	29.6	37	66.5	30.4	37	−1.59	.056
	S	64.5	25.9	39	71.8	21.6	37	−1.33	.092
14. Are Jewish?	E	16.0	25.5	47	1.07	3.03	46	3.93	.001
	J	25.3	29.6	37	1.79	3.58	34	4.59	.001
	S	16.0	24.6	39	2.92	6.43	38	3.18	.001

TABLE 2A-4. Distribution of Schools, by the Per Cent of Student Enrollment that Is White, School Level, and School SES

		Per Cent of Student Enrollment that Is White			
		0–4	5–95	96–100	All
Elementary Schools					
	Highest	—	5	42	47
School	Moderately high	—	13	34	47
SES	Moderately low	6	20	20	46
	Lowest	21	20	6	47
	All	27	58	102	187

$$\chi^2_6 = 83.4; \; p = .001_2$$

		0–4	5–95	96–100	All
Junior High Schools					
	Highest	—	9	28	37
School	Moderately high	3	22	12	37
SES	Moderately low	6	19	11	36
	Lowest	15	19	3	37
	All	24	69	54	147

$$\chi^2_6 = 50.6; \; p = .001_2$$

		0–4	5–95	96–100	All
Senior High Schools					
	Highest	—	9	30	39
School	Moderately high	2	21	16	39
SES	Moderately low	6	15	18	39
	Lowest	12	22	5	39
	All	20	67	69	156

$$\chi^2_6 = 36.5; \; p = .001_2$$

Note. For a more detailed presentation of the distribution of per cent of white enrollment by School SES, see Table 10-1.

TABLE 2A-5. Mean and Standard Deviation of School Enrollment, by School Level and School SES

		Mean	Standard Deviation	N	$t_{(H-L)}$	p
Elementary Schools						
	Highest	648	183	47		
School	Moderately high	649	262	47	-2.48	.007
SES	Moderately low	634	198	46		
	Lowest	888	639	47		
Junior High Schools						
	Highest	1210	433	37		
School	Moderately high	1206	377	37	0.45	.674
SES	Moderately low	1205	831	36		
	Lowest	1164	451	37		
Senior High Schools						
	Highest	1859	895	39		
School	Moderately high	2037	891	39	1.48	.931
SES	Moderately low	1674	801	39		
	Lowest	1601	618	39		

TABLE 2A-6. Mean and Standard Deviation of the Ratio of the Number of Pupils in a School to the Number for which the Building Was Designed, by School Level and School SES

		Mean	Standard Deviation	N	$t_{(H-L)}$	p
Elementary Schools						
	Highest	0.98	0.21	45		
School	Moderately high	0.93	0.18	47	-2.20	.014
SES	Moderately low	1.02	0.30	45		
	Lowest	1.09	0.26	44		
Junior High Schools						
	Highest	1.13	0.28	37		
School	Moderately high	1.06	0.22	36	1.77	.962
SES	Moderately low	1.04	0.20	34		
	Lowest	1.02	0.24	34		
Senior High Schools						
	Highest	1.08	0.25	38		
School	Moderately high	1.06	0.30	39	2.64	.996
SES	Moderately low	1.02	0.28	38		
	Lowest	0.92	0.28	39		

TABLE 2A-7. Number of All Teachers and Pupils in Elementary, Junior, and Senior High Schools of Highest and Lowest SES

Status	Highest SES	Lowest SES		
Elementary Schools				
Teachers	1,009	1,369	$z =$	0.23
Pupils	30,449	41,749	$p =$	.82$_2$
Total	31,458	43,118		
Junior High Schools				
Teachers	1,765	1,850	$z =$	-2.56
Pupils	44,778	43,063	$p =$	.01$_2$
Total	46,543	44,913		
Senior High Schools				
Teachers	3,012	2,692	$z =$	-1.32
Pupils	72,510	62,422	$p =$	.18$_2$
Total	75,522	65,114		

TABLE 2A-8. Distribution of Schools, by Region, School Level, and School SES

		Region				
		East	Midwest	Far West	South	All
Elementary Schools						
	Highest	10	13	11	13	47
School	Moderately high	17	14	9	7	47
SES	Moderately low	13	14	8	11	46
	Lowest	11	15	5	16	47
	All	51	56	33	47	187

$$\chi_9^2 = 8.27, p = .51_2$$

		East	Midwest	Far West	South	All
Junior High Schools						
	Highest	8	5	15	9	37
School	Moderately high	9	6	12	10	37
SES	Moderately low	13	3	6	14	36
	Lowest	13	10	5	9	37
	All	43	24	38	42	147

$$\chi_9^2 = 15.15, p = .09_2$$

		East	Midwest	Far West	South	All
Senior High Schools						
	Highest	9	10	7	13	39
School	Moderately high	12	12	9	6	39
SES	Moderately low	8	14	4	13	39
	Lowest	9	19	4	7	39
	All	38	55	24	39	156

$$\chi_9^2 = 11.59, p = .24_2$$

TABLE 2A-9. Distribution of Schools, by Size of City, School Level, and School SES

		Size of City			
		Metropolis (more than 1 million)	Large City (250 thousand to 1 million)	Medium City (50 to 250 thousand)	All
Elementary Schools					
	Highest	5	12	30	47
School	Moderately high	8	18	21	47
SES	Moderately low	7	15	24	46
	Lowest	12	17	18	47
	All	32	62	93	187

$$\chi_6^2 = 7.94, \; p = .24_2.$$

Junior High Schools					
	Highest	13	8	16	37
School	Moderately high	6	12	19	37
SES	Moderately low	9	14	13	36
	Lowest	15	13	9	37
	All	43	47	57	147

$$\chi_6^2 = 10.08, \; p = .12_2$$

Senior High Schools					
	Highest	7	18	14	39
School	Moderately high	10	15	14	39
SES	Moderately low	7	14	18	39
	Lowest	13	23	3	39
	All	37	70	49	156

$$\chi_6^2 = 15.66, \; p = .02_2$$

TABLE 3A-1.   Summary of the Family Background of Pupils in Elementary, Junior and Senior High Schools of Highest and Lowest SES (as Reported by Principals)

What per cent of the pupils in your school:		Highest SES			Lowest SES			$t_{(H-L)}$	p
		Mean	S.D.	N	Mean	S.D.	N		
1. Have emotional or	E	8.67	8.83	46	27.4	23.6	46	−5.05	.001
social problems?	J	13.2	12.4	37	29.3	22.3	37	−3.84	.001
	S	7.13	5.44	39	28.4	22.4	38	−5.76	.001
2. Have poor teeth?	E	6.05	7.45	42	33.5	23.1	46	−7.35	.001
	J	12.8	15.0	36	38.4	27.8	37	−4.88	.001
	S	13.5	14.0	35	33.7	26.4	36	−4.01	.001
3. Come from homes	E	1.24	1.49	46	26.7	23.1	46	−7.49	.001
receiving some type	J	2.97	8.23	37	25.8	21.0	37	−6.15	.001
of welfare or relief	S	2.46	2.26	39	23.3	19.8	39	−6.53	.001
payment?									
4. Have an inade-	E	12.6	26.8	44	35.4	28.9	46	−3.88	.001
quate diet at home?	J	14.4	28.5	35	41.7	26.5	36	−4.18	.001
	S	12.5	25.3	36	35.2	25.7	38	−3.83	.001
5. Have inadequate	E	0.59	0.91	46	21.0	23.5	46	−5.90	.001
clothing to wear to	J	2.19	6.67	37	9.84	13.0	37	−3.18	.001
school?	S	1.11	1.23	38	9.92	16.3	39	−3.33	.001
6. Come from a	E	9.87	12.2	47	37.4	22.6	46	−7.33	.001
broken home?	J	15.9	13.0	37	38.0	21.3	37	−5.39	.001
	S	12.8	8.03	36	33.9	20.8	39	−5.69	.001
7. Come from homes	E	20.7	15.1	47	38.7	23.4	47	−4.43	.001
where the mother	J	27.0	16.6	37	45.4	17.9	37	−4.58	.001
is employed full	S	21.9	11.7	39	49.9	21.4	39	−7.17	.001
time?									
8. Transferred into	E	10.7	8.79	40	24.0	17.6	38	−4.23	$.001_2$
your school from	J	11.5	10.9	36	18.9	17.3	31	−2.12	$.032_2$
another school dur-	S	6.89	5.99	35	12.3	10.1	34	−2.70	$.007_2$
ing the 1959–1960									
school year?									
9. Transferred out of	E	9.17	7.66	46	22.9	15.5	46	−5.39	$.001_2$
your school last	J	11.3	10.2	37	18.8	16.8	37	−2.32	$.020_2$
year to attend	S	6.13	5.42	39	9.69	6.81	39	−2.55	$.011_2$
another school?									

TABLE 3A-2. Summary of Parental Interest and Behavior in Elementary, Junior and Senior High Schools of Highest and Lowest SES (as Reported by Principals)

What per cent of the parents of the pupils in your school:		Highest SES			Lowest SES			$t_{(H-L)}$	p
		Mean	S.D.	N	Mean	S.D.	N		
1. Usually attend school events open to the public?	E	61.0	26.8	47	31.1	24.9	46	5.57	.001
	J	51.6	23.3	37	37.5	28.1	37	2.35	.009
	S	39.5	18.4	39	25.6	20.9	38	3.10	.001
2. Visit the school at least once during the school year?	E	86.5	14.0	47	48.6	31.0	47	7.64	.001
	J	75.6	17.5	37	43.6	25.5	37	6.29	.001
	S	58.7	20.0	39	33.1	25.1	39	4.98	.001
3. Come to school to talk about the problems of their children only when they are sent for?	E	19.3	25.8	44	54.3	34.3	45	−5.44	.001
	J	27.8	27.0	36	55.6	37.1	34	−3.60	.001
	S	26.0	28.0	39	58.4	35.6	38	−4.45	.001
4. If they have children with social or emotional problems, come to school on their own initiative to talk about their children?	E	52.3	37.5	46	10.1	19.5	45	6.71	.001
	J	31.1	27.9	37	9.84	15.1	37	4.08	.001
	S	23.7	25.8	39	5.49	8.80	39	4.18	.001
5. If they have children with academic problems, come to school on their own initiative to talk about their children?	E	52.5	34.9	46	13.5	17.2	46	6.80	.001
	J	46.8	27.5	37	10.5	12.4	37	7.32	.001
	S	36.3	27.5	39	9.36	12.0	39	5.60	.001
6. If they have children who are serious misbehavior problems, come to school on their own initiative to talk about their children?	E	34.2	31.9	45	8.35	17.4	46	4.80	.001
	J	15.3	24.4	37	6.73	11.5	37	1.94	.052
	S	16.6	21.9	39	3.18	4.00	39	3.77	.001
7. Are interested in the academic achievement of their children?	E	86.8	13.8	45	60.7	28.9	46	5.48	.001
	J	88.9	8.59	36	61.6	25.7	35	6.04	.001
	S	82.7	13.6	37	60.8	26.8	38	4.44	.001

TABLE 3A-2 (Continued)

What per cent of the parents of the pupils in your school:		Highest SES			Lowest SES			$t_{(H\text{-}L)}$	p
		Mean	S.D.	N	Mean	S.D.	N		
8. Are interested in the grades their children receive?	E	88.7	17.2	41	62.3	23.0	39	5.83	.001
	J	89.7	8.94	36	69.6	23.0	31	4.84	.001
	S	84.8	17.5	35	62.6	25.5	34	4.23	.001
9. Are interested in the extracurricular achievements of their children?	E	58.5	25.6	41	25.7	22.5	40	6.12	.001
	J	57.9	25.6	35	32.1	28.1	33	3.96	.001
	S	59.6	19.1	37	43.1	25.7	38	3.15	.001
10. Are interested in the athletic program of your school?	E	40.1	30.1	30	25.4	28.8	31	1.95	.026
	J	42.3	26.8	34	21.3	28.3	33	3.12	.001
	S	41.7	22.3	39	35.2	29.1	39	1.11	.134
11. Are interested in having their children acquire knowledge in areas which may be of no immediate practical use (e.g., fine arts, classics)?	E	44.3	33.4	46	15.1	22.3	45	4.89	.001
	J	59.1	30.0	37	15.8	16.0	36	7.66	.001
	S	29.6	21.5	38	24.6	21.3	37	1.01	.156
12. Are interested in having their children learn to play a musical instrument?	E	34.2	23.4	41	10.8	11.5	37	5.50	.001
	J	23.8	14.6	36	12.0	9.16	31	3.87	.001
	S	13.6	11.1	34	11.7	9.28	33	0.74	.230
13. Are interested in cooperating with the school in strengthening its program?	E	77.5	18.5	46	39.2	31.2	44	7.12	.001
	J	77.0	16.6	37	40.4	31.2	37	6.30	.001
	S	65.0	27.0	39	45.7	35.2	39	2.72	.003
14. Are able to control the behavior of their children?	E	82.5	20.9	45	68.5	23.4	46	3.01	.001
	J	87.4	8.84	36	69.7	20.9	37	4.68	.001
	S	79.3	15.3	39	70.0	19.3	39	2.36	.009
15. Expect the school to control their children when they can't do it themselves?	E	9.7	14.9	30	36.4	35.5	34	−3.83	.001
	J	18.8	24.7	18	38.1	30.6	29	−2.26	.012
	S	21.0	27.8	28	29.6	26.6	29	−1.19	.117

TABLE 3A-2 (Continued)

What per cent of the parents of the pupils in your school:		Highest SES			Lowest SES			$t_{(H-L)}$	p
		Mean	S.D.	N	Mean	S.D.	N		
16. Adequately super-	E	79.7	15.5	46	42.1	25.9	46	8.45	.001
vise their children	J	77.0	17.8	35	44.5	25.8	37	6.19	.001
during out-of-	S	67.5	20.9	36	44.7	21.5	38	4.62	.001
school hours?									
17. Are overprotective	E	27.7	25.8	47	7.83	7.11	46	5.03	.001
of their children?	J	25.4	26.6	37	8.49	8.96	37	3.67	.001
	S	24.3	24.0	39	8.26	10.0	39	3.85	.001
18. Push their chil-	E	21.2	22.0	47	7.24	7.63	46	4.06	.001
dren too hard about	J	23.2	22.7	37	3.76	4.76	37	5.09	.001
their school work?	S	16.4	13.8	39	8.64	10.3	39	2.80	.003

TABLE 3A-3. Summary of Academic and Behavioral Characteristics of Pupils in Elementary, Junior, and Senior High Schools of Highest and Lowest SES (as Reported by Principals)

What per cent of the pupils in your school:		Highest SES			Lowest SES			$t_{(H-L)}$	p
		Mean	S.D.	N	Mean	S.D.	N		
1. Have an I.Q.	E	21.9	12.6	46	3.45	4.26	47	9.46	.001
greater than 120?	J	22.9	13.6	37	4.11	3.50	37	8.13	.001
	S	20.2	12.6	39	5.46	5.75	39	6.64	.001
2. Have an I.Q. less	E	7.11	5.32	46	39.6	20.5	47	−10.4	.001
than 90?	J	8.57	4.49	37	46.0	20.7	37	−10.8	.001
	S	11.8	9.57	39	39.8	20.0	39	−7.89	.001
3. Have stayed back	E	3.7	4.4	46	20.3	14.0	45	−7.67	.001
one year or more?	J	4.2	5.6	37	17.9	17.3	36	−4.58	.001
	S	4.8	5.3	39	17.4	14.5	38	−5.09	.001
4. Are one year or	E	8.9	7.8	47	35.7	22.0	46	−7.86	.001
more below grade	J	15.0	14.6	37	51.4	22.2	36	−8.30	.001
level in arithmetic?	S	10.2	6.5	37	41.4	23.4	38	−7.82	.001
5. Are one year or	E	10.0	9.6	47	42.5	22.7	46	−9.03	.001
more below grade	J	15.1	15.1	37	52.4	23.2	36	−8.16	.001
level in reading?	S	11.5	7.7	38	43.7	24.8	38	−7.64	.001

TABLE 3A-3 (Continued)

What per cent of the pupils in your school:		Highest SES			Lowest SES			$t_{(H-L)}$	p
		Mean	S.D.	N	Mean	S.D.	N		
6. Are *not* interested in academic achievement?	E	8.8	12.3	44	22.4	20.5	46	−3.79	.001
	J	11.7	10.2	37	31.8	22.5	37	−4.95	.001
	S	9.6	7.8	38	20.6	13.7	39	−4.31	.001
7. Are interested in athletics?	E	56.3	28.8	38	53.6	30.9	40	0.40	.345
	J	58.2	27.0	36	50.1	27.5	36	1.26	.104
	S	39.3	27.2	39	42.3	26.2	39	−0.50	.692
8. Do *not* regularly do their home- work?	E	6.9	7.2	40	20.1	18.3	45	−4.28	.001
	J	15.1	14.6	37	25.6	20.5	37	−2.54	.006
	S	13.2	7.9	38	31.1	22.1	38	−4.70	.001
9. Will probably drop out of school be- fore they graduate from high school?	E	7.1	8.4	45	44.4	22.2	45	−10.5	.001
	J	12.8	18.5	37	47.8	25.8	35	−6.64	.001
	S	9.1	7.1	39	35.8	15.6	39	−9.73	.001
10. Will probably go to college?	E	63.9	20.5	47	6.8	10.4	47	17.0	.001
	J	64.2	16.5	37	6.5	4.5	37	20.5	.001
	S	61.0	21.1	39	20.3	11.5	38	10.5	.001
11. Have been truant one or more times during the last school year?	E	0.6	0.6	47	4.8	6.1	46	−4.70	.001
	J	3.2	8.0	37	9.9	8.0	37	−3.60	.001
	S	4.3	4.2	39	12.8	12.6	39	−4.00	.001
12. Have been disci- pline problems during the last school year?	E	3.5	3.6	47	8.6	8.1	46	−3.94	.001
	J	5.4	6.4	37	12.9	10.5	37	−3.71	.001
	S	4.8	3.4	39	9.3	12.0	39	−2.25	.012
13. Have been in- volved in school vandalism during the last school year?	E	0.7	0.9	46	1.2	1.2	46	−2.26	.012
	J	1.2	1.6	37	2.0	2.6	35	−1.58	.057
	S	1.1	0.8	38	1.4	1.6	39	−1.04	.149
14. Have ever been arrested?	E	0.2	0.4	44	2.6	4.9	44	−3.24	.001
	J	1.3	1.0	37	4.9	5.1	37	−4.21	.001
	S	1.5	1.0	38	4.6	8.3	39	−2.29	.011
15. Have ever been in court?	E	0.2	0.4	41	2.76	4.96	41	−3.30	.001
	J	1.4	1.6	36	5.2	5.1	31	−4.24	.001
	S	1.8	1.8	36	5.3	10.2	35	−2.03	.021

TABLE 3A-4. Summary of Academic and Behavioral Characteristics of Pupils in Elementary, Junior, and Senior High Schools of Highest and Lowest SES (as Reported by Teachers)

What per cent of the pupils you teach:		Highest SES			Lowest SES			$t_{(H-L)}$	p
		Mean	S.D.	N	Mean	S.D.	N		
1. Are one or more	E	11.8	7.14	38	39.1	17.2	39	−9.05	.001
years behind grade	J	23.2	12.6	28	53.2	15.1	25	−7.88	.001
level in reading ability?	S	23.2	13.1	31	46.9	17.0	30	−6.11	.001
2. Were not ade-	E	16.9	9.04	38	38.3	16.4	39	−7.06	.001
quately prepared to	J	25.1	10.6	28	44.7	14.5	25	−5.66	.001
do the grade level work you expected of them when they entered your class?	S	26.2	10.2	31	44.2	18.5	30	−4.73	.001
3. Are not mastering	E	11.3	5.98	38	26.9	11.9	39	−7.24	.001
the subject matter	J	15.2	7.17	28	34.3	12.3	25	−7.00	.001
or skills you teach at the minimum level of satisfactory performance?	S	15.6	7.40	31	31.4	12.6	30	−6.00	.001
4. Are *not* interested	E	13.8	7.67	38	28.6	13.2	39	−5.99	.001
in academic	J	23.4	11.9	28	41.2	14.9	25	−4.83	.001
achievement?	S	26.1	12.0	31	43.0	15.4	30	−4.79	.001
5. Work up to their	E	57.3	11.9	38	48.7	12.8	39	3.05	.001
intellectual capaci-	J	42.8	15.3	28	35.9	15.0	25	1.65	.050
ties?	S	40.3	10.5	31	36.9	11.8	30	1.19	.117
6. Will eventually go	E	48.9	18.1	38	12.6	7.81	39	11.5	.001
on to a four year	J	51.2	15.8	28	12.8	7.63	25	11.1	.001
college?	S	54.4	20.9	31	17.6	12.0	30	8.40	.001
7. Show a sense of	E	68.8	12.0	38	55.5	13.9	39	4.49	.001
self-discipline?	J	62.2	12.0	28	52.1	12.6	25	2.99	.001
	S	62.5	13.2	31	57.1	14.0	30	1.55	.061
8. Are tolerant to-	E	86.4	9.32	38	76.9	16.1	39	3.17	.001
ward fellow stu-	J	79.2	9.61	28	73.5	11.6	25	1.97	.024
dents with different social back- grounds?	S	78.3	9.18	31	75.0	12.5	30	1.17	.121
9. Appear *socially* im-	E	12.0	6.45	38	20.9	12.4	39	−3.93	.001
mature for their	J	14.7	7.10	28	24.5	9.10	25	−4.40	.001
age?	S	19.3	6.71	31	26.0	13.5	30	−2.47	.007

TABLE 3A-4 (Continued)

What per cent of the pupils you teach:		Highest SES			Lowest SES			$t_{(H-L)}$	p
		Mean	S.D.	N	Mean	S.D.	N		
10. Appear *emotionally* immature for their age?	E	14.0	6.29	38	21.2	12.1	39	−3.26	.001
	J	18.5	9.97	28	28.7	12.1	25	−3.36	.001
	S	21.3	8.47	31	25.4	13.4	30	−1.43	.076
11. Have been discipline problems during the last school year?	E	8.51	4.26	38	16.1	10.0	39	−4.31	.001
	J	8.39	4.28	28	16.5	7.20	25	−5.05	.001
	S	6.34	3.88	31	9.42	5.42	30	−2.56	.005
12. Show disrespect for teachers?	E	9.79	9.54	38	13.5	11.1	39	−1.57	.058
	J	16.1	10.0	28	21.6	13.3	25	−1.71	.044
	S	12.5	8.24	31	17.6	12.1	30	−1.93	.027
13. Have engaged in vandalism at school during the current school year?	E	1.13	1.25	38	4.82	6.93	39	−3.23	.001
	J	2.70	1.19	28	6.87	6.03	25	−3.59	.001
	S	3.89	3.58	31	4.90	4.36	30	−0.99	.161

TABLE 4A-1. Number of All Teachers in Each of Two Categories of "Sex" for Elementary, Junior, and Senior High Schools of Highest and Lowest SES

Sex	Highest SES	Lowest SES		
Elementary Schools				
Female	886	1104	$z = 4.30$	
Male	123	265	$p < .001_2$	
Total	1009	1369		
Junior High Schools				
Female	1006	889	$z = 5.63$	
Male	759	961	$p < .001_2$	
Total	1765	1850		
Senior High Schools				
Female	1418	1288	$z = -0.44$	
Male	1594	1404	$p = .66_2$	
Total	3012	2692		

TABLE 4A-2. Number of All Teachers in Each of Five Categories of "Years of Teaching Experience" for Elementary, Junior, and Senior High Schools of Highest and Lowest SES

Years of Teaching Experience	Highest SES	Lowest SES	
Elementary Schools			
Less than 1	39	152	
1–5	181	422	$d = 0.233$
6–10	169	275	$p < .001_2$
11–20	270	258	
More than 20	318	238	
Total	977	1345	
Junior High Schools			
Less than 1	152	212	
1–5	519	629	$d = 0.114$
6–10	295	408	$p < .001_2$
11–20	356	294	
More than 20	413	319	
Total	1735	1862	
Senior High Schools			
Less than 1	149	235	
1–5	542	774	$d = 0.140$
6–10	496	476	$p < .001_2$
11–20	619	513	
More than 20	1164	755	
Total	2970	2753	

TABLE 4A-3. Number of All Teachers in Each of Four Categories of "Years of Teaching Experience in Current School" for Elementary, Junior, and Senior High Schools of Highest and Lowest SES

Years of Teaching Experience in Current School	Highest SES	Lowest SES	
Elementary Schools			
Less than 1	112	274	
1–5	409	567	$d = 0.102$
6–10	300	291	$p < .001_2$
More than 10	184	224	
Total	1005	1356	
Junior High Schools			
Less than 1	345	341	
1–5	804	752	$d = 0.065$
6–10	369	395	$p < .001_2$
More than 10	239	368	
Total	1757	1856	
Senior High Schools			
Less than 1	347	382	
1–5	1126	1080	$d = 0.051$
6–10	538	494	$.001_2 < p < .005_2$
More than 10	933	707	
Total	2944	2663	

TABLE 4A-4. Number of All Teachers in Each of Five Categories of "Age" for Elementary, Junior, and Senior High Schools of Highest and Lowest SES

Age	Highest SES	Lowest SES	
Elementary Schools			
Less than 25	105	243	
25–34	206	404	$d = 0.174$
35–44	247	298	$p < .001_2$
45–54	323	259	
55 or More	128	138	
Total	1009	1342	
Junior High Schools			
Less than 25	180	210	
25–34	523	669	$d = 0.114$
35–44	438	477	$p < .001_2$
45–54	390	290	
55 or More	287	182	
Total	1818	1828	
Senior High Schools			
Less than 25	197	231	
25–34	627	764	$d = 0.074$
35–44	641	589	$p < .001_2$
45–54	704	580	
55 or More	585	502	
Total	2754	2666	

TABLE 4A-5. Number of All Teachers in Each of Four Categories of "Highest Degree" for Elementary, Junior, and Senior High Schools of Highest and Lowest SES

Highest Degree	Highest SES	Lowest SES	
Elementary Schools			
Certificate	84	78	
Bachelors	660	890	$d = 0.023$
Masters	249	315	$p > .10_2$
Doctorate	14	4	
Total	1007	1287	
Junior High Schools			
Certificate	21	15	
Bachelors	1126	1145	$d = 0.006$
Masters	615	605	$p > .10_2$
Doctorate	3	4	
Total	1765	1769	
Senior High Schools			
Certificate	35	40	
Bachelors	1227	1420	$d = 0.099$
Masters	1532	1195	$p < .001_2$
Doctorate	35	24	
Total	2829	2679	

TABLE 4A-6. Number of The Sample of Teachers in Each of Four Categories of "Quality of College Work" for Elementary, Junior, and Senior High Schools of Highest and Lowest SES

Quality of College Work	Highest SES	Lowest SES	
Elementary Schools			
Somewhat below average	0	3	
Average	102	125	$d = 0.082$
Above average	188	148	$p > .10_2$
Graduated with honors	27	41	
Total	317	317	
Junior High Schools			
Somewhat below average	1	3	
Average	65	65	$d = 0.030$
Above average	128	111	$p > .10_2$
Graduated with honors	28	29	
Total	222	208	
Senior High Schools			
Somewhat below average	2	2	
Average	70	79	$d = 0.055$
Above average	127	113	$p > .10_2$
Graduated with honors	47	39	
Total	246	233	

TABLE 4A-7. Number of The Sample of Teachers in Each of Four Categories of "Salary" for Elementary, Junior, and Senior High Schools of Highest and Lowest SES

Salary	Highest SES	Lowest SES	
Elementary Schools			
Less than $5000	102	79	
$5000–5999	91	124	$d = 0.072$
$6000–6999	72	44	$p > .10_2$
$7000 or more	52	69	
Total	317	316	
Junior High Schools			
Less than $5000	69	39	
$5000–5999	54	65	$d = 0.124$
$6000–6999	50	51	$.05_2 < p < .10_2$
$7000 or more	48	52	
Total	221	207	
Senior High Schools			
Less than $5000	49	39	
$5000–5999	68	45	$d = 0.113$
$6000–6999	53	62	$.05_2 < p < .10_2$
$7000 or more	77	87	
Total	247	233	

TABLE 4A-8. Number of the Sample of Teachers in Each of Four Categories of "Community of Youth" for Elementary, Junior, and Senior High Schools of Highest and Lowest SES

Community of Youth	Highest SES	Lowest SES	
Elementary Schools			
Farm	67	37	
Village	92	72	$d = 0.157$
Small city	44	45	$p < .001_2$
Large city	115	164	
Total	318	318	
Junior High Schools			
Farm	28	21	
Village	59	31	$d = 0.147$
Small city	36	33	$.01_2 < p < .025_2$
Large city	99	124	
Total	222	209	
Senior High Schools			
Farm	19	19	
Village	71	42	$d = 0.104$
Small city	39	41	$p > .10_2$
Large city	117	131	
Total	246	233	

TABLE 4A-9. Number of The Sample of Teachers in Each of Three Categories of "Father's Occupation" for Elementary, Junior, and Senior High Schools of Highest and Lowest SES

Father's Occupation	Highest SES	Lowest SES	
Elementary Schools			
Blue collar	93	131	$d = 0.126$
Farm owner or renter	65	39	$.01_2 < p < .025_2$
White collar	151	137	
Total	309	307	
Junior High Schools			
Blue collar	58	84	$d = 0.146$
Farm owner or renter	37	14	$.01_2 < p < .025_2$
White collar	120	104	
Total	215	202	
Senior High Schools			
Blue collar	67	97	$d = 0.142$
Farm owner or renter	31	17	$.01_2 < p < .025_2$
White collar	138	114	
Total	236	228	

TABLE 4A-10.   Number of The Sample of Teachers in Each of Seven Categories of "Father's Education" for Elementary, Junior, and Senior High Schools of Highest and Lowest SES

Father's Education	Highest SES	Lowest SES	
Elementary Schools			
Some elementary school or less	59	73	
Completed elementary school	57	60	
Some high school	67	58	$d = 0.052$
Completed high school	50	57	$p > .10_2$
Some college	38	32	
Completed college	26	19	
Graduate school	17	17	
Total	314	316	
Junior High Schools			
Some elementary school or less	34	42	
Completed elementary school	35	44	
Some high school	49	41	$d = 0.098$
Completed high school	39	31	$p > .10_2$
Some college	29	16	
Completed college	15	16	
Graduate school	19	19	
Total	220	209	
Senior High Schools			
Some elementary school or less	37	54	
Completed elementary school	41	58	
Some high school	54	42	
Completed high school	39	32	$d = 0.162$
Some college	35	14	$.001_2 < p < .005_2$
Completed college	20	15	
Graduate school	20	19	
Total	246	234	

TABLE 4A-11. Number of the Sample of Teachers in Each of Seven Categories of "Mother's Education" for Elementary, Junior, and Senior High Schools of Highest and Lowest SES

Mother's Education	Highest SES	Lowest SES	
Elementary Schools			
Some elementary school or less	32	55	
Completed elementary school	67	66	$d = 0.071$
Some high school	68	57	$p > .10_2$
Completed high school	78	79	
Some college	42	31	
Completed college	24	25	
Graduate school	4	5	
Total	315	318	
Junior High Schools			
Some elementary school or less	22	32	
Completed elementary school	25	39	$d = 0.126$
Some high school	42	38	$.05_2 < p < .10_2$
Completed high school	63	43	
Some college	34	29	
Completed college	27	21	
Graduate school	9	8	
Total	222	210	
Senior High Schools			
Some elementary school or less	29	51	
Completed elementary school	44	43	$d = 0.105$
Some high school	47	44	$p > .10_2$
Completed high school	68	50	
Some college	27	19	
Completed college	26	22	
Graduate school	5	5	
Total	246	234	

TABLE 4A-12. Number of the Sample of Teachers in Each of Four Categories of "Income Position of Family" for Elementary, Junior, and Senior High Schools of Highest and Lowest SES

Income Position of Family	Highest SES	Lowest SES	
Elementary Schools			
Lowest ¼ of community	27	49	
Moderately low ¼ of community	129	128	$d = 0.071$
Moderately high ¼ of community	113	100	$p > .10_2$
Highest ¼ of community	40	33	
Total	309	310	
Junior High Schools			
Lowest ¼ of community	23	38	
Moderately low ¼ of community	91	85	$d = 0.088$
Moderately high ¼ of community	69	58	$p > .10_2$
Highest ¼ of community	32	18	
Total	215	199	
Senior High Schools			
Lowest ¼ of community	25	42	
Moderately low ¼ of community	110	118	$d = 0.132$
Moderately high ¼ of community	80	49	$.025_2 < p < .05_2$
Highest ¼ of community	22	19	
Total	237	228	

TABLE 4A-13. Number of All Teachers in Each of Two Categories of "Race" for Elementary, Junior, and Senior High Schools of Highest and Lowest SES

Race	Highest SES	Lowest SES	
Elementary Schools			
White	999	812	$z = 22.4$
Nonwhite	10	557	$p < .001_2$
Total	1009	1369	
Junior High Schools			
White	1717	1130	$z = 26.6$
Nonwhite	48	720	$p < .001_2$
Total	1765	1850	
Senior High Schools			
White	2977	2020	$z = 27.2$
Nonwhite	35	672	$p < .001_2$
Total	3012	2692	

TABLE 4A-14. Number of All Teachers in Each of Three Categories of "Religious Affiliation" for Elementary, Junior, and Senior High Schools of Highest and Lowest SES

Religious Affiliation	Highest SES	Lowest SES	
Elementary Schools			
Protestant	746	876	$\chi_2^2 = 27.6$
Catholic	177	351	$p < .001_2$
Jewish	86	142	
Total	1009	1369	
Junior High Schools			
Protestant	1075	1180	$\chi_2^2 = 45.1$
Catholic	318	426	$p < .001_2$
Jewish	372	244	
Total	1765	1850	
Senior High Schools			
Protestant	2084	1740	$\chi_2^2 = 15.0$
Catholic	564	606	$p = .002_2$
Jewish	364	346	
Total	3012	2692	

TABLE 4A-15. Proportion of All Teachers in Each of Three Categories of "Religious Affiliation" for Elementary, Junior, and Senior High Schools of Highest and Lowest SES

Religious Affiliation	Highest SES	Lowest SES	z	p
Elementary Schools				
Protestant	.740	.640	5.18	$.001_2$
Catholic	.175	.256	-4.70	$.001_2$
Jewish	.085	.104	-1.56	$.12_2$
Number of teachers	1009	1369		
Junior High Schools				
Protestant	.609	.638	-1.80	$.07_2$
Catholic	.180	.230	-3.72	$.001_2$
Jewish	.211	.132	6.32	$.001_2$
Number of teachers	1765	1850		
Senior High Schools				
Protestant	.692	.646	3.69	$.001_2$
Catholic	.187	.225	-3.55	$.001_2$
Jewish	.121	.129	-0.92	$.36_2$
Number of teachers	3012	2692		

TABLE 4A-16. Chi-Square Test of Goodness of Fit of Sex Distribution of Teacher Sample and Population in Twelve Types of Schools

Type of School	Sex of Teacher	Population (T)	Sample (E)	Sample (O)	χ^2	p
Elementary	Male	123	39	37		
Highest SES	Female	886	310	312	0.11	$.74_2$
	Total	1009	349	349		
Elementary	Male	121	40	49		
Mod. high SES	Female	881	294	285	2.30	$.13_2$
	Total	1002	334	334		
Elementary	Male	131	44	40		
Mod. low SES	Female	859	287	291	0.41	$.53_2$
	Total	990	331	331		

TABLE 4A-16 (Continued)

Type of School	Sex of Teacher	Population (T)	Sample (E)	Sample (O)	χ^2	p
Elementary	Male	265	63	52		
Lowest SES	Female	1106	262	273	2.38	$.12_2$
	Total	1371	325	325		
Junior High	Male	759	110	117		
Highest SES	Female	1006	146	139	0.79	$.38_2$
	Total	1765	256	256		
Junior High	Male	887	118	117		
Mod. high SES	Female	914	122	123	0.02	$.86_2$
	Total	1801	240	240		
Junior High	Male	791	106	102		
Mod. low SES	Female	850	113	117	0.29	$.60_2$
	Total	1641	219	219		
Junior High	Male	961	133	134		
Lowest SES	Female	841	117	116	0.02	$.86_2$
	Total	1802	250	250		
Senior High	Male	1594	138	123		
Highest SES	Female	1418	123	138	3.56	$.06_2$
	Total	3012	261	261		
Senior High	Male	1714	117	108		
Mod. high SES	Female	1633	112	121	1.41	$.23_2$
	Total	3347	229	229		
Senior High	Male	1281	130	121		
Mod. low SES	Female	1392	141	150	1.19	$.27_2$
	Total	2673	271	271		
Senior High	Male	1404	127	122		
Lowest SES	Female	1288	117	122	0.40	$.53_2$
	Total	2692	244	244		

TABLE 4A-17. Distribution of 47 Elementary Schools of Highest SES, According to the Per Cent of Teachers and the Per Cent of Pupils Who Are Nonwhite

					Per Cent of Teachers Who Are Nonwhite								
	0	1 to 9	10 — 19	20 — 29	30 — 39	40 — 49	50 — 59	60 — 69	70 — 79	80 — 89	90 to 99	100	All Schools
100													—
90–99													—
80–89													—
70–79													—
60–69													—
50–59													—
40–49													—
30–39													—
20–29													—
10–19	3												3
1–9	20	2											22
0	20	2											22
All schools	43	4	—	—	—	—	—	—	—	—	—	—	47

Line of microcongruency

Line of macrocongruency

Per Cent of Pupils Who Are Nonwhite

TABLE 4A-18. Distribution of 47 Elementary Schools of Moderately High SES, according to the Per Cent of Teachers and the Per Cent of Pupils Who Are Nonwhite

		Per Cent of Teachers Who Are Nonwhite											
Per Cent of Pupils Who Are Nonwhite	0	1 to 9	10 — 19	20 — 29	30 — 39	40 — 49	50 — 59	60 — 69	70 — 79	80 — 89	90 to 99	100	All Schools
100													—
90–99													—
80–89													—
70–79		1											1
60–69		1											1
50–59													—
40–49													—
30–39	1												1
20–29	1	2											3
10–19	3	1											4
1–9	18	3	1	1									23
0	12	2											14
All schools	35	8	1	3	—	—	—	—	—	—	—	—	47

Line of microcongruency

Line of macrocongruency

TABLE 4A-19.   Distribution of 45 Elementary Schools of Moderately Low SES, According to the Per Cent of Teachers and the Per Cent of Pupils Who Are Nonwhite

Per Cent of Pupils Who Are Nonwhite	Per Cent of Teachers Who Are Nonwhite												
	0	1 to 9	10–19	20–29	30–39	40–49	50–59	60–69	70–79	80–89	90 to 99	100	All Schools
100												2	2
90–99		1	1		1						1	1	5
80–89		1		1									2
70–79			1										1
60–69	1												1
50–59	1		1										2
40–49													—
30–39	1		2										3
20–29		1											1
10–19	2	1											3
1–9	14	1	1										16
0	9												9
All schools	28	5	6	1	1	—	—	—	—	—	1	3	45[a]

←Line of microcongruency

←Line of macrocongruency

[a] Data on race of teachers unknown are for one of the moderately low SES schools.

TABLE 4A-20. Distribution of 46 Elementary Schools of Lowest SES, According to the Per Cent of Teachers and the Per Cent of Pupils Who Are Nonwhite

		Per Cent of Teachers Who Are Nonwhite											
	0	1 to 9	10 — 19	20 — 29	30 — 39	40 — 49	50 — 59	60 — 69	70 — 79	80 — 89	90 to 99	100	All Schools
Per Cent of Pupils Who Are Nonwhite													
100						1		1		1	2		9
90–99	3		1	2		1		2		2		1	13
80–89		2	1		1								4
70–79													—
60–69													—
50–59	1			1			1						3
40–49	1	1											2
30–39			1	1									2
20–29	1	1											2
10–19	2		1										3
1–9	4	1											5
0	3												3
All schools	15	5	4	4	1	2	1	3	—	3	3	5	46[a]

←Line of microcongruency

←Line of macrocongruency

[a] Data on race of teachers are unknown for one of the lowest SES schools

TABLE 4A-21. Distribution of 47 Elementary Schools of Highest SES, According to the Per Cent of Teachers and the Per Cent of Pupils Who Are Jewish

Per Cent of Pupils Who Are Jewish	Per Cent of Teachers Who Are Jewish												All Schools
	0	1 to 9	10–19	20–29	30–39	40–49	50–59	60–69	70–79	80–89	90 to 99	100	
100													—
90–99						1	1	1					3
80–89													—
70–79							1						1
60–69		1											1
50–59													—
40–49													—
30–39	1		2										3
20–29		2	2										4
10–19	7		1										8
1–9	17	4											21
0	5	1											6
All schools	30	8	5	—	—	1	2	1	—	—	—	—	47

Line of macrocongruency

Line of microcongruency

TABLE 4A-22. Distribution of 46 Elementary Schools of Moderately High SES, According to the Per Cent of Teachers and the Per Cent of Pupils Who Are Jewish

	Per Cent of Teachers Who Are Jewish												
Per Cent of Pupils Who Are Jewish	0	1 to 9	10–19	20–29	30–39	40–49	50–59	60–69	70–79	80–89	90 to 99	100	All Schools
100													—
90–99											1		1
80–89							1						1
70–79													—
60–69		1											1
50–59													—
40–49													—
30–39	2												2
20–29	1								1				2
10–19		2											2
1–9	11	7	4	1									23
0		7											14
All schools	18	17	6	2	—	—	1	—	1	—	1	—	46[a]

Line of macrocongruency

Line of microcongruency

[a] Data on religion of both pupils and teachers are unknown for one school of moderately high SES.

TABLE 4A-23. Distribution of 45 Elementary Schools of Moderately Low SES, According to the Per Cent of Teachers and the Per Cent of Pupils Who Are Jewish

		Per Cent of Teachers Who Are Jewish											
Per Cent of Pupils Who Are Jewish	0	1 to 9	10–19	20–29	30–39	40–49	50–59	60–69	70–79	80–89	90 to 99	100	All Schools
100													—
90–99													—
80–89													—
70–79													—
60–69													—
50–59													—
40–49													—
30–39													—
20–29				1									1
10–19			1										1
1–9	7	1	1	3		2							14
0	22	5		1	1								29
All schools	29	6	2	5	1	2	—	—	—	—	—	—	45[a]

Line of macrocongruency

Line of microcongruency

[a] Data on religion of both pupils and teachers are unknown for one school of moderately low SES.

TABLE 4A-24. Distribution of 45 Elementary Schools of Lowest SES, According to the Per Cent of Teachers and the Per Cent of Pupils Who Are Jewish

		Per Cent of Teachers Who Are Jewish											
		0	1 to 9	10 — 19	20 — 29	30 — 39	40 — 49	50 — 59	60 — 69	70 — 79	80 — 89	90 to 99	100	All Schools
Per Cent of Pupils Who Are Jewish	100													—
	90–99													—
	80–89													—
	70–79													—
	60–69													—
	50–59													—
	40–49													—
	30–39													—
	20–29													—
	10–19		1					1	1					3
	1–9	2	4	1	1									8
	0	20	10	4										34
All schools		22	15	5	1	—	—	1	1	—	—	—	—	45[a]

Line of macrocongruency

Line of microcongurency

[a] Data on religion of both pupils and teachers are unknown for two schools of lowest SES.

TABLE 5A-1. Means and Standard Deviations of Responses of Elementary, Junior, and Senior High School Teachers in Schools of Highest and Lowest SES to Questions about Their Level of Aspiration

How desirous are you [I would not want to (1), I am not especially anxious to (2), I have some desire to (3), I would very much like to (4), I am extremely anxious to (5)] of doing the following?		Highest SES			Lowest SES			$t_{(H\text{-}L)}$	p
		Mean	S.D.	N	Mean	S.D.	N		
1. Become an assistant principal.	E	1.58	0.90	344	1.82	1.09	324	−3.11	.001
	J	2.01	1.19	252	2.18	1.26	245	−1.55	.061
	S	1.75	1.06	256	1.98	1.28	242	−2.19	.014
2. Become the principal of an elementary school.	E	1.62	1.14	346	1.78	1.17	324	−1.79	.037
	J	1.56	0.97	252	1.69	1.10	245	−1.40	.081
	S	1.34	0.75	254	1.58	0.99	242	−3.05	.001
3. Become the principal of a junior high school.	E	1.19	0.64	343	1.38	0.83	324	−3.32	.001
	J	1.90	1.27	252	2.09	1.32	245	−1.64	.051
	S	1.53	0.96	254	1.80	1.14	242	−2.86	.002
4. Become the principal of a senior high school.	E	1.16	0.58	343	1.24	0.63	324	−1.71	.044
	J	1.65	1.07	252	1.92	1.24	245	−2.60	.005
	S	1.76	1.13	256	1.98	1.33	242	−1.99	.023
5. Become a staff specialist attached to a central office.	E	1.92	1.21	345	1.97	1.15	324	−0.55	.291
	J	2.30	1.30	251	2.45	1.29	244	−1.29	.098
	S	2.28	1.27	254	2.41	1.35	241	−1.10	.136
6. Become an assistant superintendent of schools.	E	1.23	0.72	344	1.29	0.70	322	−1.09	.138
	J	1.52	0.99	252	1.69	1.10	245	−1.81	.035
	S	1.51	1.00	255	1.74	1.23	242	−2.29	.010
7. Become an associate superintendent of schools.	E	1.20	0.66	344	1.30	0.71	322	−1.88	.030
	J	1.50	0.97	252	1.65	1.05	245	−1.65	.050
	S	1.53	0.99	256	1.75	1.23	242	−2.20	.014
8. Become a school superintendent.	E	1.17	0.60	344	1.27	0.70	322	−1.98	.024
	J	1.49	1.00	252	1.58	1.02	245	−0.99	.161
	S	1.46	0.97	256	1.65	1.18	245	−1.97	.024
9. Remain a teacher in this *school* for the remainder of my educational career.	E	3.24	1.39	344	2.61	1.32	322	5.99	.001
	J	2.88	1.37	253	2.27	1.26	245	5.17	.001
	S	3.20	1.28	255	2.68	1.25	242	4.58	.001
10. Remain a teacher in this *school system* for the remainder of my educational career, but move to a school in a "better neighborhood."	E	1.78	0.97	328	2.44	1.18	318	−7.78	.001
	J	1.97	1.10	250	2.52	1.18	244	−5.36	.001
	S	1.71	0.93	242	2.41	1.16	240	−7.31	.001

TABLE 5A-2. Means and Standard Deviations of Responses of Elementary, Junior, and Senior High School Teachers in Schools of Highest and Lowest SES to Questions about Their Job Satisfaction

How do you feel [very satisfied (6), moderately satisfied (5), slightly satisfied (4), slightly dissatisfied (3), moderately dissatisfied (2), very dissatisfied (1)] about the following items?	Highest SES			Lowest SES			$t_{(H\text{-}L)}$	p
	Mean	S.D.	N	Mean	S.D.	N		
1. The level of competence of most of the other teachers in the school. E	5.07	0.90	344	4.78	1.14	322	3.66	.001
J	4.74	1.07	252	4.45	1.20	243	2.84	.002
S	4.72	1.11	259	4.58	1.13	243	1.40	.081
2. The method employed in this school for making decisions on curriculum matters. E	4.56	1.23	333	4.52	1.32	319	0.40	.345
J	4.39	1.39	249	4.13	1.33	239	2.11	.017
S	4.23	1.34	256	4.30	1.33	240	−0.58	.719
3. The method employed in this school for making decisions on pupil discipline matters. E	4.41	1.44	342	4.18	1.65	324	1.92	.027
J	4.20	1.53	253	4.02	1.67	244	1.25	.106
S	4.30	1.44	259	4.43	1.48	244	−1.00	.841
4. The attitude of the students toward the faculty in this school. E	4.81	1.21	345	4.34	1.40	324	4.65	.001
J	4.55	1.32	253	3.80	1.46	244	6.01	.001
S	4.37	1.39	259	4.52	1.30	244	−1.25	.894
5. The manner in which the teachers and the administrative staff work together in this school. E	4.92	1.15	345	4.75	1.39	324	1.73	.042
J	4.71	1.32	252	4.36	1.41	244	2.85	.002
S	4.55	1.28	259	4.63	1.37	244	−0.68	.752
6. The cooperation and help which I receive from my superiors. E	4.96	1.25	345	4.96	1.32	325	−0.00	.500
J	4.97	1.27	253	4.78	1.38	244	1.60	.055
S	4.76	1.38	258	4.88	1.33	243	−0.99	.839
7. The educational philosophy which seems to prevail in this school. E	4.99	1.09	345	4.73	1.29	324	2.82	.002
J	4.75	1.24	253	4.20	1.45	243	4.55	.001
S	4.58	1.30	258	4.41	1.47	242	1.37	.085

How do you feel [very satisfied (6), moderately satisfied (5), slightly satisfied (4), slightly dissatisfied (3), moderately dissatisfied (2), very dissatisfied (1)] about the following items?		Highest SES			Lowest SES				
		Mean	S.D.	N	Mean	S.D.	N	$t_{(H-L)}$	p
8. The evaluation process which my superiors use to judge my effectiveness as a teacher.	E	4.72	1.31	335	4.75	1.36	319	−0.29	.614
	J	4.67	1.30	248	4.36	1.45	241	2.49	.006
	S	4.37	1.39	255	4.46	1.40	241	−0.72	.764
9. The level of competence of my superiors.	E	5.06	1.11	345	5.01	1.21	322	0.56	.288
	J	5.09	1.07	253	4.89	1.26	243	1.91	.028
	S	4.81	1.27	257	4.79	1.40	242	0.17	.432
10. The adequacy of the supplies available for me to use in my teaching in this school.	E	4.88	1.35	342	4.22	1.67	324	5.62	.001
	J	4.48	1.52	251	3.90	1.70	244	4.00	.001
	S	4.15	1.63	258	4.29	1.56	244	−0.98	.836
11. The amount of time which is available to me while I am at school for my personal professional growth.	E	3.43	1.57	337	3.43	1.48	323	0.00	.500
	J	3.59	1.52	248	3.72	1.53	244	−0.95	.671
	S	3.16	1.60	256	3.60	1.50	241	−3.16	.999
12. The extent to which I am informed by my superiors about school matters affecting me.	E	4.70	1.37	343	4.78	1.30	325	−0.77	.779
	J	4.71	1.25	250	4.51	1.41	244	1.67	.048
	S	4.43	1.46	256	4.59	1.36	244	−1.27	.898
13. The academic performance of the students in this school.	E	5.01	1.03	343	3.45	1.48	324	15.87	.001
	J	4.69	1.24	249	2.97	1.43	244	14.28	.001
	S	4.53	1.27	256	2.94	1.46	244	13.01	.001
14. The extent to which the professional growth of teachers is subsidized by this school system.	E	3.74	1.56	329	3.59	1.53	314	1.23	.109
	J	3.66	1.56	242	3.29	1.54	236	2.61	.004
	S	3.14	1.58	250	3.15	1.54	239	−0.07	.528

TABLE 5A-3.   Means and Standard Deviations of Responses of Elementary, Junior, and Senior High School Teachers in Schools of Highest and Lowest SES to Questions about Their Career Satisfaction

How do you feel [very satisfied (6), moderately satisfied (5), slightly satisfied (4), slightly dissatisfied (3), moderately dissatisfied (2), very dissatisfied (1)] about the following items?		Highest SES			Lowest SES				
		Mean	S.D.	N	Mean	S.D.	N	$t_{(H\text{-}L)}$	p
1. The state of	E	4.38	1.60	344	4.51	1.61	325	−1.05	.853
teaching as a	J	4.02	1.66	253	4.03	1.70	243	−0.07	.528
"profession."	S	3.63	1.67	257	4.14	1.59	243	−3.49	.999
2. The top salary	E	3.25	1.69	346	3.15	1.63	324	0.78	.218
available for	J	2.70	1.59	254	2.83	1.58	246	−0.92	.821
teachers.	S	2.65	1.56	259	2.84	1.58	244	−1.36	.913
3. My chances for	E	3.82	1.55	344	3.90	1.55	324	−0.67	.749
receiving salary	J	3.43	1.53	253	3.70	1.50	245	−1.99	.977
increases as a	S	3.28	1.56	259	3.74	1.47	242	−3.39	.999
teacher.									
4. The amount of	E	4.61	1.12	341	4.42	1.22	324	2.09	.018
progress which I	J	4.40	1.09	252	4.28	1.30	246	1.12	.131
am making in my	S	4.26	1.26	259	4.34	1.19	244	−0.73	.767
professional									
career.									
5. The amount of	E	3.29	1.50	346	3.12	1.50	325	1.47	.071
recognition which	J	3.05	1.54	253	2.77	1.41	246	2.12	.016
teachers are given	S	2.91	1.46	257	3.09	1.41	244	−1.40	.919
by society for									
their efforts and									
contributions.									
6. The capabilities	E	4.25	1.13	345	4.16	1.22	324	0.99	.161
of most of the	J	4.03	1.31	254	3.95	1.26	245	0.69	.245
people who are in	S	3.83	1.32	259	3.97	1.21	244	−1.24	.892
teaching.									
7. The effect of a	E	4.37	1.29	342	4.40	1.21	320	−0.31	.622
teacher's job on	J	4.26	1.26	253	4.51	1.18	245	−2.28	.989
his family life.	S	4.08	1.39	258	4.35	1.20	240	−2.31	.990
8. The effect of a	E	4.33	1.29	343	4.45	1.21	324	−1.24	.892
teacher's job on	J	4.30	1.26	253	4.47	1.28	243	−1.49	.932
his social life.	S	4.10	1.73	259	4.33	1.19	242	−1.72	.957

TABLE 5A-3 (Continued)

How do you feel [very satisfied (6), moderately satisfied (5), slightly satisfied (4), slightly dissatisfied (3), moderately dissatisfied (2), very dissatisfied (1)] about the following items?		Highest SES			Lowest SES				
		Mean	S.D.	N	Mean	S.D.	N	$t_{(H-L)}$	p
9. The possibilities for a teacher advancing to a position of greater responsibility in teaching.	E	4.26	1.30	341	4.35	1.16	323	−0.94	.826
	J	3.88	1.35	252	3.89	1.39	245	−0.08	.532
	S	3.70	1.46	259	3.94	1.37	242	−1.89	.971
10. The amount of recognition which teachers are given by members of other professions.	E	3.37	1.49	345	3.40	1.44	323	−0.26	.603
	J	3.22	1.54	253	3.17	1.45	245	0.37	.355
	S	3.09	1.47	258	3.32	1.37	244	−1.81	.965
11. The level of professional standards maintained by most teachers.	E	4.09	1.28	345	4.09	1.34	324	−0.00	.500
	J	3.86	1.30	254	3.79	1.20	245	0.62	.268
	S	3.78	1.27	259	3.93	1.26	243	−1.33	.908
12. The opportunity which teachers have for associating with other professional people.	E	3.79	1.38	345	4.07	1.27	325	−2.73	.997
	J	3.68	1.45	252	3.88	1.40	246	−1.57	.942
	S	3.70	1.41	257	3.97	1.33	243	−2.20	.986
13. The amount of recognition which noneducators give to teachers as compared to what they give to other professionals.	E	2.88	1.39	344	2.99	1.36	324	−1.03	.848
	J	2.73	1.48	252	2.83	1.37	245	−0.78	.782
	S	2.71	1.35	254	3.06	1.35	243	−2.89	.998
14. The amount of time for leisure activities which teaching affords.	E	3.93	1.56	344	3.89	1.47	325	0.34	.367
	J	3.97	1.65	253	4.13	1.48	245	−1.14	.873
	S	3.71	1.68	257	4.00	1.52	242	−2.02	.978

TABLE 5A-4. Means and Standard Deviations of Responses of Elementary, Junior, and Senior High School Teachers in Schools of Highest and Lowest SES to Questions about Their Work Satisfaction

To what degree do you enjoy each of the following aspects [a great deal (5), very much (4), somewhat (3), very little (2), not at all (1)] of a teacher's role?		Highest SES			Lowest SES			$t_{(H-L)}$	p
		Mean	S.D.	N	Mean	S.D.	N		
1. Preparing lessons.	E	3.73	0.81	348	3.87	0.90	324	−2.12	.983
	J	3.59	0.92	253	3.75	0.93	246	−1.93	.973
	S	3.72	0.88	257	3.71	0.89	240	0.13	.448
2. Correcting papers.	E	2.92	0.90	334	2.99	0.88	313	−1.00	.841
	J	2.56	0.96	250	2.73	1.00	242	−1.92	.973
	S	2.38	0.92	253	2.59	0.96	237	−2.47	.993
3. Attending teachers' meetings.	E	2.97	0.90	348	3.01	0.91	324	−0.57	.716
	J	2.80	0.84	255	2.92	0.92	248	−1.53	.937
	S	2.44	0.91	260	2.72	0.96	241	−3.35	.999
4. Supervising large groups of children.	E	2.68	1.08	338	2.81	1.08	319	−1.54	.938
	J	2.67	1.12	249	2.85	1.14	243	−1.77	.962
	S	2.60	1.07	240	2.85	1.11	229	−2.48	.993
5. Supervising small groups of children.	E	4.17	0.75	342	4.28	0.72	323	−1.93	.973
	J	3.99	0.89	250	4.18	0.77	245	−2.54	.994
	S	3.86	0.94	242	4.00	0.87	233	−1.68	.954
6. Working with pupils in extra-curricular activities.	E	3.72	0.94	291	3.80	0.91	300	−1.05	.853
	J	3.82	0.91	248	4.04	0.92	242	−2.66	.996
	S	3.73	1.06	252	3.91	0.97	233	−1.95	.974
7. Talking with individual parents about a problem concerning their child.	E	3.93	0.84	348	3.99	0.85	324	−0.92	.821
	J	3.74	0.87	255	3.95	0.84	248	−2.75	.997
	S	3.58	0.98	258	3.84	0.90	237	−3.07	.999
8. Talking with a group of parents about a mutual problem.	E	3.59	0.94	331	3.66	0.95	306	−0.93	.824
	J	3.57	0.96	235	3.69	0.95	223	−1.34	.910
	S	3.38	0.98	229	3.70	0.94	207	−3.47	.999
9. Working with youngsters who are having a hard time adjusting to a school situation.	E	3.86	0.89	340	3.91	0.89	321	−0.72	.764
	J	3.77	0.89	249	3.92	0.96	246	−1.80	.964
	S	3.75	0.85	250	3.85	0.84	237	−1.31	.905

TABLE 5A-4 (Continued)

To what degree do you enjoy each of the following aspects [a great deal (5), very much (4), somewhat (3), very little (2), not at all (1)] of a teacher's role?		Highest SES			Lowest SES			$t_{(H\text{-}L)}$	p
		Mean	S.D.	N	Mean	S.D.	N		
10. Working primarily with children rather than with adults.	E	4.39	0.74	342	4.35	0.80	320	0.67	.251
	J	3.95	0.88	247	4.06	1.04	239	−1.26	.896
	S	3.70	1.09	244	3.83	0.96	231	−1.38	.916
11. Working with "exceptionally able" pupils.	E	4.36	0.73	340	4.22	0.85	307	2.25	.012
	J	4.58	0.67	254	4.45	0.73	236	2.06	.020
	S	4.50	0.73	254	4.42	0.70	233	1.23	.109
12. Working with "average" pupils.	E	4.25	0.60	348	4.29	0.63	323	−0.84	.800
	J	4.18	0.67	255	4.20	0.63	244	−0.34	.633
	S	4.10	0.69	260	4.19	0.60	240	−1.55	.939
13. Working with "slow" pupils.	E	3.34	0.99	346	3.29	1.05	325	0.63	.264
	J	3.21	1.12	253	3.32	1.10	246	−1.11	.866
	S	2.89	1.04	259	3.03	1.03	241	−1.51	.934
14. Handling administrative paper work.	E	2.36	1.03	331	2.43	1.00	311	−0.87	.808
	J	2.24	1.03	251	2.39	1.10	243	−1.57	.942
	S	2.08	0.99	249	2.25	1.05	236	−1.84	.967
15. Evaluating pupil progress.	E	3.67	0.86	346	3.86	0.84	323	−2.89	.998
	J	3.59	0.86	252	3.66	0.92	247	−0.88	.811
	S	3.41	0.91	254	3.64	0.75	241	−3.06	.999
16. Working with guidance personnel.	E	3.67	0.86	271	3.80	0.87	259	−1.73	.958
	J	3.70	0.91	247	3.79	0.97	241	−1.06	.855
	S	3.53	0.94	253	3.76	0.94	239	−2.71	.997
17. Working with curriculum specialists.	E	3.44	0.90	295	3.63	1.01	260	−2.34	.990
	J	3.52	1.00	227	3.53	1.02	205	−0.10	.540
	S	3.36	1.02	230	3.53	0.95	214	−1.81	.965
18. Having a different group of pupils to work with each year.	E	4.28	0.73	344	4.15	0.92	321	2.03	.021
	J	4.07	0.82	250	3.84	1.01	245	2.78	.003
	S	3.96	0.83	253	3.88	0.86	240	1.05	.147
19. Having a different group of pupils to work with periodically during the day.	E	2.80	1.32	190	3.04	1.39	211	−1.77	.962
	J	4.28	0.73	250	4.09	0.78	245	2.80	.003
	S	4.22	0.69	256	4.15	0.73	239	1.10	.136

TABLE 5A-4 (Continued)

To what degree do you enjoy each of the following aspects [a great deal (5), very much (4), somewhat (3), very little (2), not at all (1)] of a teacher's role?		Highest SES			Lowest SES				
		Mean	S.D.	N	Mean	S.D.	N	$t_{(H\text{-}L)}$	p
20. Having to discipline problem children.	E	1.82	0.88	341	1.81	0.93	323	0.14	.444
	J	1.74	0.87	252	1.98	1.03	246	−2.81	.998
	S	1.57	0.77	249	1.95	0.98	240	−4.78	.999
21. Having a vacation from work periodically during the school year.	E	4.34	0.77	342	4.39	0.78	314	−0.83	.797
	J	4.46	0.73	252	4.36	0.92	242	1.34	.090
	S	4.47	0.69	259	4.33	0.86	242	2.02	.022
22. Having a long summer vacation every year.	E	4.33	0.88	342	4.26	0.96	324	0.98	.164
	J	4.29	1.00	251	4.23	1.03	246	0.66	.255
	S	4.17	1.09	255	4.00	1.19	240	1.66	.048
23. Having a work routine which changes periodically during the day.	E	4.16	0.87	309	4.10	0.92	301	0.83	.203
	J	4.22	0.88	250	4.19	0.85	242	0.38	.352
	S	4.20	0.84	259	4.13	0.83	241	0.94	.174
24. Having to schedule one's time carefully.	E	2.89	1.07	343	3.06	1.08	321	−2.04	.979
	J	3.18	0.98	254	3.24	0.94	241	−0.69	.755
	S	3.07	1.04	257	3.34	0.96	239	−3.00	.999
25. Having to follow specified curricula.	E	3.03	0.83	339	3.07	0.92	317	−0.59	.724
	J	2.88	0.86	247	2.87	0.79	241	0.13	.448
	S	2.76	0.92	245	2.92	0.86	234	−1.96	.975
26. Working with a committee of teachers on a common problem.	E	3.61	0.85	337	3.75	0.85	312	−2.10	.982
	J	3.65	0.86	252	3.76	0.80	243	−1.47	.929
	S	3.49	0.94	254	3.58	1.00	240	−1.03	.848

TABLE 5A-5. Summary of the Morale of Teachers in Elementary Schools of Highest and Lowest SES (as Reported by Principals)

What per cent of the teachers in your school:	Highest SES			Lowest SES			$t_{(H-L)}$	p
	Mean	S.D.	N	Mean	S.D.	N		
1. Complain about how hard their students are to work with?	7.3	10.9	46	19.3	24.8	46	−3.00	.001
2. Complain about the physical plant of the school?	5.76	12.4	45	13.7	27.8	46	−1.75	.040
3. Complain about the lack of stimulation in their work?	3.2	7.2	45	9.4	19.9	43	−1.96	.025
4. Act as if they get real enjoyment from their work?	90.7	10.6	47	79.7	22.3	46	3.05	.001
5. Have a sense of per-personal loyalty to you?	90.7	13.6	44	81.9	23.3	45	2.17	.015

TABLE 5A-6. Summary of the Morale of Teachers in Elementary Schools of Highest and Lowest SES (as Reported by Teachers)

What per cent of the teachers in your school:	Highest SES			Lowest SES			$t_{(H-L)}$	p
	Mean	S.D.	N	Mean	S.D.	N		
1. Enjoy working in the school?	87.6	7.0	43	79.0	13.4	41	3.71	.001
2. Display a sense of pride in the school?	89.1	6.9	43	80.5	14.0	41	3.60	.001
3. Display a sense of loyalty to the school?	90.0	6.1	43	82.7	12.3	41	3.47	.001
4. Accept the educational philosophy underlying the curriculum of the school?	88.2	6.6	43	84.5	11.7	41	1.80	.036
5. Respect the judgment of the administrators of the school?	82.4	7.9	43	79.0	15.4	41	1.28	.100
6. Work cooperatively with their fellow teachers?	87.5	7.7	43	86.7	8.9	41	0.44	.330
7. Have a sense of personal loyalty to the principal?	83.3	10.9	43	74.5	19.1	41	2.61	.004

TABLE 6A-.1   Summary of the Performance of Teachers in Elementary Schools of Highest and Lowest SES (as Reported by Principals)

What per cent of the teachers in your school:	Highest SES			Lowest SES			$t_{(H-L)}$	p
	Mean	S.D.	N	Mean	S.D.	N		
1. Have mastered the skills necessary to present their subject matter with high competence?	84.9	14.6	47	68.8	21.2	46	4.27	.001
2. Waste a lot of time in their classroom activities?	5.2	6.6	45	12.8	22.7	46	−2.16	.015
3. Lack self-confidence?	4.4	5.5	40	10.3	13.0	38	−2.63	.004
4. Are not able to control the students in their classrooms?	1.9	3.0	43	7.1	14.3	46	−2.34	.010
5. Maintain a professional attitude toward their work?	93.4	6.3	47	87.9	16.1	46	2.18	.015
6. Competently carry out their teaching assignments?	91.3	15.1	47	85.7	15.4	47	1.78	.038
7. Consistently try out new ideas in their classrooms?	63.7	25.6	47	49.5	29.2	45	2.48	.007
8. Attempt to improve their teaching skills?	87.7	12.9	47	76.9	21.5	46	2.94	.002
9. Do textbook teaching only?	5.5	7.3	45	12.2	15.5	46	−2.63	.004
10. Make themselves available to students at some sacrifice of their own free time?	81.6	23.0	47	70.2	28.7	46	2.12	.017
11. Plan their courses so that different types of students can benefit from them?	90.1	11.6	47	78.7	23.6	45	2.96	.002

TABLE 6A-1 (Continued)

What per cent of the teachers in your school:	Highest SES			Lowest SES			$t_{(H-L)}$	p
	Mean	S.D.	N	Mean	S.D.	N		
12. Get real satisfaction out of devoting their time and energy to the problems of young people?	87.9	13.9	47	79.2	23.7	46	2.16	.015
13. Agree with your philosophy of education?	88.4	10.1	40	79.5	19.9	36	2.50	.006
14. Would stand behind you if you were unfairly criticized?	94.3	8.7	46	89.4	15.5	46	1.87	.031
15. Cooperate with your efforts to improve your school program?	93.6	7.0	47	89.6	12.7	47	1.89	.029
16. Help new teachers to the school become acclimated to the ways that things are done?	93.5	12.0	47	85.6	22.3	46	2.14	.016
17. Get along amicably with their supervisors?	96.2	4.3	46	91.7	15.7	46	1.87	.031

TABLE 6A-2. Summary of the Performance of Teachers in Elementary Schools of Highest and Lowest SES (as Reported by Teachers)

What per cent of the teachers in your school:	Highest SES			Lowest SES			$t_{(H-L)}$	p
	Mean	S.D.	N	Mean	S.D.	N		
1. Waste a lot of time in their classroom activities?	11.7	8.4	43	16.7	9.1	41	−2.62	.004
2. Do everything possible to motivate their students?	81.2	8.9	43	77.5	13.4	41	1.50	.067
3. Are committed to doing the best job of which they are capable?	87.0	6.2	43	82.0	10.4	41	2.69	.004
4. Take a strong interest in the social or emotional problems of their students?	83.7	9.3	43	76.1	12.5	41	3.17	.001
5. Plan their classes so that different types of students can benefit from them?	83.7	8.0	43	80.9	11.4	41	1.31	.095
6. Maintain an interest in improving the educational program of the school?	82.9	8.6	43	79.0	11.6	41	1.76	.039
7. Try new teaching methods in their classrooms?	73.3	9.6	43	67.7	16.3	41	1.93	.027
8. Provide opportunities for students to go beyond the minimum demands of assigned work?	80.6	10.3	43	73.0	15.0	41	2.72	.003
9. Maintain effective discipline in their classes?	84.3	7.7	43	80.5	11.8	41	1.76	.039

TABLE 7A-1. Summary Table of the Characteristics of Teachers and Principals in Schools of Highest and Lowest SES

	Teacher[a]		Principal[a]	
	Highest SES	Lowest SES	Highest SES	Lowest SES
Mean Experience				
Years teacher	$15_{(977)}$	$11_{(1345)}$	$11_{(47)}$	$12_{(46)}$
Years administrator	—	—	$6_{(47)}$	$3_{(46)}$
Years principal	—	—	$13_{(47)}$	$10_{(47)}$
Years in education	$15_{(977)}$	$11_{(1345)}$	$30_{(47)}$	$25_{(46)}$
Years in school	$7_{(995)}$	$6_{(1356)}$	$8_{(47)}$	$6_{(47)}$
Mean Age	$42_{(1009)}$	$39_{(1369)}$	$55_{(47)}$	$50_{(47)}$
Mean Per Cent				
Above average college work	$68\%_{(317)}$	$60\%_{(317)}$	$81\%_{(47)}$	$72\%_{(47)}$
MA or doctorate	$23_{(1009)}$	$25_{(1323)}$	$92_{(47)}$	$94_{(47)}$
Male	$11_{(1009)}$	$19_{(1369)}$	$47_{(47)}$	$58_{(47)}$
Mean Salary	$\$5711_{(317)}$	$\$5854_{(316)}$	$\$9032_{(47)}$	$\$9202_{(47)}$

[a] The subscripted values associated with each statistic represent the number of cases on which the statistic was based. For the teachers there were two sources of data. Numbers around 300 represent the sample of teachers in each school who returned the teacher questionnaire. Numbers around 1000 represent data for all teachers in these schools of different SES. Data for them were obtained from a report of the principal to the personal and background questionnaire.

TABLE 8A-1. Means, Standard Deviations, and Correlation Coefficients for the Reports of the Average Teachers in 158 Elementary Schools as to Their Principals' Performance in 23 Aspects of Administrative Behavior

Aspect of Administrative Behavior[a]	1	2	3	4	5	6	7	8	9	10	11
1.	—	.68	.33	.55	.53	.56	.69	.61	.49	.64	.58
2.		—	.50	.53	.62	.64	.73	.65	.64	.69	.70
3.			—	.38	.58	.37	.46	.42	.46	.44	.30
4.				—	.52	.53	.55	.55	.62	.69	.68
5.					—	.62	.56	.62	.56	.63	.49
6.						—	.68	.64	.59	.65	.65
7.							—	.66	.63	.66	.63
8.								—	.65	.66	.54
9.									—	.73	.62
10.										—	.75
11.											—
12.											
13.											
14.											
15.											
16.											
17.											
18.											
19.											
20.											
21.											
22.											
23.											

[a] See Table 8-2 for the wording of each aspect.

12	13	14	15	16	17	18	19	20	21	22	23	Mean	S.D.
.55	.68	.60	.54	.56	.35	.60	.64	.57	.62	.54	.68	4.45	0.76
.65	.70	.79	.51	.72	.43	.61	.66	.63	.67	.69	.69	4.43	0.76
.36	.40	.44	.38	.49	.58	.37	.47	.40	.44	.48	.45	4.66	0.62
.70	.77	.58	.79	.55	.50	.44	.62	.66	.70	.62	.70	4.27	0.64
.53	.58	.60	.51	.78	.58	.58	.64	.59	.57	.64	.65	4.61	0.71
.62	.66	.60	.53	.75	.46	.63	.69	.66	.63	.56	.71	4.19	0.89
.66	.73	.63	.58	.64	.44	.64	.69	.66	.69	.62	.72	4.47	0.64
.56	.64	.69	.60	.63	.48	.53	.68	.60	.69	.57	.66	4.37	0.87
.67	.68	.68	.66	.62	.56	.54	.70	.70	.74	.65	.71	4.33	0.68
.77	.81	.69	.71	.68	.52	.65	.76	.75	.74	.66	.80	4.61	0.66
.83	.79	.68	.66	.64	.43	.55	.66	.76	.74	.61	.73	4.18	0.70
—	.82	.68	.70	.63	.43	.54	.64	.76	.75	.67	.76	4.19	0.67
	—	.72	.78	.68	.51	.62	.75	.78	.79	.68	.80	4.39	0.78
		—	.63	.65	.48	.57	.70	.65	.72	.74	.70	4.25	0.90
			—	.53	.52	.47	.66	.66	.70	.65	.74	4.38	0.66
				—	.57	.70	.75	.72	.64	.65	.76	4.76	0.67
					—	.45	.55	.47	.53	.54	.52	4.40	0.67
						—	.84	.64	.59	.54	.68	4.80	0.71
							—	.73	.78	.68	.79	4.80	0.66
								—	.79	.66	.82	4.50	0.71
									—	.75	.81	4.30	0.62
										—	.75	4.31	0.74
											—	4.64	0.68

TABLE 8A-2. Means, Standard Deviations, and Correlation Coefficients for the Reports of the Average Teachers in 158 Elementary Schools as to Eight Indices of Teacher Performance

Index of Teacher Performance[a]	1	2	3	4	5	6	7	8	Mean	S.D.
1.	—	.48	.38	.46	.55	.33	.49	.47	70.75	14.90
2.		—	.53	.55	.58	.58	.57	.54	77.82	13.21
3.			—	.55	.52	.57	.56	.59	82.74	10.67
4.				—	.73	.59	.60	.59	79.45	12.81
5.					—	.65	.62	.64	80.63	11.87
6.						—	.66	.58	83.84	10.39
7.							—	.77	82.09	12.14
8.								—	77.31	14.51

[a] See Table 8-1 for the wording of each index.

TABLE 8A-3. Factor Weights Resulting from the Principal Components Analysis of the Correlation Matrix of the Eight Indices of Teacher Performance

Index of teacher performance[a]	Factor							
	I (Teacher performance factor)	II	III	IV	V	VI	VII	VIII
1.	.77	−.35	.45	.22	−.05	.15	.09	.02
2.	.82	−.10	.15	−.18	.41	−.26	−.12	−.03
3.	.71	.62	.25	.08	−.17	−.13	−.01	.00
4.	.84	−.17	−.10	−.29	−.26	−.17	.19	.18
5.	.87	−.11	−.05	−.20	−.25	.16	−.30	−.15
6.	.83	.25	−.10	−.15	.25	.36	.09	.11
7.	.88	−.01	−.24	.16	.02	−.06	.21	−.29
8.	.84	−.06	−.27	.39	.02	−.06	−.16	.19
Latent root	5.41	0.62	0.44	0.41	0.40	0.30	0.23	0.19
Cumulative per cent of trace	67.62	75.33	80.83	86.02	90.96	94.73	97.58	100.00

[a] See Table 8-1 for the wording of each index.

TABLE 8A-4. Means and Standard Deviations for the Reports of the Average Teachers in 158 Elementary Schools of High and Low SES as to Their Principals' Performance in 23 Aspects of Administrative Behavior

Aspect of Administrative Behavior[a]	High SES ($N = 79$)		Low SES ($N = 79$)	
	Mean	S.D.	Mean	S.D.
1.	4.37	0.78	4.53	0.74
2.	4.44	0.69	4.42	0.82
3.	4.68	0.52	4.64	0.70
4.	4.21	0.66	4.33	0.63
5.	4.76	0.62	4.45	0.76
6.	4.18	0.85	4.20	0.92
7.	4.44	0.63	4.50	0.66
8.	4.31	0.90	4.43	0.85
9.	4.30	0.66	4.36	0.71
10.	4.54	0.64	4.69	0.67
11.	4.09	0.68	4.27	0.72
12.	4.11	0.66	4.27	0.68
13.	4.32	0.77	4.45	0.79
14.	4.27	0.88	4.23	0.93
15.	4.31	0.70	4.45	0.60
16.	4.80	0.61	4.71	0.74
17.	4.42	0.67	4.38	0.69
18.	4.80	0.68	4.81	0.75
19.	4.78	0.62	4.82	0.71
20.	4.50	0.67	4.50	0.74
21.	4.26	0.56	4.34	0.67
22.	4.38	0.64	4.24	0.82
23.	4.61	0.69	4.67	0.68

[a] See Table 8-2 for the wording of each aspect.

Appendix B

SPECIMEN RESEARCH INSTRUMENTS

The research instruments used by the National Principalship Study to obtain data from the principals, teachers, and higher administrators number 192 pages. Approximately one-half of these instruments are relevant to the general concern of the School SES Study. Given the massive nature of these materials, it is impractical to attempt to present more than just a few specimen instruments here. Included below are sections from the teachers' questionnaire designed to measure: the background of the teachers, teacher job aspiration, teacher career and job satisfaction, teacher work satisfaction, teacher morale and classroom performance, and the administrative behavior of principals.

Other instruments of the National Principalship Study have been presented by Gross and Herriott,[1] by Gross and Trask,[2] by Dreeben and Gross,[3] and by Dodd.[4]

[1] Neal Gross and Robert E. Herriott, *Staff Leadership in Public Schools* (New York: John Wiley and Sons, 1965).

[2] Neal Gross and Anne E. Trask, *The Sex Factor and the Administration of Schools* (New York: John Wiley and Sons, forthcoming, title tentative).

[3] Robert Dreeben and Neal Gross, *The Role Behavior of School Principals,* Final Report No. 3, Cooperative Research Project No. 853 (Cambridge, Massachusetts: Graduate School of Education, Harvard University, 1965).

[4] Peter C. Dodd, *Role Conflicts of School Principals,* Final Report No. 4, Cooperative Research Project No. 853 (Cambridge, Massachusetts: Graduate School of Education, Harvard University, 1965).

B-1: Section of the Teacher Questionnaire Used to Measure the Background of Teachers

Instructions

Our purpose here is to obtain background characteristics of teachers. This information will be used to compare the backgrounds of teachers and principals and to examine factors related to the views held by teachers about the principal's role. Please answer the following questions by checking the *ONE* answer which *best specifies* your reply.

11. How many years have you been a teacher?

_____ 1) 1 year   _____ 6) 6–10 years
_____ 2) 2 years   _____ 7) 11–15 years
_____ 3) 3 years   _____ 8) 16–20 years
_____ 4) 4 years   _____ 9) 21–25 years
_____ 5) 5 years   _____ 0) 26 years or more

12. How many years have you taught in this *school system?*

_____ 1) 1 year   _____ 6) 6–10 years
_____ 2) 2 years   _____ 7) 11–15 years
_____ 3) 3 years   _____ 8) 16–20 years
_____ 4) 4 years   _____ 9) 21–25 years
_____ 5) 5 years   _____ 0) 26 years or more

13. How many years have you taught in *this school?*

_____ 1) 1 year   _____ 6) 6–10 years
_____ 2) 2 years   _____ 7) 11–15 years
_____ 3) 3 years   _____ 8) 16–20 years
_____ 4) 4 years   _____ 9) 21–25 years
_____ 5) 5 years   _____ 0) 26 years or more

14. In how many *schools* in this system have you taught?

_____ 1) 1 school   _____ 4) 4 schools
_____ 2) 2 schools   _____ 5) 5 schools
_____ 3) 3 schools   _____ 6) 6 or more schools

15. At what time do you customarily arrive at school for work?

_____ 1) before 7:30 AM
_____ 2) between 7:30 and 8:00 AM
_____ 3) between 8:01 and 8:30 AM
_____ 4) between 8:31 and 9:00 AM
_____ 5) between 9:01 and 9:30 AM

16. At what time do you customarily leave school?

_____ 1) before 2:00 PM
_____ 2) between 2:00 and 3:00 PM
_____ 3) between 3:01 and 4:00 PM
_____ 4) between 4:01 and 5:00 PM
_____ 5) between 5:01 and 7:00 PM
_____ 6) after 7:00 PM

17. *On the average* how frequently do you work on school activities at home?

_____ 1) zero nights per week
_____ 2) one night per week
_____ 3) 2 to 3 nights per week
_____ 4) 4 to 5 nights per week
_____ 5) more than 5 nights per week

18. *On the average,* how much of your weekend is taken up with school work?

_____ 1) none
_____ 2) very little
_____ 3) some
_____ 4) a great deal

19. *On the average,* how frequently are you contacted at home about school matters?

_____ 1) once a week or less
_____ 2) 2 to 4 times a week
_____ 3) 5 to 10 times a week
_____ 4) more than 10 times a week

20. When were your born?

_____ 1) 1891–1895   _____ 6) 1916–1920
_____ 2) 1896–1900   _____ 7) 1921–1925
_____ 3) 1901–1905   _____ 8) 1926–1930
_____ 4) 1906–1910   _____ 9) 1931–1935
_____ 5) 1911–1915   _____ 0) 1936–1940

21. Are you:

_____ 1) Female
_____ 2) Male

22. Where were your parents born?

_____ 1) both in the United States
_____ 2) one in U.S. and one foreign born
_____ 3) both foreign born

23. What was your *father's* MAJOR lifetime occupation?

_____ 1) education
_____ 2) professional (other than education), of scientific
_____ 3) managerial, executive, or proprietor of large business
_____ 4) small business owner or manager
_____ 5) farm owner or renter
_____ 6) clerical or sales
_____ 7) skilled worker or foreman
_____ 8) semi-skilled worker
_____ 9) unskilled worker or farm laborer
_____ 0) other (specify _____)

24. What was your *mother's* MAJOR lifetime occupation (other than housewife)?

_____ 1) none
_____ 2) education
_____ 3) professional (other than education), or scientific
_____ 4) secretarial, clerical
_____ 5) small business owner or manager
_____ 6) skilled worker
_____ 7) domestic worker or unskilled worker
_____ 8) semi-skilled worker
_____ 0) other (specify _____)

25. What was your *father's* highest educational attainment?

_____ 1) no formal education
_____ 2) some elementary school
_____ 3) completed elementary school

B-1: (Continued)

_____ 4) some high school, technical school or business school
_____ 5) graduated from high school, technical school or business school
_____ 6) some college
_____ 7) graduated from college
_____ 8) graduate or professional school

26. What was your *mother's* highest educational attainment?

_____ 1) no formal education
_____ 2) some elementary school
_____ 3) completed elementary school
_____ 4) some high school or business school
_____ 5) graduated from high school or business school
_____ 6) some college
_____ 7) graduated from college
_____ 8) graduate or professional school

27. In what type of a community did you spend the MAJOR part of your youth?

_____ 1) farm
_____ 2) village or town (under 10,000)
_____ 3) small city (10,000–50,000)
_____ 4) city (50,000 or more)

28. In what type of schools did you receive *MOST* of your *elementary* school education?

_____ 1) public
_____ 2) parochial
_____ 3) private

29. In what type of schools did you receive *MOST* of your *secondary* education?

_____ 1) public
_____ 2) parochial
_____ 3) private

30. In general, what was the quality of your work when you were in *secondary* school?

_____ 1) way above average
_____ 2) above average
_____ 3) average
_____ 4) somewhat below average

31. In general, how active were you in extracurricular activities when you were in *secondary school?*

_____ 1) far more active than average
_____ 2) more active than average
_____ 3) about average
_____ 4) somewhat less active than average

32. What was the *income* position of your parents at the time of your graduation from *high* school?

_____ 1) highest 25% of our community
_____ 2) second highest 25% of our community
_____ 3) third highest 25% of our community
_____ 4) lowest 25% of our community

33. At what type of college did you do *MOST* of your undergraduate work?
_____ 1) state university
_____ 2) state teachers' college or normal school
_____ 3) other public college or university
_____ 4) private university
_____ 5) private teachers' college or normal school
_____ 6) other private college

34. In general, what was the quality of your work when you were in *college?*

_____ 1) graduated with honors
_____ 2) above average
_____ 3) average
_____ 4) somewhat below average

35. In general, how active were you in extracurricular activities when you were in *college?*

_____ 1) far more active than average
_____ 2) more active than average
_____ 3) about average
_____ 4) somewhat less active than average

36. At what type of college did you do *MOST* of your graduate work?

_____ 0) I have not done graduate work
_____ 1) state university
_____ 2) state teachers' college or normal school
_____ 3) other public college or university
_____ 4) private university
_____ 5) private teachers' college or normal school
_____ 6) other private college

37. When you were in undergraduate college what per cent of your expenses did you personally earn?

_____ 1) 0 to 25%
_____ 2) 26 to 50%
_____ 3) 51 to 75%
_____ 4) 76 to 100%

38. In what way did you do *MOST* of your *undergraduate* college work?

_____ 1) full-time study
_____ 2) part-time study

39. In what way did you do *MOST* of your *graduate study?*
_____ 1) full-time study
_____ 2) part-time or summer study

40. What plans do you have for future formal education?

_____ 1) I have no plans
_____ 2) I plan to take courses, but not toward a specific degree
_____ 3) I plan to study for a master's but not a doctorate
_____ 4) I plan to study for a doctorate

41. How many semester hours of education courses did you have as an *undergraduate?*

_____ 1) none _____ 5) 31 to 40
_____ 2) 1 to 10 _____ 6) 41 to 50
_____ 3) 11 to 20 _____ 7) 51 to 60
_____ 4) 21 to 30 _____ 8) more than 60

42. How many semester hours of *graduate work* have you taken?

_____ 1) none _____ 5) 31 to 40
_____ 2) 1 to 10 _____ 6) 41 to 50
_____ 3) 11 to 20 _____ 7) 51 to 60
_____ 4) 21 to 30 _____ 8) more than 60

B-1: (Continued)

43. What is the *highest* academic degree which you have received?

_____ 1) certificate
_____ 2) bachelor's
_____ 3) master's
_____ 4) master's plus 30 hours
_____ 5) doctor's

44. What is your marital status?

_____ 1) single
_____ 2) married
_____ 3) separated
_____ 4) divorced
_____ 5) widow or widower.

45. Which category best represents your *current* salary?

_____ 1) Less than $4,000
_____ 2) $4,000 through $4,999
_____ 3) $5,000 through $5,999
_____ 4) $6,000 through $6,999
_____ 5) $7,000 through $7,999
_____ 6) $8,000 through $8,999
_____ 7) $9,000 through $9,999
_____ 8) $10,000 through $10,999
_____ 9) More than $11,000

46. When did the idea *FIRST* occur to you that you might enter teaching?

_____ 1) Before entering high school
_____ 2) In high school
_____ 3) After completing high school, but before graduating from college
_____ 4) After graduating from college

47. When did you make the *FINAL* decision to enter teaching?

_____ 1) Before entering high school
_____ 2) In high school
_____ 3) After completing high school, but before graduating from college
_____ 4) After graduating from college

48. At the time you made the *FINAL* decision, did you prefer teaching over any other occupation?

_____ 1) Yes, I preferred teaching
_____ 2) No, I preferred another occupation, but was not able to enter it

49. Which *one* of the following persons was most influential in your decision to enter teaching?

_____ 1) A member of my family who was a teacher
_____ 2) A friend who was a teacher
_____ 3) Someone else who was a teacher
_____ 4) A member of my family who was *not* a teacher
_____ 5) A friend who was *not* a teacher
_____ 6) Someone else who was *not* a teacher
_____ 7) No one

50. What grade level(s) do you teach? [If more than one, indicate your MAJOR grade level with a double check (√√).]

_____ 1) K or 1st grade   _____ 7) 7th grade
_____ 2) 2nd grade   _____ 8) 8th grade
_____ 3) 3rd grade   _____ 9) 9th grade
_____ 4) 4th grade   _____ 0) 10th grade
_____ 5) 5th grade   _____ 11) 11th grade
_____ 6) 6th grade   _____ 12) 12th grade

(FOR JUNIOR HIGH AND SENIOR HIGH TEACHERS, AND DEPARTMENTALIZED ELEMENTARY TEACHERS)

51. What subject area(s) do you teach? [If more than one, indicate your MAJOR area with a double check (√√).]

_____ 1) English
_____ 2) History; social studies
_____ 3) Science
_____ 4) Mathematics
_____ 5) Foreign languages
_____ 6) Home economics
_____ 7) Business or commercial subjects
_____ 8) Physical education; health
_____ 9) Fine arts (music, art, etc.)
_____ 0) Industrial arts
_____ 11) Other (specify_____)

B-2: Section of the Teacher Questionnaire used to Measure the Job Aspiration of Teachers

---

Instructions

At the heading of the column below is Question 13. Please answer this question for each of the statements found below. In answering the question, *write* in the *one* code letter which best represents your answer.

Question 13

How desir- A = I would not want to . . .
ous are you of B = I am not especially
doing the fol-   anxious to . . .
lowing? C = I have some desire to
                . . .
         D = I would very much like
                to . . .
         E = I am extremely anxious
                to . . .

Statements

11. Become an assistant principal.

12. Become the principal of an elementary school.

13. Become the principal of a junior high school.

14. Become the principal of a senior high school.

15. Become a staff specialist attached to a central office.

16. Become an assistant superintendent of schools.

17. Become an associate superintendent of schools.

18. Become a school superintendent.

19. Remain a teacher in this *school* for the remainder of my educational career.

20. Remain a teacher in this *school system* for the remainder of my educational career, but move to a school in a "better neighborhood."

21. Remain a teacher at my present grade level(s) for the remainder of my educational career.

22. Obtain a higher paying teaching job in another school system.

23. Obtain a higher paying position *outside* the field of education.

B-3: Section of the Teacher Questionnaire used to Measure the Career and Job Satisfaction of Teachers

Instructions

Please answer Question 12 for each of the items found below. In answering this question, *write* in the *one* code letter which best represents your answer.

Question 12

How do you feel about the following items?   I feel . . . with . . .

A = Very satisfied
B = Moderately satisfied
C = Slightly satisfied
D = Slightly dissatisfied
E = Moderately dissatisfied
F = Very dissatisfied

Items

11. The state of teaching as a "profession."

12. The top salary available for teachers.

13. My chances for receiving salary increases as a teacher.

14. The amount of progress which I am making in my professional career.

15. The amount of recognition which teachers are given by society for their efforts and contributions.

17. The capabilities of most of the people who are in teaching.   x

18. The effect of a teacher's job on his family life.

19. The effect of a teacher's job on his social life.

20. The possibilities for a teacher advancing to a position of greater responsibility in teaching.

21. The amount of recognition which teachers are given by members of other professions.

23. The level of professional standards maintained by most teachers.   x

24. The opportunity which teachers have for associating with other professional people.

25. The amount of recognition which noneducators give to teachers as compared to what they give to other professionals.

26. The amount of time for leisure activities which teaching affords.

14. The level of competence of most of the other teachers in this school.   xxx

15. The method employed in this school for making decisions on curriculum matters.

16. The method employed in this school for making decisions on pupil discipline matters.

17. The attitude of the students toward the faculty in this school.

18. The manner in which the teachers and the administrative staff work together in this school.

19. The cooperation and help which I receive from my superiors.

20. The educational philosophy which seems to prevail in this school.

21. The evaluation process which my superiors use to judge my effectiveness as a teacher.

23. The level of competence of my superiors.   x

24. The adequacy of the supplies available for me to use in my teaching in this school.

26. The amount of time which is available to me while I am at school for my personal professional growth.   x

27. The extent to which I am informed by my superiors about school matters affecting me.

28. The academic performance of the students in this school.

29. The extent to which the professional growth of teachers is subsidized by this school system.

B-4: Section of the Teacher Questionnaire used to Measure the Work Satisfaction of Teachers

Instructions

The role of the *TEACHER* is a varied one, involving many different tasks and calling for the application of many different skills. Most teachers find that they enjoy these different aspects of their role to varying degrees.

Please answer Question 10 below for each aspect of the teacher's role listed. In answering this question, *write* in the *one* code letter which best represents your answer.

Question 10

To what degree do you enjoy each of the following aspects of a teacher's role?

I enjoy . . .
↑

A = A great deal
B = Very much
C = Somewhat
D = Very little
E = Not at all
N = Aspect not relevant in my particular situation

Aspects of a Teacher's Role

11. Preparing lessons.

12. Correcting papers.

13. Attending teachers' meetings.

14. Supervising large groups of children.

15. Supervising small groups of children.

16. Working with pupils in extracurricular activities.

17. Talking with individual parents about a problem concerning their child.

18. Talking with a group of parents about a mutual problem.

19. Working with youngsters who are having a hard time adjusting to a school situation.

20. Working primarily with children rather than with adults.

21. Working with "exceptionally able" pupils.

22. Working with "average" pupils.

23. Working with "slow" pupils.

24. Handling administrative paper work.

25. Evaluating pupil progress.

26. Working with guidance personnel.

27. Working with curriculum specialists.

28. Having a different group of pupils to work with each year.

29. Having a different group of pupils to work with periodically during the day.

30. Having to discipline problem children.

31. Having a vacation from work periodically during the school year.

32. Having a long summer vacation every year.

33. Having a work routine which changes periodically during the day.

34. Having to schedule one's time carefully.

35. Having to follow specified curricula.

36. Working with a committee of teachers on a common problem.

B-5: Section of the Teacher Questionnaire used to Measure the Morale and the Performance of Teachers

C. Of the *TEACHERS* in your school, what *per cent* . . .

(M)	11. Display a sense of loyalty to the school?	_____%
(M)	13. Enjoy working in the school?	_____%
(M)	15. Respect the judgment of the administrators of the school?	_____%
(M)	17. Work cooperatively with their fellow teachers?	_____%
(M)	19. Display a sense of pride in the school?	_____%
(M)	21. Accept the educational philosophy underlying the curriculum of the school?	_____%
(P)	23. Try new teaching methods in their classrooms?	_____%
(P)	25. Waste a lot of time in their classroom activities?	_____%
(P)	27. Do everything possible to motivate their students?	_____%
(P)	29. Maintain effective discipline in their classes?	_____%
(P)	31. Maintain a professional attitude towards their work?	_____%
(P)	33. Do "textbook teaching" only?	_____%
(P)	35. Usually "drag their feet" when new ideas are introduced into the school program?	_____%
(P)	37. Take a strong interest in the social or emotional problems of their students?	_____%
(P)	39. Maintain an interest in improving the educational program of the school?	_____%
(P)	41. Are committed to doing the best job of which they are capable?	_____%
	43. Have a sense of personal loyalty to the principal?	_____%
(P)	45. Plan their classes so that different types of students can benefit from them?	_____%
(P)	47. Provide opportunities for students to go beyond the minimum demands of assigned work?	_____%
	49. Would stand behind the principal if he were unfairly criticized by a group of parents?	_____%
	51. Support the principal when he is being criticized by elements in the community?	_____%
	53. Support the principal when he is under pressure from the higher administration of the school system?	_____%
(P)	55. Willingly contribute some extra time in working on a new program that the principal feels will benefit the students?	_____%

Key: (M) = Morale item; (P) = Performance item

B-6: Section of the Teacher Questionnaire Used to Measure the Administrative Behavior of Principals

Instructions

The purpose here is to explore how *teachers* view the PRINCIPAL'S performance on various aspects of his job. Please answer Question 7 by *writing* in the *one* letter which best represents your feeling.

Question 7

How do you view the performance of your principal in each of the following areas?	A = Outstanding
	B = Excellent
	C = Good
	D = Fair
	E = Poor
	F = Very poor

Areas of Administrative Behavior

11. Running meetings or conferences.

12. Handling delicate interpersonal situations.

13. Working with community agencies.

14. Getting teachers to use new educational methods.

15. Obtaining parental cooperation with the school.

16. Resolving student discipline problems.

17. Directing the work of administrative assistants.

18. Cutting red tape when fast action is needed.

19. Maximizing the different skills found in the faculty.

20. Communicating the objectives of the school program to the faculty.

21. Improving the performance of *inexperienced* teachers.

22. Getting *experienced* teachers to upgrade their performance.

23. Giving leadership to the instructional program.

24. Developing *esprit de corps* among teachers.

25. Revising school procedures in the light of modern educational practices.

26. Handling parental complaints.

27. Publicizing the work of the school.

28. Keeping the school office running smoothly.

29. Planning generally for the school.

30. Knowing about the strengths and weaknesses of teachers.

31. Getting teachers to coordinate their activities.

32. Attracting able people to the school staff.

33. Knowing about the strengths and weaknesses of the school program.

34–37. In which *two* of the areas listed above is your principal the *strongest?* (Please write the two numbers in the boxes to the right.)

38–41. In which *two* of the areas listed above is your principal the *weakest?* (Please write the two numbers in the boxes to the right.)

NAME INDEX

Abrahamson, Stephen, 5, 8
Amerman, Helen E., 9, 10
Antonovsky, Aaron, 182

Barber, Bernard, 15
Barton, Allen H., 6, 47
Bates, Delbert, 98
Becker, Howard S., 8, 9, 12, 84, 85, 86, 206
Bendix, Reinhard, 40
Berreman, Joel V., 181, 182
Blalock, Hubert M., 146, 181, 184, 191, 203
Bloom, Benjamin S., 144
Blue, John T., Jr., 183, 184, 185
Bogue, Donald J., 2
Bond, Horace M., 5
Brookover, Wilbur B., 8
Brown, Bert, 183
Brown, James A. C., 98
Burchinal, Lee G., 36
Burton, William H., 7, 56

Canady, Herman G., 183
Chandler, Bobby J., 3, 9, 10, 39
Charters, W. W., Jr., 8
Clark, Kenneth B., 7
Cloward, Richard A., 40, 43
Coleman, Hubert A., 5
Coleman, James S., 161
Conant, James B., 4, 6, 38, 198

Corwin, Ronald G., 98
Croft, Don B., 200

Davidson, Helen H., 8, 9
Davie, James S., 5
Davis, Allison, 7, 40, 56, 144, 181
Deutsch, Martin, 8, 38, 183
Dodd, Peter C., 13, 270
Dornbusch, Sanford M., 182
Dreeben, Robert, 13, 270
Duncan, Beverly, 2
Duncan, Otis D., 2
Durant, Henry, 98

Eels, Kenneth, 1, 17, 46
Epps, Edgar G., 182

Fauman, S. Joseph, 3
Frazier, E. Franklin, 24

Gage, Nathaniel L., 8, 104, 201
Galdston, Iago, 98
Gans, Herbert J., 8, 44, 161
Gardner, Bruce, 36
Gerth, Hans H., 16
Ginzberg, Eli, 24, 161
Goldberg, Miriam L., 4
Gordon, C. Wayne, 6
Gottlieb, David, 104
Grigg, Charles M., 182
Grodzins, Morton, 2

Trask, Anne E., 13, 208, 270
Turner, Ralph H., 7

Uzell, O., 183

Vontress, Clemmont E., 84

Warner, W. Lloyd, 1, 8, 17
Watson, Goodwin B., 98
Wayland, Sloan R., 8

Weaver, Robert C., 3
Weber, Max, 16
Whitla, Dean K., 19
Wilder, David E., 6, 47
Wilder, Eleanor W., 104
Willis, Benjamin C., 39
Wilson, Alan B., 6, 7, 182
Winget, John A., 9
Wolf, Eleanor P., 3
Wolfle, Dael L., 65

SUBJECT INDEX